Praise for
THIS ISN'T WORKING

"We talk a lot about leadership, but we rarely talk about the cost of the way we lead. This book is a must-read for anyone serious about fixing the broken leadership model and building a better future for us all."

—Rose Marcario, former CEO, Patagonia; partner, ReGen Ventures

"This book is a rallying cry for ambitious leaders to redefine what it truly means to reach success. It gives us permission to be human, to prioritize our needs, and to make an impact without sacrificing ourselves. It will leave you feeling empowered to do things differently and build a career that fuels you instead of depletes you—a must-read!"

—Kristen Hadeed, author of *Permission to Screw Up*

"Too many brilliant leaders are burning out because the system wasn't built for them to succeed. *This Isn't Working* is a game-changer for leaders who want to build high-impact careers without burning out themselves. The book provides the roadmap for better leadership and better workplaces that don't just demand performance, but genuinely support it."

—Morra Aarons-Mele, author of *The Anxious Achiever*

"A timely and necessary book that challenges outdated success norms and provides a bold, refreshing approach to leadership that is both ambitious and sustainable. If you're tired of playing by rules that weren't built for you, this book will show you a better way."

—Deepa Purushothaman, author of *The First, the Few, the Only*

"In *This Isn't Working*, Meghan French Dunbar sets the record straight on why traditional models of work set women up to fail and offers a step-by-step guide for how women can chart their own path by rewriting the rules of leadership, reimagining work, and redefining career success. If you've ever said to yourself, 'there's got to be a different way to have a successful career,' this book is for you."

—Marianne Cooper, senior research scholar, VMware Women's Leadership Innovation Lab, Stanford University

"For too long, ambitious women have been told to change who they are to succeed in business. This book exposes why business itself is the problem and, more importantly, shows women how to lead on their own terms—without sacrificing themselves—and actually *improve* their results. A must-read for every working woman, and really all people working in business."

—Sheryl O'Loughlin, cofounder and founding CEO, Plum Organics; author of *Killing It*

"Finally! A business book that acknowledges the unique realities for women leaders, that's thoroughly readable and enjoyable, with lots of relatable anecdotes and 'aha' moments. If you want to feel both seen and uplifted, read this book!"

—Morgan Simon, founding partner, Candide Group

THIS ISN'T WORKING

How Working Women Can Overcome Stress, Guilt, and Overload to Find True Success

MEGHAN FRENCH DUNBAR

VENTURE

New York

Copyright © 2025 by Meghan French Dunbar
Cover design by Ann Kirchner
Cover image © Bjarte Rettedal via Getty Images; © Andrey_Popov / Shutterstock.com
Cover copyright © 2025 by Hachette Book Group, Inc.

Hachette Book Group supports the right to free expression and the value of copyright. The purpose of copyright is to encourage writers and artists to produce the creative works that enrich our culture.

The scanning, uploading, and distribution of this book without permission is a theft of the author's intellectual property. If you would like permission to use material from the book (other than for review purposes), please contact permissions@hbgusa.com. Thank you for your support of the author's rights.

Basic Venture
Hachette Book Group
1290 Avenue of the Americas, New York, NY 10104
www.basic-venture.com

Printed in the United States of America

First Edition: August 2025

Published by Basic Venture, an imprint of Hachette Book Group, Inc. The Basic Venture name and logo is a registered trademark of the Hachette Book Group.

The Hachette Speakers Bureau provides a wide range of authors for speaking events. To find out more, go to hachettespeakersbureau.com or email HachetteSpeakers@hbgusa.com.

Basic Venture books may be purchased in bulk for business, educational, or promotional use. For more information, please contact your local bookseller or the Hachette Book Group Special Markets Department at special.markets@hbgusa.com.

The publisher is not responsible for websites (or their content) that are not owned by the publisher.

Print book interior design by Amy Quinn.

Library of Congress Control Number: 2024057623

ISBNs: 9781541704862 (hardcover), 9781541704886 (ebook)

LSC-C

Printing 1, 2025

To the women on whose shoulders we stand, the ones who endured, persevered, and refused to settle so we no longer have to abide by the status quo but can, instead, redefine it

CONTENTS

	Introduction	1
Chapter 1:	It's Not You. It's the System.	9

Part I: Rewriting the Rules of Leadership

Chapter 2:	From Imbalanced "Masculine" Leadership to Holistic Leadership	31
Chapter 3:	From Assimilated Leadership to Authentic Leadership	49
Chapter 4:	From Overextended Leadership to Optimized Leadership	81
Chapter 5:	From Sacrificial Leadership to Sustained Leadership	107

Part II: Reimagining the Workplace

Chapter 6:	From Harmful Workplaces to Beneficial Workplaces	137
Chapter 7:	From Disenfranchised Workplaces to Dignified Workplaces	161
Chapter 8:	From Individualistic Workplaces to Unified Workplaces	189

Part III: Redefining Success

Chapter 9:	From Social Success to Soul Success	211
Chapter 10:	From Short-Term Profit Maximization to Long-Term Value Creation	239
	Conclusion	267
	Acknowledgments	*271*
	Notes	*275*
	Index	*285*

INTRODUCTION

To anyone on the outside, it seemed like I had it all. I'd started, scaled, and sold a business by age thirty-three. I was well-known in the business community, gave keynotes to business leaders twice my age, and was invited to events with high-profile CEOs. By any measure, I was "successful." However, behind the scenes, I was struggling. Burnout, constant stress, depression. I'd contended with these issues for much of my journey. I felt like I was doing everything right, though. I went to yoga, read self-help books, tried to meditate, and worked with a coach. I power posed, put affirmations on my desk, and had a vision board. Yet, in the rare moments when I stopped the relentless busyness of my life, something just didn't feel . . . right.

In 2014, my co-founder and I crowdfunded the launch of *Conscious Company* magazine. We were the first nationally distributed print publication in the United States dedicated to businesses that positively impact the world. Our first issue was picked up for distribution at Whole Foods Markets worldwide. We leveraged this success to close an investment round and build a media organization with a massive online presence, events, podcasts, and a membership community of thousands of progressive business leaders. It seemed like the business was thriving, but, similar to my situation, appearances were deceiving.

In early 2017, I reviewed our company's financial projections and found that, barring a miracle, we would run out of money by the end of the year. I'd given my all to the company and done everything I was "supposed" to do to succeed. I was gutted. I couldn't stop thinking about our first employee, Cia. Her family's health insurance, including coverage for her sons, Oliver and Isaac, depended on our company. I thought about Laurie, one of our twenty-one investors, who'd invested $125,000 because she believed in the vision *I'd* painted for her. I felt like I was failing female business leaders everywhere. It would be another data point for investors to justify why women hold less than 10 percent of CEO roles worldwide.

The pressure was too much. Overwhelmed by a rising sense of panic, I started feeling chest pains and shortness of breath. I was forced to lie down on the hardwood floor, where I screamed into a pillow and felt like my world was crumbling around me. I wasn't okay. Through sobs, I yelled for my husband, Scott, and heard him taking the stairs two at a time. He threw the door open and wrapped himself around me. I will never forget the look in his eyes when he found me on that floor. Later, when I'd calmed down, Scott said, "I can't watch you suffer like this anymore. Nothing is worth this."

I'd allowed things to deteriorate to this point because it just felt *normal* to suffer. Every successful businesswoman I knew was struggling in some way. Between the events I hosted, industry conferences I spoke at, and interviews I did for our magazine, I'd heard similar stories from CEOs, founders, executives, partners, managers, consultants, associates, and others.

Fellow CEO Emily Lutyens had an undiagnosable medical issue triggered by stress that sporadically paralyzed both of her legs. Deepa Purushothaman, one of the youngest partners ever at Deloitte, had an undiagnosable illness caused by extreme stress that forced her to take eight months of medical leave. Sheryl O'Loughlin, former CEO of Clif Bar, co-founder of Plum Organics, and then CEO of REBBL, had to walk away from her career after years of stress-related anorexia and depression.

These brilliant, ambitious, high-achieving women were "successful" yet barely holding it together. Maybe some of this resonates with you. You're driven. You aspire to lead. You excel. You achieve. Yet what you've worked so hard for isn't what you expected. The career you once strove for has become a source of anxiety, stress, and depletion. Something doesn't feel *right*, but you can't quite put your finger on it. You read books on leadership, mindfulness, stress reduction, personal development, and anything that might provide an answer. You exercise, take an occasional spa day, and try to be proactive about your well-being. But nothing sticks. You wonder if you're missing something. Maybe you're the exception—the only one who constantly questions whether you're doing it right and is spread too thin? Because everyone around you seems *just fine*.

I felt the same way but slapped on the shiny, confident veneer and pretended all was well. I had to, right? I couldn't show any cracks in my armor, especially after we sold our business in December 2017 and the new parent company asked me to remain as CEO. I felt that admitting I was struggling meant I wasn't cut out for the role. My silence perpetuated a lie.

June 6, 2018, was the first day of our Conscious Company Leaders Forum. We had more than two hundred business leaders flying in from all over the world. I'd share the stage with business titans like Justin Rosenstein of Asana, CNN Hero Chad Houser, and best-selling author Lynne Twist. However, I woke up that morning to the news that Kate Spade had lost her life to suicide the night before. To outsiders, it made little sense. Spade was living the dream of businesswomen worldwide. She founded her namesake brand in 1993, became a household name, and sold her company to Neiman Marcus for nearly $100 million. Even though it seemed like she had it all—intelligence, talent, wealth, acclaim, fame—I wondered how many people knew she was struggling. Or, like me, had she put on a brave face, hiding her struggles behind her success?

While reflecting on Spade's death, I decided to drop my facade. I opened our event by speaking about my mental health struggles, including the panic attack I'd experienced the previous year. I spoke of the immense pressure I felt, how I'd tied my identity to my work and prioritized my work over all else to the detriment of my well-being. Over the next two days, attendee after attendee—primarily women—sought me out to share similar stories. Burnout, exhaustion, depression, stress, mental health issues, medical challenges—the stories just kept coming.

I continued opening up about my mental health over the next two years and experienced similar responses everywhere I went. So many high-achieving businesspeople were struggling—people of all gender identities. These experiences tracked with statistics I'd seen, like the fact that more than 75 percent of workers have experienced burnout at their current work or that three out of five workers experience negative mental or physical health issues as a result of work-related stress.[1] But as more and more people connected with me about their suffering, I noticed that a disproportionate number of them were women. I looked into this dynamic further and found that research supported my observations.

Women consistently report much higher levels of stress than men. Working women's well-being is declining faster than men's, regardless of whether they have children.[2] An estimated 43 percent of women report feeling burned out, compared to 31 percent of men at the same level.[3] Additionally, women's symptoms of depression significantly *increase* as their authority increases, while symptoms of depression in men tend to decrease.[4]

Unfortunately, these statistics hit a little too close to home. In 2019, when I returned from maternity leave after having my first child, Jack, the stress, burnout, and depression were just too much. In February 2020, I resigned as CEO from the company I'd co-founded and loved. My last day was March 13. Four days later, we

INTRODUCTION

were in a statewide lockdown due to COVID-19. Instead of launching my next venture—an *in-person* events company for women—I unexpectedly became a full-time mom to our nine-month-old son. Over the next eighteen months, between social isolation, no longer working full-time, and having complications during my second pregnancy requiring weeks of bed rest, I had a lot of time to think. I knew I wanted to work again, but no part of me wanted to return to the world where I felt that I had to destroy myself in the name of success.

I desperately wanted to understand *why* working women were disproportionately struggling and if there was a better way. I read about the history of business and systems change. I pored over articles, podcasts, and books by other successful businesswomen and reviewed interviews I'd done throughout my career. I captured anything relevant I found. Ultimately, I discovered clear issues that explained why we're struggling. As we'll explore in Chapter 1, contemporary business sets women up for failure. The game is not just rigged; it's actively harming us. Yet, with no clear alternative, we keep trying to force ourselves to succeed in the status quo, and it's destroying us. Once I uncovered these dynamics, I felt deeply validated, like I'd been struggling to swim my whole life, only to realize that someone had tied a weight to my ankle that I'd never noticed. I hope as you explore these issues, you'll feel something similar.

After identifying the fundamental problems, I sought solutions. The best place to begin was studying the business leaders I knew who seemed to be successful and thriving. They do exist. I'd met them. Co-founder and co-CEO of EO Products Susan Griffin-Black; founder of her namesake brand and fashion icon Eileen Fisher; co-founder and CEO of Rising Tide Capital Alfa Demmellash; co-founder and chief visionary of Dermalogica skincare Jane Wurwand; thought leader and author Akaya Windwood. It wasn't like these women didn't face challenges or work hard; the difference was, they somehow remained grounded, healthy, and deeply content amidst it all. Moreover, the people who worked at their organizations seemed to feel the same way.

These leaders appeared to have realized that the status quo business playbook wasn't working and found the courage to write their own playbook instead. That courage had paid off. Not only were they thriving as people, but their careers were hugely successful by any measure. They weren't succeeding *despite* forging their own path; they were succeeding *because* they'd done so. They showed me that you don't have to compromise your health, values, or life in the name of success—you can succeed by bringing the best of yourself to the table, prioritizing the most essential things in life, and building a career that truly matters. Each woman felt like she'd unlocked something that could transform *everything* and had paved a path for the rest of us to follow.

As I investigated each woman's essential practices, I noticed trends. They shared common leadership approaches, workplace practices, and beliefs about success and the role of business in society. The deeper I went, the more I found, ultimately revealing an entirely new playbook that transforms work, improves lives, and begins repairing the entire system for good. This is the playbook I've detailed in this book. And while this book details issues specifically impacting women—meaning women and girls in all their intersecting identities—and addresses that audience, it's intended for everyone because contemporary business harms us all. Regardless of gender identity, you'll benefit from understanding these issues and incorporating the book's practices into your life.

In Part I, you'll untangle your limiting beliefs about leadership by highlighting what extraordinary leaders do to flourish at work and in life. You'll reimagine leadership through four essential practices: being holistic, authentic, optimized, and sustained. In Part II, you'll examine the most harmful workplace practices that hold us back and uncover the power of beneficial, dignified, and unified workplaces that make work better for everyone (including you). In Part III, you'll explore how your definition of success may be standing in the way of leading the life you genuinely love and causing more harm than you realize.

In each section, you'll be presented with concrete solutions to extricate yourself from the harmful status quo and begin transforming your work and life for good. With these new practices, you'll move from feeling overwhelmed, depressed, and burned out to feeling supported, energized, and fulfilled. What's more, your workplace can transform from a place of stress and depletion to a place of healing and joy.

Now, if you read all that and feel incapable of such change—I promise you, you can do this. The women who've led the way come from all backgrounds and experiences, are of different ages, went to different schools, and work in various industries. Many of them felt trapped in previous roles and doubted themselves. However, at some point in every woman's story, she decided to stop settling. One of these women, Hannah Drain Taylor, says, "I always wondered if I was an idealist. I felt like I had my head in the clouds, believing a company like ours could exist or that I could feel so good at work. But I had to try. I kept at it, and it finally materialized."

You have everything you need to follow in the footsteps of women like Hannah. That said, it will require change, and change can be uncomfortable. But haven't we already established that what you're doing right now is also uncomfortable? The difference is that any discomfort you feel while trying the practices in this book is temporary *and* will lead to lasting solutions. The discomfort of the status quo has no clear end in sight.

Doing what's needed to improve business is mission-critical because work has become one of the most significant influences on our lives. A full 60 percent of workers claim their job has a larger impact on their mental health than anything else in their life.[5] Can you even imagine if we could begin to shift business for good? If work wasn't soul-sucking and stressful but became a place where we found care, did fulfilling work, and were supported in becoming the highest version of ourselves? My deepest hope is to show you that this world is possible. We can start making this change. Together. The choice is yours. You can either maintain the status quo or help business become one of the most impactful vehicles we have to solve the societal issues of our time. I don't know about you, but I'm sick to death of watching extraordinary women suffer. I'm *done* watching contemporary business dim the light of people I love—of constantly hearing about extraordinary, hardworking people barely surviving or seeing brilliant women doubt their greatness, their worth, and what they're capable of. It's time for change. Shall we?

Chapter 1

IT'S NOT YOU. IT'S THE SYSTEM.

As CEO of Conscious Company Media, I was part of a women's mastermind group with six fellow CEOs. We met monthly to talk shop and support each other. One woman in our group was struggling with a debilitating medical issue triggered by stress. At her doctor's request, she planned to step down as CEO to address her health. She told us, "I feel like such a failure, like I'm letting everyone down. I guess I don't have what it takes." As this woman—a graduate of Brown with an MBA from Berkeley who'd co-founded and run a successful international company—blamed *herself* for this situation, I knew something was wrong but couldn't articulate the problem.

What I know now that I wish I could've told my friend then is that there was nothing wrong with her. Instead, she was struggling because there are hugely problematic issues in the business world that hold all women back.

To understand the fundamental issues that women are contending with, we must begin by exploring patriarchy. Now, if the dreaded "p" word just made you worry that this book is about to get all sorts of political/philosophical/polarizing and are questioning whether it's for you, I ask you to stay with me a little longer. I've been there. I resisted this word for a good chunk of my life. It felt too controversial. I didn't want to be seen as one of "those women" who made others uncomfortable by talking about *it*.

I was raised to believe I could be anything I wanted. I saw women reaching the highest levels: Oprah, Sandra Day O'Connor, Condoleezza Rice, Madeleine Albright. I could sing every word of Carly Simon's "Let the River Run" after watching *Working Girl* for the hundredth time. I felt I'd had the same opportunities as men for much of my life because I was successful at the same things boys were. I excelled in school and was often at the top of my class. I played sports with boys and could keep up, if not dominate. In college, I did as well as or better than the men in my classes and took on the same roles as the guys at the restaurant where I worked. I equated the fact that I *could* succeed alongside men with the idea that I was having the same experience as them.

So when I first started hearing words like "patriarchy" and "feminism," I felt like we'd made enough progress to claim men and women were equal and questioned whether patriarchy was even still a thing. Maybe the "radical" women who used these words weren't trying hard enough?

Yet, as my career progressed, I noticed things that didn't quite fit my "we're all equal now" script: being on a leadership team and seeing that junior men were being paid more than I was; my male business partner telling me he should take the investor meeting so he could talk to the investor "man to man"; a competitor launched by men raising $2.4 million in a matter of months *before* they had a product on shelves, while it took us eighteen months to raise $700,000 as two female founders with a successful product on shelves (by the way, the competitor went out of business in nine months). With experiences like these added to the stories I'd heard from other women in business who'd contended with similar issues, I was finally ready to admit that maybe, just maybe, things weren't *quite* as equal as I'd once believed. Even so, I was uncomfortable discussing the concept of patriarchy.

So in 2017, at my company's large annual event, the Conscious Company Leaders Forum, when one of my co-hosts—the extraordinary Jocelyn Macdougall—casually mentioned "smashing the patriarchy" onstage in front of a co-ed audience of 150 impact-driven business leaders, I was . . . *uncomfortable*. I felt like Jocelyn had crossed some invisible line and worried about the potential backlash.

As our event wrapped up, we asked the audience about their most meaningful moments from our three-day gathering. Surprising no one, one of the men stood up and referenced the "smashing the patriarchy" comment. He said he felt attacked but couldn't articulate why. I assumed we were about to end our event on a sour note, but then this man said he didn't know what Jocelyn meant by "Smash the patriarchy" and asked her to explain her comment. Wait, what? Did that man admit to not knowing something? Did he ask to talk about it as a group? We weren't just going to sweep our discomfort under the rug because we were all scared to have an uncomfortable conversation? Was this seriously about to happen? Yes, yes, it was.

Jocelyn acknowledged the discomfort in the room with ease and humor. Then, she clarified a common misconception: patriarchy isn't about *judgment*. It doesn't imply that men are wrong or inherently evil. Patriarchy describes the factual state of societies where men have disproportionate power, influence, and authority, which is true of nearly all present-day societies and has been true for millennia. Jocelyn clarified that "Smash the patriarchy" didn't mean "Down with all men!" Instead, her comment was about desiring a future where people of all genders have an equitable power distribution.

Given that this was an audience of leaders striving to positively impact the world through business, the audience shared Jocelyn's hope for a more equitable world. Many of us just didn't know how "smashing the patriarchy" fit in with that. We had an incredible discussion, ending the event on a beautiful note.

The Influence of Patriarchy

For clarity's sake, let's build on Jocelyn's explanation and get on the same page about the definition of patriarchy. Renowned cultural critic bell hooks defines patriarchy as a "political-social system that insists that males are inherently dominating, superior to everything and everyone deemed weak, especially females, and endowed with the right to dominate and rule over the weak and to maintain that dominance through various forms of psychological terrorism and violence."[1]

When people hear the definition of patriarchy, someone almost always asks, "Haven't men always dominated women? Isn't it just the natural order of things?" Nope. Out of the more than two million years humans have existed, patriarchal societies became the norm only in the last ten thousand years or so. Before that, research has found that smaller, nomadic societies varied in structure, with women and men often equitably sharing power. As a result of all sorts of factors like agriculture, currency, and the adoption of monotheistic religions, women's societal roles changed around 8000 BCE. Since then, most women have lived in patriarchal societies.[2]

Patriarchy's foundational belief is that men are superior to women. On that foundation, patriarchal societies put pressure on women to focus their lives around serving, pleasing, and obeying men. Women are expected to be physically attractive, take on all domestic labor, provide and care for children, and care for others. Marriages are expected to be between a man and a woman, and women are expected to obey their husbands or any other men in their families. To this end, women are conditioned to be gentle, nurturing, agreeable, docile, and subservient. Men are viewed as natural leaders who have full autonomy to do as they please, including feeling justified in controlling women, being violent, and feeling entitled to women's bodies. Women are seen as weak, overly emotional, and not suited for specific roles or serious work and are frequently reminded that they're secondary to and worth less than men.

Excluding some rare gender-equitable or matriarchal societies like the Mosuo of China or the Minangkabau of Indonesia, nearly all present-day societies are considered patriarchal. Depending on where you live, the severity of patriarchal beliefs and practices varies, but that doesn't change the fact that nearly all of us live under patriarchy.

In patriarchal societies, many men feel pressured to adopt certain behaviors to prove their "manliness," known as toxic masculinity. The Anxiety and Depression Association of America defines toxic masculinity's three core tenets as toughness (showing strength by dominating others, not showing emotions, and not asking for help), antifemininity (being hostile to or objectifying women, viewing anything "feminine" as weak), and power (viewing the world as a competition, winning at all costs, and equating money and influence with success).[3] These beliefs shape many men's sense of self-worth, ideas of success, and overall character, harming both men and the people around them.

The Trauma of Patriarchy

It's a struggle to live with the realities of being a woman in a patriarchal society and not internalize the beliefs in some way. Common expressions of internalized patriarchal beliefs that you might relate to include feeling guilty when you take care of yourself, unnecessarily apologizing, feeling shame about your body, feeling embarrassed if your home isn't spotless, letting men speak first, avoiding causing anyone discomfort, quieting yourself when you're in a group of men, and never feeling good enough. Any of this sound familiar?

Whether you realize it or not, internalized patriarchy informs what you believe you're capable of as well as your judgment, sense of self-worth, safety, freedom, and sense of control over your life. Given how pervasive and deeply rooted patriarchy is in cultures worldwide, it's nearly impossible to go through life without somehow experiencing its impact.

The influence of patriarchy and toxic masculinity is all around us. Of course, your exposure to and acceptance of patriarchy vary depending on factors such as where you live and your religious tradition, upbringing, family, media consumption, and peers, but that doesn't change the fact that patriarchy and toxically masculine beliefs influence your life: the fear of realizing that you're alone with a man you don't know in an elevator or parking garage or that a man is following you down the street; the extreme discomfort of having a man stare at you too long, demand your attention, or try to touch you without permission; the terror of realizing that a man is about to become violent or overly aggressive toward you; the feeling of being diminished by men at the table not making eye contact with you, talking over you, patronizing you, or ignoring you; the anger of having a man interrupt you, take credit for your idea, or doubt your work. It's not that all men do these things; rather, it's that all women have experienced them.

At one of our women-only business events, someone asked why we hosted events exclusively for women. I asked everyone to raise their hand if they had ever *not* been diminished, threatened, harmed, taken advantage of, dominated, harassed, or assaulted by a man. Not one woman raised her hand. Dr. Valerie Rein describes this dynamic as "collective trauma," defining trauma as "any experience that made you feel unsafe in your fullest expression and led to developing trauma adaptations to keep you safe."[4] Every woman has had individual traumatic experiences where she has been made to feel unsafe in her fullest expression of herself based on her gender identity, and women collectively share an understanding of what it feels like to be marginalized as a group.

Women are constantly reminded that we're unsafe, undervalued, and secondary. We see Brock Turner being caught in the act of sexually assaulting a woman, convicted of three counts of felony sexual assault, and sentenced by a male judge to *six months* in jail. We watch a presidential nominee be found liable for sexual abuse and brag about sexually assaulting women by "grabbing them by the pussy" and then go on to win the US presidency . . . twice. We see women banned from schools in Afghanistan, arrested by morality police for not wearing headscarves in Iran, and being raped by soldiers in war zones. Everywhere we look, we're reminded that women are considered worth less than men. And we just learn to live with it. We adapt. We get small. We hold back. We question ourselves. We appease. We sacrifice. We do what we need to do to survive in a culture that constantly tells us we're not as valuable as the dominant group.

While we may normalize the constant reminders of women's oppression, it's causing untold damage to our health. Per Dr. Emily Nagoski and Amelia Nagoski, external stressors, like cultural norms and experiences of discrimination, and internal stressors, like self-criticism, body image, and identity, can all be perceived in your body as threats. Stress is "the neurological and physiological shift that happens in your body when you encounter one of these threats." In response to stress, your blood pressure rises, your immune and digestive systems slow down, and your ability to grow and repair tissue decreases.[5] In short, stress degrades your mental and physical health. And living in a patriarchal society is *stressful*.

Women are pressured to constantly worry about social acceptability: our behavior, our appearance, our identity, our children, and our accomplishments. Researchers Dr. Gabor Maté and Daniel Maté found that excessive concern about social acceptability was one of the three traits that predispose us to disease more than any other, in addition to repressing anger and compulsive self-sacrificing behavior, which are also common behaviors of women living under patriarchy. It follows that women suffer disproportionately from chronic disease. We're at higher risk of chronic pain, fibromyalgia, irritable bowel syndrome, and autoimmune disorders like lupus and rheumatoid arthritis; have higher incidences of non-smoking-related malignancies than men; and have anxiety, depression, and PTSD at double the rates of men.[6] None of these statistics point to women being weaker than or inferior to men. Instead, they demonstrate the impact of living in cultures where we're constantly stressed because we're treated as though we're inferior to men.

Now that we have the context of patriarchy and how it manifests in everyday life, let's explore its influence on business.

Business + Patriarchy + Toxic Masculinity = <3

The first known currency was invented an estimated five thousand years ago, resulting in the advent of business—selling something for a profit—and the first known organizations that could enter into contracts emerged roughly three thousand years ago.[7] As business proliferated worldwide, most societies had already fully adopted patriarchal beliefs. As a result, from generation to generation, from the creation of contracts and the first issuance of stock to the invention of machines and workers' rights, one thing remained constant over thousands of years: business was—and still is—almost exclusively defined and led by men. Nearly all of these men were influenced by patriarchal and toxically masculine beliefs, which they then brought into the business world.

Yes, there were exceptions, and women have recently made significant strides in business. However, we're still excluded from most leadership roles that influence the contemporary business world. As of this writing, a whopping 95 percent of CEOs worldwide are men, while men lead 448 companies in the Fortune 500.[8] Men lead the ten largest private equity firms in the world—KKR, Blackstone, EQT, CVC Capital Partners, Thomas Bravo, Carlyle Group, General Atlantic, Clearlake Capital Group, Hellman and Friedman, and Insight Partners—as well as the ten largest companies in the world—Apple, Saudi Aramco, Microsoft, Alphabet, Amazon, Tesla, Berkshire Hathaway, NVIDIA Corporation, Taiwan Semiconductor Manufacturing, and Meta Platforms.[9]

It's fair to say that men have defined almost every aspect of business since its inception and typically still do. As a result, the design of the system is fundamentally flawed. This is not because men are inherently flawed, deficient, or "bad" in any way. I'll say that again for those in the back: the problem with contemporary business design is not *men*. The problem is that men who've been steeped in patriarchal and toxically masculine beliefs (and colonialism, white supremacy, ableism, and heteronormativity—all critical topics that would require additional books to unpack) have designed business through those lenses, resulting in seven issues that work directly against women.

1. Gender Discrimination

Patriarchy's foundational belief that women are inferior to men is baked into the business world. This belief results in women being discriminated against, held to higher standards, and valued less than men. The United Nations found that nine out of ten people worldwide still hold fundamental biases against women.[10] These biases are translated to the workplace, where more than 40 percent of women report experiencing gender-based discrimination. Both men and women are twice as likely to hire a male candidate as a female one.[11] In the tech world, 94 percent of people feel that women are held to higher standards than men.[12]

Perhaps the most glaring example of continued gender discrimination is the simple fact that women are still paid less than men for the *same work*. In the United States, on average, white women earn 16 percent less than men, earning 84 cents for every dollar a man makes. For women with additional marginalized identities, it's even worse: Latinas earn 55 percent of what non-Hispanic white men are paid; Black women are paid 64 percent of what non-Hispanic white men are paid; and Native American women earn 59 cents for every dollar paid to white, non-Hispanic men.[13] And it's not because we don't advocate for ourselves. Men and women ask for pay raises at the same rate, but women receive them 7 percent less often than men.[14]

Women also experience microaggressions—statements or actions that demean someone based on their identity. Women are more likely than men to have their work questioned or have someone else take credit for their ideas. Additionally, women are twice as likely as men to be mistaken for someone more junior or have someone comment on their emotional state and are two and a half times more likely than men to have someone comment on their appearance. Women with additional marginalized identities are disproportionately on the receiving end of microaggressions like these and more.[15]

2. Exclusion from Leadership

Continuing with the impact of women's assumed inferiority on business, women often aren't considered leadership material. Globally, roughly 40 percent of people feel that men make better business executives than women based solely on gender identity.[16] Research has shown that female candidates for leadership roles are consistently judged as having less leadership potential than men, making them 14 percent less likely to be promoted.[17]

The aversion to women in leadership runs so deep that research has found that even the experience of reporting to a female supervisor makes some men feel that their masculinity is being questioned. These men then attempt to reassert control "by engaging in harmful behaviors like lying, cheating, stealing, breaking rules, undermining colleagues, and withholding help."[18] Another study found that the mere idea of a female president made more than a quarter of the respondents feel angry or upset.[19] Such biases help to explain why women hold less than 30 percent of C-suite roles worldwide—with 22 percent of those roles held by white women and only 7 percent held by women of color—and less than 30 percent of senior management roles.[20]

Beyond the patriarchal belief that women don't belong in leadership, toxic masculinity also influences how we think about leadership. Antifeminine beliefs have resulted in "feminine" traits—compassion, vulnerability, listening, intuition, flexibility, etc.—being seen as a sign of weakness that don't belong in business or as "soft skills" that are still inferior to "masculine" traits. Toxically masculine beliefs about toughness also influence leadership norms. Business leaders feel that showing emotions or asking for help are signs of weakness and feel pressured to be stoic, self-sufficient, and unflappable. Anyone who shows emotions at work is labeled "volatile," "dramatic," or "unstable."

3. Expected Gender Roles and Double Standards

The patriarchal belief that women should take care of home life and behave according to patriarchal ideals shows up in the business world as well. Patriarchy pressures women to be demure, agreeable, pleasant, gentle, and submissive. However, the business world values "masculine" traits, like aggression, dominance, confidence, and strength, because the business world was designed solely by men who were pressured to embody these characteristics. Women are told to behave "like men" at work and are then penalized for violating gender norms when they do. The result? A lose-lose situation.

When we assert ourselves or speak up, we're criticized for being too loud or abrasive. When we're competitive, we're called a bitch. When we're focused, we're told to smile more. When we prove a man wrong, we're a pretentious know-it-all. The traits viewed as desirable for men and expected in business are questioned, judged, or shunned when expressed by a woman. This may help explain why more than 75 percent of high-performing women receive negative feedback from their superiors compared to the 2 percent of high-performing men who do. Or why almost 90 percent of high-performing women receive feedback about their personalities compared to 12 percent of high-performing men.[21] These dynamics are even more intense for women of color. Social psychologist Cydney Hurston Dupree's research showed that when women use powerful and dominant language, others view them as cold and less likable. While these findings applied to all women, Dupree found that the effects were strongest for Black and Latina women.[22]

In addition to being judged based on behavioral double standards, we're often subjected to judgmental comments about not being at home. "Who's taking care of your kids right now?" "How do you juggle being a mom and working?" "Is your husband 'babysitting' your kids?" No one asks working men about family life, but it's a common experience for working women. The subtle (or not-so-subtle) message is clear: you're *supposed* to be at home. And these judgments aren't just in our heads. Research has shown that when women achieve success at work, we're liked less and penalized for violating traditional gender roles.[23]

Adding to this, Eve Rodsky, author of *Fair Play*, found that even in what would be considered the most equitable heterosexual households, women still take on more household responsibilities and emotional labor than their male partners. Working women often undertake what Rodsky deems "the second shift," meaning taking on extra work like caring for aging parents, packing school lunches, making family health appointments, keeping track of social calendars, and additional responsibilities of home and social life.[24]

4. Male-Centered Workplaces

Patriarchal beliefs have also resulted in workplaces and professional spaces being designed for men. For example, even though most women feel more comfortable in warmer temperatures than men, the formula for the standard temperature for office spaces is based on the metabolic rate of a forty-year-old man, established in the 1960s. While the debate over the office thermostat might seem petty, one study found that reducing the temperature from 77°F to 72°F in a room of women cut their productivity in *half* and doubled their mistakes.[25]

Women contend with additional workplace challenges, like not having safe places to pump breast milk in privacy or comfort or on-site workplaces that don't take women's bodily needs into account. Each time you're forced to put on your coat at work, feel your feet dangle from a chair that's too tall for you, hide from coworkers to address your body's needs, or are forced to navigate challenges that your male colleagues don't deal with, some part of you remembers that this world wasn't made for you. You're the exception here. You don't belong.

5. Barriers for Working Parents

Another patriarchal influence on business is the assumption that everyone is in a heteronormative partnership where the man works and the woman stays home to take care of the children. As a result, business norms don't account for parents' needs even though, in many homes, both parents now work at least part-time.

Barriers for working parents include parental leave policies that extend only to women, don't include same-sex couples or adoption, are contingent on company tenure, or don't even exist; strict working hours that don't align with school hours; being asked to work outside working hours; and not having the flexibility to leave the workplace during the day. Former Ellevate Network CEO Kristy Wallace detailed her struggle with this dynamic, saying, "I had a CEO of a company tell me, 'We need you in the office at least until 10:00 p.m. one night a week.' I told him, 'I can't be here at 10:00 p.m. I have a family.' It was seen as like I was choosing between my family and my career when in reality, that should never have been a choice asked of me."

The contemporary business landscape makes it nearly impossible for two working parents to succeed without help or someone being forced to make sacrifices.

6. Objectification and Victimization

Under patriarchy, many men feel entitled to women's bodies. Unfortunately, this dynamic has infiltrated the business world, with men abusing positions of authority to coerce women into sexual situations and feeling confident in their ability to get away with it.

Between 54 and 81 percent of women report experiencing sexual harassment in the workplace. Three-quarters of those women report being harassed by someone in a more senior role, and nearly one-third said they were harassed directly by their boss. Unfortunately, more than half of women don't report instances of sexual harassment, fearing the potential loss of their job, being labeled a troublemaker, or having their concerns not taken seriously.[26] Roughly 50 percent of women report that sexual harassment has hurt their careers, causing them to quit their jobs, have lower job engagement and satisfaction rates, and suffer from increased financial stress.[27]

7. Toxic Definitions of Success

The toxically masculine beliefs about power—that everything is a competition, winning is everything, and success is defined by money—have had a profound impact on the business world. So much so that the entire contemporary premise about the purpose of business is the culmination of thousands of years of toxic masculinity, all climaxing in one completely messed-up theory: shareholder supremacy.

On September 13, 1970, Milton Friedman published his now infamous *New York Times* piece in which he proposed that "there is one and only one social responsibility of business—to use its resources and engage in activities designed to increase its profits so long as it stays within the rules of the game."[28]

Friedman's article popularized the idea of shareholder theory, meaning business leaders have a *responsibility* to do everything in their power, as long as it's not technically illegal, to make as much money as possible for company shareholders. Friedman took this so far as to vilify business leaders who attempted to make a positive societal impact or did anything to negate the harm caused by their company's actions because to him, the sole purpose of business was to maximize profit at all costs.

When you compare shareholder theory to toxic masculinity's core beliefs, it's really *something*: the responsibility of business is to maximize individual wealth and power; individual leaders are pressured to win at all costs by doing anything necessary to maximize profit regardless of the impact on others; business leaders who demonstrate "feminine traits," like compassion, empathy, or care for any stakeholders beyond shareholders, are "irresponsible"; business leaders should be cutthroat and strive to dominate competitors; the only measure of worth for a company is to make money and gain power—it's a winner-take-all game.

Good ol' Friedman successfully took toxic masculinity's greatest hits, tied them up in a bow, called it economic theory, and (checks notes) . . . won the Nobel Prize six years later for his contributions to the field of economics.

When Friedman's article came out, the men who were in power were gifted with the perfect justification for taking toxic masculinity and their perceived "manliness" to the extreme. Now they actually had a fiduciary responsibility to do so! Think of the 1980s and 1990s. Think hostile takeovers, leveraged buyouts, Gordon Gekko, and *The Wolf of Wall Street*. Pure, unfettered toxic masculinity parading as "success" in business. Shareholder theory was like a siren song to many business leaders worldwide, but the consequences couldn't have been more severe.

If you tell a company leader that (1) their sole responsibility is to make money, (2) they can do whatever they need to do to accomplish that goal so as long as it's legal(ish), (3) their job security depends on their ability to maximize revenue and perform better than their competitors, and (4) their performance will be analyzed and publicly tracked every three months (assuming they're publicly traded), what in the fresh hell do you think is going to happen? Yeah, that leader's going to make some pretty sketchy decisions. They're going to reduce worker pay below poverty levels while the founders become one of the wealthiest families in history (Walmart);[29] cut corners on employee safety measures, working employees to the bone, resulting in more than 40 percent of employees being injured on the job (Amazon);[30] deny climate change and their company's role in it despite internally acknowledging all of it since 1977 (Exxon);[31] use aggressive and deceptive marketing to get doctors to prescribe company products they know are highly addictive and destroy people's lives (Purdue Pharma);[32] or suppress research that demonstrates that their products are literally *killing* people (Monsanto).[33] Purely profit-driven business decisions like these have caused immeasurable harm to society.

Business decisions to cut costs through wage stagnation, employee reduction, and outsourcing work to the lowest bidder while increasing executive pay to exorbitant levels have drastically increased income inequality. Since the introduction of shareholder supremacy, the bottom 90 percent of income earners in the United States have had annual earnings gains of just 24 percent, while the top 1 percent of income earners have seen their annual earnings more than double; the middle class has decreased from more than 60 percent to less than 50 percent of the US population;[34] and the top 1 percent of American earners now have more wealth than the entire middle class combined.[35]

High-pressure, win-at-all-cost business cultures are destroying people's well-being as well. More than 85 percent of workers report having experienced moderate, high, or extreme stress in the last year, with four out of five workers who experienced extreme stress saying their primary source of stress was work.[36] And stress kills. Chronic stress increases people's blood pressure, promotes artery-clogging deposits in the body, and changes the brain in ways that can lead to increased depression, anxiety, and addiction.[37]

The profit-at-all-cost mentality has also led to environmental destruction. Since the introduction of shareholder supremacy, the population sizes of mammals, fish, birds, reptiles, and amphibians have declined by almost 70 percent, while more than five hundred land animals are on the brink of extinction. The primary cause of species loss has been profit-driven land-use change, such as deforestation and the conversion of habitats into agricultural systems.[38] Deforestation. Climate change. Pollution. These issues and many more have only worsened in the past fifty years at the hands of business.

Shareholder supremacy *incentivizes* business leaders to be as creative and ruthless as possible in taking advantage of others and exploiting resources. Leaders are pressured to look into the eyes of humans they've worked with for years and cut their pay or put them out of a job for profit's sake. They're asked to treat humans as numbers on a balance sheet rather than honor their humanity and to lie to people in their community about the safety of their products for the sake of the bottom line.

Business leaders are pressured to compromise their very humanity for "success," either forced to become comfortable abandoning the best parts of themselves time and time again or becoming complete psychopaths. And no, I'm not exaggerating. While only 1 percent of the general population is classified as psychopathic—meaning they entirely lack a conscience, empathy, and remorse—research has shown that *more than 20 percent of CEOs are*.[39] That's one in five, my friend. And for those who aren't psychopaths, the ramifications of being forced to behave this way are severe. CEOs are twice as likely to be depressed as the general population, while suicide is also more likely for those in the C-suite.[40]

Take a second to let that sink in. The system has become so toxic and demands such abhorrent behavior from those in positions of power that many of its leaders are contending with significant mental health issues or are succeeding because they lack a damn conscience. *This* is why it doesn't matter how many women get into positions of power—the system is so harmful that it's chewing up and spitting out anyone who makes it into a leadership role.

Taking all of this into account—chronic stress outside work, discrimination, exclusion, extra work, double standards, noninclusive workplaces, barriers for parents, objectification and victimization, and toxic ideas about success—can you start to see why maybe, just *maybe*, you're not the problem here?

You're not just attempting to succeed in a system that harms most of the people working within it regardless of gender identity; you're trying to succeed in this system *on top of* all the additional barriers that hold women back as well! And these barriers aren't insignificant—many of them correlate with the strongest known predictors of declining health and well-being.

When it comes to burnout, the six primary causes are (1) unfairness, (2) lack of community, (3) excessive workload, (4) perceived lack of control, (5) not being rewarded properly, and (6) feeling out of alignment with your values.[41] When it comes to mental health issues—aside from biological factors, trauma, chronic medical conditions, and substance abuse—some of the key predictors are social isolation, discrimination, loneliness, long-term stress, and social expectations.[42] All of these elements track with one or multiple of the barriers facing businesswomen. Take unfairness: how fair does it feel when you are discriminated against, excluded from leadership, paid less for the same work, objectified, or doubted for no reason? Or how about feeling a lack of community and social isolation? How isolating does it feel when you work in a male-centered workplace, are the only woman in the room, or can tell people don't like you because of behavioral double standards? We take on excessive workloads to "prove" ourselves. We abandon our values to align with toxic ideas about success. We don't have time for self-care because of additional work at home. Every barrier you face in the business world *directly* relates to increased physical and mental health concerns. And you're expected to *over*perform in this system under increased scrutiny, suppress your true self, and somehow do it all with a smile on your face every working day of every month of every year.

Do I have that right? This has to be a joke. It's no wonder we're suffering! Frankly, I'm surprised the sheer force of one thousand black holes isn't causing us to regularly implode with rage. Now do you understand why I said it's not your fault? It has nothing to do with *you*. You're not struggling because you're deficient in any way. You're friggin' spectacular. Business is the problem. The fact that you've been succeeding *despite* all of this is astounding.

As I peeled back the layers of this situation, not only did I feel validated, but I started to feel . . . powerful. I mean, any woman who's even a marginally productive member of society in the face of all this is a warrior. Those who've gone further and entered the business world, where the entire game is rigged against us, and had a modicum of success are bona fide queens. And those of you who've done this while holding multiple marginalized identities are, quite simply, miraculous.

Can you imagine what we could do if we began to fix this? If we worked toward building a better system that not only removed these barriers but also added to our health and well-being? If we helped build businesses that didn't destroy society but made it better?

Fortunately, I didn't set out to write a book to highlight problems without providing concrete solutions. Repairing business is not just possible; it's actively happening.

The trailblazing leaders who've pioneered better business practices have started to move the needle. It's up to us to keep the momentum going: to adopt healthier practices and model them for others, to refuse to abide by the toxic status quo, to stand up for ourselves and future generations, to build on what has already been done and inspire an even greater change that will begin to repair business worldwide. This book will show you how.

Part I

Rewriting the Rules of Leadership

Chapter 2

FROM IMBALANCED "MASCULINE" LEADERSHIP TO HOLISTIC LEADERSHIP

I ONCE WALKED INTO DAY ONE OF A JOB AND OVERHEARD MY NEW boss yelling at an employee, "Just get it done! I honestly don't know how this could take you so long!" As I settled into my role, I discovered this was how he treated everyone. He lashed out, micromanaged us, and punished anyone who couldn't meet his impossibly high standards.

I learned to keep my head down and isolate myself to stay out of his line of fire. Others tried to impress him by matching his energy, even if it meant throwing colleagues under the bus. It was a mess. Going through a day without an "incident," where someone wasn't upset about something the boss said or the team wasn't squabbling among ourselves, was rare. At one point, when the boss asked us for feedback and then retaliated against anyone who dared criticize him, I decided I'd had enough. I gave the boss six weeks' notice. He responded by collecting my computer that *same day*, cutting off my email access, and never speaking to me again.

This particular leader illustrates the traditional playbook's imbalanced "masculine" leadership approach.

The Traditional Playbook: Imbalanced "Masculine" Leadership

When I ask you to imagine a leader or a manager, what immediately comes to mind? If you pictured a man or someone demonstrating "masculine" traits, you're not alone. Research on the "think manager, think male" phenomenon has shown that most people, regardless of gender identity, picture a man or think of someone with "masculine" qualities—confidence, strength, ambition, dominance, etc.—when asked about leadership.[1] There's a clear reason why: good ol' patriarchy and toxic masculinity.

See, all of us have access to the entire range of human character traits regardless of our gender identity. *But*, under patriarchy, society decided to split these traits up to set us up for success with our expected gender roles.

As young girls, we're typically conditioned to express traits that please men in our future roles as perfect, respectable, subservient wives and mothers. We're told to care for others, be quiet and demure, avoid conflict, obey the rules, defer to men, and put others' needs ahead of our own—characteristics that became labeled as "feminine." We're given baby dolls, kitchen sets, dollhouses, and makeup kits. We're surrounded by examples of women being saved by men and valued for their appearance: Cinderella, Barbie, beauty pageants, *The Real Housewives*. We're discouraged from expressing "masculine" traits and told we're "too bossy" or "too loud" when we do.

Conversely, young boys are often encouraged to express a suite of "masculine" traits that align with their expected gender roles as providers, protectors, and decision-makers. Boys are conditioned to compete, speak up, be confident, fight, assert themselves, and dominate others. They're given toy guns, footballs, monster trucks, and superhero action figures. They grow up seeing men taking risks, saving the day, and wielding violence and intimidation to express what it means to be a man: think *Die Hard*, the NFL, *Top Gun*, WWE. They're told to "man up," to "take it like a man," and that "boys don't cry" and can even be belittled for demonstrating any traits that are considered "feminine."

Those young boys who've been conditioned to only feel comfortable expressing "masculine" traits grow up to become the same men who've been leading the business world for the last three thousand years. As a result, leadership has become synonymous with all things "masculine." It's not that "masculine" traits are the most *effective*; rather, these are the only traits that have been *available* to most business leaders over time. Unfortunately, this dynamic has led too many leaders to equate any "masculine" trait—aggression, intimidation, dominance, hypercompetitiveness—with effective leadership. Yet not all "masculine" traits are created equal. Many "masculine" traits will actually *degrade* your leadership. Dominant or hyperindividualist managers have proven to decrease employee's collaboration and desire to be helpful, and the number-one predictor of employee turnover is a toxic workplace culture created by managers who are biased, cutthroat, dishonest, disrespectful, or abusive.[2] At present, more than 70 percent of people feel that the traditional leadership approach has contributed to the societal problems we're currently facing.[3]

The most effective leadership has proven to be a blend of healthy "feminine" and "masculine" traits. This means the traditional purely "masculine" approach is akin to showing up without *half* (or more) of the tools you need to do the job. When an employee comes to a leader struggling with a family emergency, but the leader can't or doesn't know how to respond with compassion because it's "feminine," everyone suffers. The employee feels unsupported; the leader feels callous, guilty, or disconnected; and the business suffers when the unsupported employee becomes disengaged or leaves the job.

A holistic approach is being called for in the place of traditional imbalanced leadership.

The New Playbook: Holistic Leadership

In the first year running *Conscious Company* magazine, we landed a huge interview for the cover of our third issue: Eileen Fisher. Fisher is the founder and former CEO of her namesake fashion brand. At that time, she rarely gave interviews. She made an exception for our publication because we focused on telling the stories of businesses that did good for the world, an ethos that aligns with Fisher's brand.

I made the journey to Irvington, New York, for the interview at Fisher's home, and I was a nervous wreck. Here I was, a thirty-year-old mountain girl from Colorado whose sense of "fashion" meant whatever I could afford at T.J. Maxx, walking up to the front door of a famous fashion designer. I couldn't find much about her on the internet, so I jumped to the entirely rational conclusion that she would be like Miranda Priestly from *The Devil Wears Prada* and destroy my very soul with a cutting remark in the first five minutes of the interview.

I rang Fisher's doorbell and was greeted by her assistant, who welcomed me inside. She showed me to the room where we'd do our interview, and I found Fisher quietly sitting at the table. She welcomed me with a warm smile and gently introduced herself. She was grounded, kind, and almost seemed a little . . . shy? My nerves evaporated entirely.

As I got settled, Fisher told me how much she loved my magazine and asked how we had gotten started. I told her the short version of our harrowing founders' journey, and she followed up with more questions. Knowing we had only a certain amount of time together, I finally said, "Eileen, I think I'm supposed to be interviewing *you* here!" To this day, it is one of my favorite interviews of my career.

Fisher spoke of the importance of listening to her team, her passion for sustainability, and why it's important to create a workplace where everyone feels safe. She said the leadership traits that she found most effective were authenticity, vulnerability, deep listening, and humility—all things I saw her express during our time together—while also talking about "traditional" leadership skills such as being strategic and bold.

I left the interview feeling inspired, excited, and a little perplexed. I'd been so conditioned to believe that the "feminine" traits she spoke of didn't belong in the business world that I couldn't comprehend what I was seeing. Founder and former CEO of MontiKids Zahra Kassam expressed a similar sentiment about leadership: "I haven't seen many women who are leading at high levels in a 'feminine' way. I don't even think it's clear what this could look like for many of us because we lack models of it." Since I hadn't seen a leader like Fisher before, I initially assumed that she was a bit of a fluke (she runs a fashion empire, *and* she's kind?). I felt like I must be missing something. Yet I soon began noticing other successful leaders openly expressing both "feminine" and "masculine" traits.

I met Alfa Demmellash, co-founder and CEO of Rising Tide Capital, who was compassionate, appreciative, and deeply authentic while also being visionary, decisive, and ambitious. I met Susan Griffin-Black, co-founder and co-CEO of EO Products, who was intuitive, attentive, and emotionally intelligent *and* honest, driven, and clear. I met Akaya Windwood, who showed me what it looked like to be strong and compassionate, confident and grounded, clear and joyful. These women had moved beyond the gender binary and understood that exceptional leadership requires a wide range of both "masculine" and "feminine" traits, tracking with a huge swath of contemporary leadership research showing that this is the most effective leadership strategy. Currently, an estimated 83 percent of people think the leaders who will most successfully navigate current societal crises will be "able to access a wide range of skills simultaneously."[4] This new-playbook approach is called holistic leadership.

Holistic leaders wield numerous healthy "feminine" and "masculine" traits and discern which trait to lean on based on the circumstances while also working to move away from as many toxic traits as possible. The following practices can help you follow in their footsteps to cultivate a more holistic leadership approach in your own work.

Holistic Leadership Practice #1: Cultivate Numerous Healthy Traits

My first big-kid job after college was as a development assistant at the Environmental Defense Fund. Three weeks into my new role, I came home early from an evening out with my brother to the apartment I shared with my then boyfriend to a cliché scene from a bad Lifetime movie: two empty wineglasses on the coffee table, my boyfriend's shorts on the floor, and a small pink bra (not mine) in the hallway to our bedroom. I made the totally rational decision to throw all of the unknown woman's clothes over the railing of our third-floor balcony, confronted my boyfriend, and left to sleep at my friend's house.

After a night of barely sleeping, I was a train wreck when I arrived at work the next day. My new boss, Whitney, instantly knew something was wrong. I figured I should tell her why so she wouldn't assume my disheveled state was a common occurrence. When she asked me what was going on, I stammered out a few words before bursting into tears. Even though it was my first time working in an office, I was confident that crying at work was *not* okay. I apologized immediately, fearing that I was about to be fired for my brazen display of, you know, genuine human emotion. Whitney shocked me by saying, "Everything's okay. Take a deep breath and start from the beginning."

While I choked out the story, Whitney gave me her full attention. She empathized with me, telling me she'd gone through something similar at my age. When I told her that I didn't know where I was going to stay while I figured out new housing, she slid her spare key across the desk and invited me to stay at her place while she was on a business trip for the rest of the week.

Because Whitney met my grief with compassion and generosity, I became her biggest fan. I mean, it was week three, and I already would have run through a plate-glass window for the woman. Whitney proved to be an exceptional leader. In addition to this initial instance of going above and beyond with compassion, she never

FROM IMBALANCED "MASCULINE" LEADERSHIP TO HOLISTIC LEADERSHIP

forgot my birthday, helped me build a flexible schedule without using my PTO to help my brother through a health crisis, and advocated for my advancement to the higher-ups. I was one of the lucky 25 percent of workers who genuinely felt that my manager cared about my well-being.[5]

But I didn't just appreciate Whitney's caring and supportive leadership style. I watched her walk into a room and own the space with the confidence of a lioness. Anytime she had a big win, she'd be sure to acknowledge my contributions. She openly and vulnerably told me about a personal struggle she was contending with that pulled her away from work for a bit. She gave me hard, honest feedback to help me improve my work and set clear boundaries with me. She somehow seemed capable of both wielding tons of "masculine" traits that I typically associated with business leaders—having strong boundaries and being direct, ambitious, and confident—and expressing "feminine" traits—being caring, supportive, vulnerable, empathetic, and appreciative.

Unbeknownst to me at the time, I was experiencing the impacts of working for a leader who'd cultivated a wide range of healthy "masculine" and "feminine" traits, which contemporary research has found to be the most effective way to lead. As a result, while Whitney's peers struggled to keep their associates for longer than a year, she and I became one of the highest-performing teams in the organization for nearly five years.

Whitney's leadership illustrates the first practice of holistic leadership: understand what healthy leadership traits are, value them equally, and cultivate as wide of a range of them as possible. Table 2.1 on the next page shows the most effective healthy leadership traits per contemporary research and the many interviews done for this book.

Even with this robust list of effective leadership traits staring you in the face, you may feel uncomfortable expressing some "feminine" traits in the workplace. You're not alone. The traditional "masculine" leadership approach is all many of us have ever known. And even when people are open to "feminine" traits, they're often still

Table 2.1: Most Effective Healthy Leadership Traits

Accountable	Confident	Inspiring
Adaptable	Decisive	Intentional
Ambitious	Emotionally Intelligent	Intuitive
Appreciative	Empowering	Relational
Attentive	Generous	Resilient
Authentic	Grounded	Strategic
Caring/Compassionate	Honest	Supportive
Collaborative	Humble	Transparent
Communicative	Innovative	Vulnerable

labeled as "soft skills" because anything "feminine" is, of course, still defined as secondary, right? But here's the thing: *all* of these healthy traits are hugely valuable.

Regarding the impact of just some of these traits on your leadership, a whopping *75 percent of the workforce* wants their manager's leadership style to be rooted in empathy and support.[6] Feeling cared for at work is currently the number-one driver of employee engagement.[7] Employees who feel that their employer genuinely cares about their well-being are 69 percent less likely to look for a new job, three times more likely to be engaged in their work, 71 percent less likely to experience burnout, and 36 percent more likely to feel that they're thriving outside work as well.[8] Intuition benefits complex decision-making, helps us perceive deception more accurately, and enables us to make quicker and often more accurate decisions.[9] Employees who regularly witness their leader being vulnerable are 5.3 times more likely to trust that leader, leading to increased innovation, creativity, and growth of team members.[10] Leading with compassion reduces employees' emotional exhaustion and absenteeism.[11] Last but not least, in every interview completed for this book, the trait leaders most commonly identified as being important to their success was being attentive and listening. None of these traits are secondary.

To be clear, being a holistic leader doesn't mean you have to embody every single healthy trait. Your leadership style should focus on embodying a combination of traits that resonates with you—some that you already possess and others that you aspire to wield. The more traits you cultivate for your tool belt, the more effective your leadership will be.

Tips for Cultivating Healthy Leadership Traits

1. Lean Into Your Strengths

One way to cultivate greater holistic leadership is by increasing awareness of the healthy traits you already lean on to understand their impact. You can start by taking five minutes at the end of every week to write down instances throughout the week where you successfully expressed any of the healthy traits. The more you identify, the better. This will ensure that you're expressing these traits consistently. It's one thing to *be able to* wield them and another to *actually* wield them in the workplace. Look for patterns as you perform this exercise. Are there certain traits that you lean on more heavily than others? Are there traits that you're holding back from the workplace for some reason? If you regularly can't find times when you expressed healthy traits, write down one way you could express each of your healthy traits the following week and practice following through.

2. Address Growth Opportunities

The beauty in having many healthy traits that can enhance your leadership is that you can continually uplevel your leadership by cultivating more traits. To help you incorporate new traits into your leadership, review the healthy traits and identify the ones you feel inspired to wield but don't quite feel comfortable with yet. From this list, choose *one* to focus on for the next month. Feel free to answer any of the following questions to help you explore how this trait shows up for you:

- What makes me uncomfortable about expressing this trait?
- Are there certain circumstances where I am more uncomfortable than normal expressing this trait? Why?
- What resources exist to help me better express this trait?
- What is one concrete way that I could genuinely practice expressing this trait in the next week?

Once you've explored how this trait shows up for you, it's time to practice wielding it. Set a small, concrete goal to get started. For example, in week one, practice expressing this trait once. In week two, practice it twice. Week three, three times. And so on. At the end of each week, keep yourself accountable by reviewing your goals and reflecting on the instances where you successfully practiced your new trait. How did it feel? What surprised you? Was there anything you learned to help you express the trait more cohesively in the future? If you're struggling, enlist the help of topical experts. You don't have to do this alone. There are myriad thought leaders out there who've explored what's needed to successfully wield all of these traits. Take the time to find them and obtain guidance on your journey.

Holistic Leadership Practice #2: Release Toxic Traits

During coursework for my MBA program, we were asked to take an assessment to determine our conflict style. My result? The turtle. At the first sign of conflict, I retreated into my shell, hoping the conflict would resolve without my having to engage with anyone or anything. Yep, that tracked.

I took my turtle conflict style into my leadership approach as CEO of my first company. I'd never learned to healthily navigate conflict, and do you know what has *a lot* of conflict? Start-ups. My go-to approach to said conflict was to shut down, complain about it to someone else afterward, and become increasingly resentful without telling the person I was experiencing the conflict with how I felt because I didn't want to "hurt anyone's feelings." Then, I'd hope the issue would magically resolve itself if I ignored it long enough. Suffice to say, my approach wasn't . . . ideal.

At one point, I was speaking to a leadership coach about a persistent issue I had with a co-worker. The coach kept urging me to talk to the co-worker directly. Yet whenever I thought about having the conversation, I'd conveniently find a reason why it wasn't the right time: "She's in a bad mood. I don't think she'll be receptive to it right now." "Her dog is sick, and I don't want to add any more stress to her plate." After yet another bogus excuse for not having this conversation, the coach called me out: "Don't you think you're being a little deceitful here?" She may as well have slapped me in the face with a brick. I mean, couldn't she see how incredibly compassionate I was by how well I understood my co-worker's made-up needs?

I said something like "I'm not intentionally being deceitful here. I know how hard this conversation will be, and I don't want to hurt her!"

The coach replied, "You've withheld your truth from this person for months. Even if you feel you have good intentions behind why you've done so, you're still being dishonest and insincere with her by saying one thing to me and something else to her face."

Gulp.

I'd love to say I changed my ways at this point, but shifting lifelong patterns of destructive behavior isn't easy. Who knew? That said, based on this coach's feedback and far too many examples where I could tell my tendency to withhold my truth was holding my leadership back, I committed to *practicing* changing my behavior. I researched healthy conflict approaches and found prompts to help me with challenging conversations, such as "I feel like we might be having different experiences here. I'd love to understand your experience and help you understand mine. Do you have a few minutes to chat?" Once I understood what to do, I started small with people I trusted. The first few times I practiced these conversations, I honestly felt like I was going to puke. But as I got through these conversations, I realized they weren't that bad. I often felt closer to the person I'd talked to as a result of working through the issue together. I felt the difference between letting an issue fester and breed resentment and compassionately addressing a conflict head-on and feeling the tremendous relief of resolution on the other side.

The more comfortable I became with having hard conversations, the more people I was willing to try my fledgling skills with and the stronger I became. I still shied away from some issues or specific people, but I did my best to give myself grace when that happened. It wasn't about perfection; it was about progress. The more progress I made toward releasing this toxic trait, the more my leadership evolved. I could see how I was helping co-workers grow and develop by having hard conversations about ways they were falling short of their potential. Issues I once would have stewed over for months became things I addressed immediately and let go of the same day. Learning to stop withholding my truth and have hard conversations was a game changer for me, professionally and personally.

While I didn't know it at the time, I was engaging with the second practice of holistic leadership: identifying and releasing toxic traits. Toxic traits undermine your leadership, negatively impacting you, those around you, or both. Table 2.2 shows some of the most common toxic leadership traits.

Many of these toxic traits are part of the traditional "masculine" leadership playbook, which is why so many of us have worked for leaders who are aggressive, authoritative, cutthroat, controlling, dominant, exploitative, hypercompetitive, prideful, threatening,

Table 2.2: Toxic Leadership Traits

Abusive	Dominant	Passively aggressive
Accusatory	Exploitative	Perfectionist
Aggressive	Harsh	Prideful
Angry	Hypercompetitive	Resentful
Authoritative	Hyperindependent	Rigid
Arrogant	Indecisive	Risky
Biased	Insincere	Self-sacrificial
Cutthroat	Jealous	Selfish
Controlling	Judgmental	Unemotional
Defensive	Manipulative	Victim mentality
Dishonest	Narcissistic	Vindictive
Disrespectful	Needy	Violent

unemotional, etc. Leaders who express toxic traits like these may feel that they're doing so in the name of driving results, but research has shown that the opposite is true. For example, when leaders control and micromanage others, they decrease employee morale, reduce employee productivity, and are cited as one of the top three reasons employees resign.[12]

While many toxic traits are traditionally considered "masculine" in the business world, the answer isn't to lean solely on "feminine" traits. Some toxic traits are the result of taking "feminine" traits too far as well. As I experienced, taking empathy for others to the extreme can become dishonesty and insincerity. Being compassionate in the absence of boundaries can become self-sacrifice.

All toxic traits—both "masculine" and "feminine" ones—degrade your leadership. Your work is to identify the ones that show up in your life and practice releasing them as much as possible.

Tips for Releasing Toxic Traits

1. Game-Tape Review

Following any conflict, take the time to review what role you played in the issue. And be honest. There's no shame here. Leadership requires growth, not perfection (see "perfectionism" as a toxic trait). You can answer the following questions to help you dig in:

- How might my behavior have contributed to this issue?
- Did I display any toxic traits during this interaction?
- Was there anything I would have done differently as my highest and best self?
- How do I imagine the other people involved in this issue experienced my behavior?

2. Solicit Feedback

Your toxic traits might be in your blind spot. To help you find them, solicit honest feedback from trusted people in your life: friends, co-workers, coaches, therapists, partners—anyone who can help you *honestly* hold up a mirror for yourself in a compassionate way. Of course, you need to make it safe for anyone to give you feedback, meaning avoiding becoming angry, defensive, or resentful about what they reflect back to you. Remember, their feedback is a gift, and they're being brave and generous enough to give it to you. The following prompts may help:

- If there was one thing you wish I did less of, what would it be?
- Do you feel that any of my behaviors are standing in the way of me being my best?
- What's one issue you recommend I address to uplevel my leadership or strengthen our relationship?

3. Seek Professional Guidance

Let's be real here—sometimes addressing toxic traits isn't as simple as identifying them and saying you're going to release them. You might need professional help to work through long-standing patterns of behavior. I sure did. My therapist has been instrumental in my journey toward releasing my toxic traits, as have professional resources (like the ones on healthy conflict resolution that I found online). Seek out thought leaders, therapists, coaches, courses, resource centers, or anything else from experts in the field that can support your journey.

Holistic Leadership Practice #3: Cultivate Balance and Discernment

When Ayla Schlosser, co-founder and former CEO of Resonate, first launched her leadership training program in Kigali, Rwanda, she wanted her team to feel egalitarian. Ayla decided that everyone on her new team would make decisions together. If they were hiring someone new, they had an all-team meeting to talk through the options. Deciding on sales strategy? All-team meeting. Marketing material? All-team meeting.

Within a few months, one of her new teammates pulled Schlosser aside to tell her that the team was struggling. The problem was that the process felt *too* collaborative. Schlosser's team appreciated having their voices heard, and they felt that they lacked direction and couldn't complete their work because they were included in everything.

Schlosser took the feedback to heart. She worked on a concrete vision and presented it to everyone. As a team, they decided which decisions felt large enough that everyone should be involved. They identified other decisions that required only some of the team and clarified which decisions Schlosser should make on her own. This brought a much-needed balance to the organization, which operated much more efficiently from that point forward.

Schlosser's experience highlights the last element of holistic leadership: understanding complementary healthy traits and discerning which traits should be deployed based on the circumstances.

Many of the healthy traits work together to balance one another—the whole yin-yang thing—and can become toxic without that balance. Someone who is driven without being able to be present and attentive to others can become callous or selfish. Or, in Schlosser's case, she needed to balance collaboration with being clear and decisive.

The most adept holistic leaders intentionally do not lean too heavily on any single trait and work to wield complementary traits together as needed to provide a healthy balance. Table 2.3 shows some key complementary healthy traits.

As you cultivate more healthy traits and understand how they work together, your leadership will expand. As it does so, discerning which trait is called for and how healthy traits complement each other will become your superpower. As former leadership coach and Talent to Team Co-CEO Hannah Drain Taylor says, "The best leaders I've ever worked with don't have a default mode. They have tons of tools in their tool belt and can figure out which one they need based on the circumstance, easily switching between traits."

Table 2.3: Examples of Balanced Traits

Adaptable and Focused	Creative and Clear
Analytical and Creative	Direct and Nurturing
Ambitious and Generous	Honest and Caring
Attentive and Driven	Passionate and Strategic
Collaborative and Decisive	Logical and Intuitive
Confident and Humble	Flexible and Stable

Tips for Cultivating Balancing Traits

1. Identify the Yin to Your Yang

Review the list of healthy traits and write down the ones that you feel you regularly lean on. Once you've done so, review each one and write down any traits you think complement your healthy traits. The simple process of doing so will help you be more aware of any imbalance in your leadership, especially when you identify a balancing trait that you don't feel comfortable wielding yet.

2. Monthly Review

Building on the first tip from practice #1, at the end of each week, write down as many instances you can think of where you expressed a healthy trait. Review your notes at the end of the month to see whether certain traits show up more than others. If so, do you see any instances where you also expressed the balancing trait? Simply being aware of this dynamic will help you be more conscious of any unintentional imbalance in your approach.

WITH AN ESTIMATED 70 PERCENT OF PEOPLE SAYING THEIR MANager has as much of an impact on their mental health as their spouse does, it's more important than ever that all of us are intentional about how we show up in the workplace.[13] Fortunately, the pioneering leaders who've come before us have shown us that holistic leadership is not only more effective but reduces harm—to those working with a leader and to the leader themself. Additionally, the holistic leadership approach helps break down some anti-"feminine" leadership beliefs that hold women back. Each time you effectively wield "feminine" traits with your team, you demonstrate their power and chisel away at ingrained toxically masculine beliefs that anything "feminine" doesn't belong in the workplace. Every day, your words, energy, and actions impact the people around you. It's up to you what impact you want to make and what kind of leader you want to be.

Key Chapter Insights

- The traditional leadership playbook, centered solely on both healthy and toxic "masculine" traits, is not the most effective leadership approach. Many of the toxic "masculine" traits commonly accepted in the business world actually harm organizations by reducing collaboration, decreasing employee satisfaction and desire to help, and increasing employee turnover.
- A holistic leadership approach blending numerous healthy "masculine" and "feminine" traits has been proven to be far more effective, driving better employee engagement and retention; decreasing the likelihood of burnout; increasing employees' feeling of thriving outside work; building more trust with the team; and increasing innovation, creativity, and team member growth.
- Holistic leaders strive to avoid toxic traits as much as possible. They can discern which healthy traits complement each other and which are needed based on circumstances, never relying too much on one trait over another.

Chapter 3

FROM ASSIMILATED LEADERSHIP TO AUTHENTIC LEADERSHIP

IN 2015, I WAS INVITED TO AN INVITATION-ONLY EVENT FOR CEOs. Before the event, I looked at the attendee lookbook and noticed that about 80 percent of the 250 attendees were men. As a young, first-time CEO, I immediately started doubting myself. Maybe you've experienced something similar. You're heading into a room where very few people reflect your experience, so you start questioning *everything*: How should I dress? What should I talk about? Should I prepare something in advance? What if someone says something offensive? Will anyone take me seriously?

I'd never been in a room with hundreds of successful male CEOs. I imagined everyone wearing expensive suits with cigars dangling from their lips as they compared financial returns and sports highlights. So I did my best to follow suit—literally. I showed up in an ill-fitting gray power suit and attempted to pulverize every man's metacarpal bone with my handshake. I brought our recent capital raise into every conversation and threw business cards out like it was Mardi Gras. If I discovered that I was talking to someone who wasn't a potential revenue opportunity, I excused myself to try to find someone who was.

I left the two-day event with no new sales and felt confused and embarrassed as I made my way to the airport. I'd played the part perfectly, dressing professionally, projecting confidence, and talking financials. I'd shown everyone I was a "serious" businessperson. Yet it wasn't enough. *I* wasn't enough. Deep down, some part of me wondered if I ever would be. I was experiencing the trap of assimilated leadership.

The Traditional Playbook: Assimilated Leadership

When Kathy Bolhous, CEO of Charter Next Generation (CNG), started her career forty years ago, she was the first woman in her role at her company. So she was thrilled when her boss asked her to join a colleague for a sales trip to Detroit to meet with one of their biggest clients. Bolhous prepared for the big meeting and traveled to the Motor City. Her colleague made dinner reservations for the client meeting, but there was one small problem: the restaurant didn't allow women. Her colleague went to the meeting while she stayed in the car for more than two hours. She says, "I wish I could say I spoke up for myself, but I had to fit in. If you made a big deal about anything, they would make sure you didn't succeed. It was assimilate or die. So I sat in the car and behaved. I couldn't give them any reason to go against me."

As Bolhous experienced, with women being excluded from business for the first *three thousand* years, when we began entering the workforce in earnest in the last fifty years, we were the minority group entering a dominant culture. To have any chance of success, we had to assimilate, meaning adopting the well-established norms, values, and beliefs created by the dominant group to "prove" ourselves. At this point, business culture revolved around men—its dominant group—and these men had firmly entrenched patriarchal and toxically masculine beliefs in the business world. So we tried our best to conform to these norms. We changed how we dressed, spoke, and behaved to be more like men while never rocking the boat or doing anything that highlighted our differences or angered men in hopes of being accepted. Fifty years later, we often still feel this pressure.

Stephanie Nadi Olson, founder of We Are Rosie, says, "I think I've bent, flexed, and thwarted myself into all sorts of knots and shapes to try to conform and assimilate in the business world. It's dehumanizing. It chips away at your soul little by little. I even pretended I didn't have children at one point because I didn't want to be penalized, have people expect less from me, or exclude me because I was a mom." Founder and former CEO of MontiKids Zahra Kassam says, "I often felt like I was dressing up because I felt like I had to play a role. Instead of coming into my power, I was trying on leadership models I'd seen in the past." Like Kassam and Nadi Olson, many of us feel pressured to change ourselves at work. In the name of "success," we conform, hide, placate, hold back, compromise, appease, defer, and still . . . it's never enough. It's also traumatizing.

Last year, I hosted a women's CEO retreat with leaders of companies backed by private equity groups, including Bolhous. Many women in attendance were in their fifties and sixties and had been the first women in their industry, role, or office when they started their careers. I asked them what it was like to pave the way for many of us. One woman said through a stifled sob, "They went out of their way to actively humiliate us," and then couldn't go on. Bolhous told us she can still barely think about that time, given how traumatic it was for her. The amount of unprocessed trauma still lingering a full thirty to forty years later was heartbreaking. These women's experiences track with research finding that the trauma of assimilation leads directly to depression, loss of identity, and mental illness.[1]

Dr. Gabor Maté and Daniel Maté's research helps explain why assimilation is so traumatizing. We all have two essential core needs: attachment and authenticity. We all crave attachment, meaning a sense of belonging and acceptance, and we crave authenticity, meaning being true to ourselves. Assimilation, then, is a clash between two of our fundamental needs. We can either change ourselves to try to belong or stay true to ourselves and be excluded. Either way, we suffer. Even worse, many working women abandon their true selves in an attempt to fit in and are *still* excluded from the "boys' club."

When we change ourselves to try to fit in, the Matés found, "the suppression of individual authenticity plays havoc with biology, breeding illness; even greater mayhem will ensue for bodies belonging to groups whose self-suppression has been systemically imposed, often with great violence."[2] For working women, self-suppression is constantly systemically imposed. For women with multiple marginalized identities—women of color, queer women, women with different abilities—this is even more true.

Government and community consultant VaShone Huff speaks of this dynamic: "For a Black woman to achieve marked success in the corporate arena usually means that we have to be stripped of any semblance of our Blackness as well." Founder and CEO of Tribal Good Twanna Harris says, "At the end of the day, you're exhausted, you're worn out. You're in the car in tears because that's the one time throughout the day that you were actually able to lift the mask and breathe. You have to wear this person and suppress your emotions to, in my opinion, a very unhealthy state all day long."

So while some point to the increasing numbers of women entering the workforce—from 38 to 58 percent between 1960 and the present—as proof that present-day business has become more balanced, our forced assimilation means that women often don't provide a balancing force. Some women even end up *over*assimilating. They take "masculine" business norms to the extreme to try to prove themselves, pushing the imbalance even further. This is why we hear of women who are "worse than the men." Women such as restaurateur Barbara Lynch, who was filmed threatening to shove one of her employees' heads through a window, or Away co-founder Stephanie Korey, who was accused of bullying employees via Slack and building a toxic, cutthroat culture.[3] It doesn't excuse these women's behavior, but it might help us understand why they've felt the need to behave this way. It's what they thought they had to do to survive and succeed.

To see assimilation in action, take a look at many of the most popular business books written by women in the last decade that echo a familiar sentiment: the way women are supposed to succeed in business is by adopting toxically masculine traits (see "smash," "break," "dominate," "power," and "kill," which are all actual words on the covers of popular women's business books) and accruing as much money and power as possible. Oh, and they need to be as attractive and "feminine" as possible while doing so. Notice all the pink covers, the stilettos, or the common use of the word "girl"? You can actually see the dueling pressures imposed on women by business and society on some of these covers, and this pressure is everywhere we look—books, magazines, television, social media. Thought leader Akaya Windwood says of this constant pressure, "As business leaders, we're constantly pulled back by the expectations of patriarchy. It's almost like gravity."

Genuine, authentic leadership is being called for in place of this assimilated version of leadership.

The New Playbook: Authentic Leadership

In 2016, I was invited to speak at a conference on a small island off the coast of Canada. I arrived and discovered that I didn't know anyone. I awkwardly stood alone as the conference opened outside on a large grassy area. Just as I started to feel like the middle school girl eating lunch by herself, I heard a powerful voice begin singing, "Birds flying high, you know how I feel. Sun in the sky, you know how I feel. . . . " I watched, dumbstruck, as a gorgeous, larger-than-life woman rocking a pompadour-mohawk-esque hairstyle, flowing pink dress, and gigantic gold earrings walked to the front of the group and belted out Nina Simone's classic "Feeling Good." Two thoughts hit me at once: (1) *Who is this queen? I need to be her best friend,* and (2) *Did no one tell this poor soul this is a business conference? Like, there are* CEOs *here!*

Assuming that she was the performer brought in to open the conference, I told myself it was fine that she wasn't buttoned-up and "professional." But then she stopped singing and introduced herself as Jocelyn Macdougall, our host and facilitator for the event. Wait, what? This woman who'd just sung in front of us all by herself, the one wearing Birkenstocks, was going to be our facilitator? Didn't she know the rules?! Did the organizers give her permission to show up like this?

Over the next three days, I watched Jocelyn endear herself to every attendee there without donning a single heel or suit jacket. She expertly facilitated the event with a level of grace I'd never seen before. She held challenging conversations with levity, spoke openly of her wife and her experiences in the queer community, and cracked jokes that made the entire audience laugh. She spoke her truth and built a space where all of us felt brave. There was no denying that Jocelyn showed up as her authentic self. I was enamored and, honestly, a little envious. Why was she allowed to be her true self while the rest of us were forced to hide behind masks of conformity to succeed? How did she find the courage to be so . . . herself?

The next year, when I had the idea to create a women's conference for business leaders to talk about the real stuff—failure, mental health, pressure and expectation, funding support, and more—I knew just whom to call.

Jocelyn agreed to help me design and facilitate this new event, the World-Changing Women's Summit. In doing so, I gained inside perspective on what made Jocelyn tick. When I wanted to shy away from something because I felt we "shouldn't," Jocelyn encouraged me to reexamine why I felt that way. In one case, we had a panel with women who'd contended with serious challenges such as having their business close or being on the receiving end of online hatred. We wanted to show that it's possible to face adversity like this and find success on the other side. As we talked to the panelists before the event, many of them told us they didn't know if they could talk about the traumatic event without crying. Following the call, I asked Jocelyn if we should just scrap the panel, worried that panelists openly crying onstage would be viewed as "unprofessional" and undermine our credibility. Jocelyn listened to my concerns and then asked me what I hoped our attendees would get out of the event. "Well, I guess I want to have a space for women leaders to connect around the real issues—somewhere these women don't feel alone and can let their guard down." As the words came out of my mouth, I realized the point she was making. We couldn't build a new type of space for women to feel brave and seen by doing things the assimilated way. We had to do things differently. We moved forward with that session as well as many other topics that pushed the boundaries, and the results were astounding. Women admitted things onstage they'd never said aloud before. One attendee was so moved by a session that she decided to ask her husband for a divorce. Women met at that event and started businesses together. It was an absolute dream. Attendee Andrea Walker from Beneficial State Bank described the event as follows: "For the first time in my life, I felt comfortable in a room full of women I didn't know, to be brutally honest and open. It was a pivotal moment for me that I'll never forget and has propelled me into action."

This experience showed me how powerful it is when someone shows up in their full authenticity, but it's worth mentioning that Jocelyn isn't some magical being who has always felt comfortable in her skin. She intentionally cultivated her authentic leadership: "Earlier in my professional life, I worked at a very fancy-dancy executive recruiting firm. I wore a pencil skirt and kitten heels every day, which is the furthest anyone who knows me now can imagine that I would ever be." Of her progression toward showing up more authentically, she says, "I started with little experiments and would gauge the feedback. I noticed that the more vulnerable and authentic I was with groups, the more positive the response would be. There were definitely times that required courage, but every time I received positive feedback, it gave me permission to take just one more step toward more authenticity or vulnerability. At some point, I was no longer doing it from a place of courage; I was doing it from a place of conviction because I had so much data that showed my authentic approach works."

Jocelyn's data highlights the beauty of authentic leadership: not only does it feel good to show up authentically, but it genuinely enhances your leadership. Research has shown that team members who work with authentic leaders have a greater emotional attachment to their organization and produce better results. Authentic leaders increase their employees' positive emotions, which encourages employees to explore new ideas, develop their potential, and discover fresh information, all of which increase their overall creativity and ability to innovate.[4]

Every woman I'd met who was thriving and inspired me to imagine a better way of doing business was authentic. She'd moved beyond societal expectations to cultivate her own unique way of showing up as her highest and best self that made her feel inspired and alive. So, a little to my disappointment, I'm not advocating streaking through your office while burning your employee handbook en route to your boss's office to unload the pent-up rage you've been harboring for seven years because that feels "authentic." We're talking about something deeper—leaning into the *best* version of you.

While it's easy to spot authentic leadership, it might feel harder to actually articulate it so that you can practice it yourself. This is because authenticity is personal; it's being true to yourself. Given the personal nature of authenticity, I can't prescribe a precise formula that will resonate with everyone. That said, there are common elements that I've experienced with every authentic leader I know.

As Table 3.1 shows, authentic leaders strive to consistently lean into their values, honor their truth, question the norm, respond to circumstances in alignment with the highest version of who they *are* and *aspire* to be, and seek environments where they can flourish.

Table 3.1: Assimilated Leadership vs. Authentic Leadership

	Assimilated Leadership	**Authentic Leadership**
Values	Guided by what others value, appearances, and others' definition of success	Guided by their own values, the impact they hope to have on the world, and their personal definition of success
Truth	Hold back their truth in fear of judgment from others, regularly deferring to others	Honor the worth of their personal experience and speak their truth regardless of who's in the room
Status Quo	Comply, obey, and do things the way they've always been done	Regularly question their actions and the status quo, especially when something doesn't feel right
Emotional Regulation	Operate on autopilot, reacting to situations with little to no self-awareness	Self-aware enough to regulate emotions and respond intentionally
Environment	Settle for working in environments and with people who don't align with their values	Seek environments and people whose values align with their own

Let's look at how to cultivate authentic leadership in your own work.

Authentic Leadership Practice #1: Identify and Lead from Your Values

Growing up in Hawaii, Steph Speirs watched her single mother try to support three kids as an immigrant working jobs that paid below the poverty line. After she landed a scholarship to a prestigious private school where she studied alongside kids from wealthy families, her perspective on poverty changed. She realized that the only difference between her and the other students was access to opportunity.

Later in life, Speirs became the co-founder and CEO of Solstice Energy, and her formative experience in a low-income community informed her values. As the business grew, she insisted that at least half of their customers come from low-income communities. She didn't want renewable energy to be accessible only to the wealthy. With Speirs's vision, Solstice Energy became one of the few providers in the country that catered to low-income communities.

Eventually, the company needed to fundraise to support its growth. During Speirs's investment pitches, numerous potential investors told her that the low-income market wouldn't be big enough or would be unreliable. Some investors went so far as to tell her they'd invest only if she abandoned her commitment to low-income customers. Speirs held strongly to her values, even if it meant walking away from potential investors. While fundraising was an uphill battle, she was able to scrape enough capital together from investors who truly believed in her story and her values.

In 2022, Speirs's dedication to her values paid off. The US government passed the largest climate bill in its history, and, wouldn't you know it, part of the bill mandated the inclusion of low-income communities. Overnight, the energy industry began focusing on serving this market because it now received tax benefits for doing so. Speirs's company was one of *three* in the entire country that already had a track record of working with low-income communities in the community solar space. She says, "For years, working with low-income customers was perceived by many as our weakness because we were so stubborn about it. So much so that we became known for it, and then it became our strength." Speirs's steadfast commitment to her values resulted in the company growing at seven times its previous growth rates and ended in her company being acquired in October 2022.

Speirs's story illustrates how values help you stay rooted in your authenticity, a topic that came up at a women's leadership workshop that we hosted in 2022. As woman after woman detailed the numerous pressures in life—caregiving for an elderly father, supporting a child with special needs, crippling financial stress because a partner had been laid off, HR issues with their teams, navigating divorce—I had the strangest vision in my head. I pictured one of those wind-sock people outside car dealerships. You know, those inflatable dancing-tube things that flail around to grab your attention? I realized that each of us is like one of these flailing people. All the challenges and pressure we face—the societal expectations, family responsibilities, workplace stress—are akin to constant sixty-mile-per-hour gusts blowing us all over the place. While we thrash around in every direction trying to keep up, the only thing tethering us to the ground are the sandbags we're tied to. These sandbags are our values. If you're disconnected from your values, you're at the mercy of the winds. And for women, the winds are *fierce*.

When we talk about values, we're looking at the personal beliefs and principles you hold sacred and aspire to. Your nonnegotiables. Having clarity about your values is critical to authentic leadership. Co-founder and co-CEO of EO Products Susan Griffin-Black says, "You have to know what your values are. You have to know what the deal-breakers are, and you have to be able to express that in a business setting where the rules can be different than what your values are. If you hold your values as most important, then there's guidance into what is the next right thing. And the next right thing isn't necessarily making the most amount of money, overworking people, making twenty times from the bottom, or any of those sorts of evil tendencies." Libby Rodney, chief strategy officer of research firm the Harris Poll, finds, "Of all the research I've done on authenticity, the values you commit to from a long-term point of view are what establish authenticity."

For example, authentic leader Jane Wurwand, co-founder and chief visionary of Dermalogica, used her values to help her decide whom to sell her hugely successful brand to after thirty years. She had tons of interested parties, so she asked all of them to pitch her and her co-founder and husband, Raymond. Unbeknownst to their potential suitors, Wurwand was looking for values alignment.

Raised by a single mother in a working-class family in the United Kingdom, Wurwand values creating opportunities for others, building meaningful connections, and having a purpose that goes far beyond just making money. She was determined to find a parent company that shared a similar ethos for her beloved company. One party flew the Wurwands on a private jet to New York, took them to an exclusive restaurant, and tried to entice them with the promise of luxury. Another brought them to the prospective purchaser's office and had a huge team try to win them over with the company's size and scale. Presentation after presentation, yet none of the interested parties resonated with Wurwand's values. Then Paul Polman from Unilever showed up.

Polman flew to LA, took a Lyft to Dermalogica's headquarters outside the city, and asked to have a brown-bag lunch in the company cafeteria. He asked the Wurwands about their purpose, their family, and their dreams. He spoke openly about his life and his vision for Unilever centered on sustainability. He walked around the Dermalogica offices and met the employees, talking to people of all levels. Wurwand instantly knew that Polman and the Unilever team were the right choice. The deal was made later that year.

For much of my career, I felt that I knew what my values were somewhere in the back of my mind, but I wouldn't have been able to clearly articulate them. You might feel the same way. Fear not: getting clarity on your values simply requires a bit of intention.

Tips for Leading from Your Values

1. Get Clear on Your Values

Of course, the first tip for leading from your values is ensuring that you're clear on what your values are. If you feel clear on your values, write them down, trying to limit your list to five values or fewer. If you need help articulating your values, reflect on the following:

- How do you hope to be remembered?
- What characteristics do you hope others use to describe you when you're not in the room?
- What traits are you expressing when you feel that you're the highest and best version of yourself?
- What qualities do you *aspire* to embody as you move through the world?

Review your answers to these prompts and reflect on the characteristics with which you most want to align your actions, words, behavior, decisions, and life. Write down everything that comes up and then work to distill your list to five values or fewer that feel most important to you. If you need help further articulating your values, you can find worksheets and exercises on this book's website.

2. Make a Reference Sheet

Keep your list of values somewhere that you easily can see and reference it. Kathy Bolhous keeps hers on her phone. Ayla Schlosser has hers on a spreadsheet on her computer. I've printed mine out and have them on the wall by my desk. Use whatever medium works best for you; the important part is that your values are written down somewhere you can easily access and see them regularly.

3. Do a Weekly High/Low Check-In

At the end of each week, either in a notebook or with a friend or partner, review your values and reflect on any time during the week that you feel you embodied one of your values (your high) and/or any time you didn't (your low). You don't need to go through all of your values. Simply finding one example where you either did well or fell short will help you embed your values further in your consciousness. I recommend recording your answers somewhere to review them and look for patterns or potential blind spots. Is there one value that you consistently ignore? Is there a value that you have a hard time tapping into? If you're regularly embodying some of your values but not all of them, why?

4. Values Alignment Check-In

Last year, I found myself having dinner with three men at a business conference. Not only was I the only woman at the table and much younger than everyone else, but I realized that they'd all served on the board of a large organization and had worked together for years. I felt myself shrinking as the outsider. I took a breath and reflected on my values: love, impact, exploration, joy, and connection. By doing so, I became curious about what brought these men joy and asked the group, "What are some of the things that made you feel happiest this year?" This question changed the entire dynamic. Instead of talking *around* me, these men started talking *to* me. They lit up as they spoke of their wives, their kid's wedding, travel, grandchildren, creating art, and working at nonprofits. At the end of the conversation, I felt a genuine connection to these men that I hadn't felt before, all because my values had helped center me in who I am and aspire to be.

Before heading into significant meetings, presentations, events, or even one-on-one conversations, review your values and reflect on how they could guide you in this interaction. What would it look like to lean into your values in this situation? Is there one value you want to focus on specifically?

Authentic Leadership Practice #2: Honor Your Truth

In 2019, while working as the CEO of Conscious Company Media, I had the idea to build a women's platform across the other three brands owned by our parent company. We could create events and content together, reaching a much larger audience of women among all four brands than any of our companies could reach alone. One of the male executives of our parent company loved the idea. He told me he had a top-notch marketing contact who'd worked with big-name people who could mock up a deck for us that would draw tons of sponsorship interest. He said it would be expensive but worth it. I was stoked. Not only was my idea getting traction, but they were going to invest significant company resources to get it off the ground.

A few weeks later, our whole team met virtually with the fancy marketing team to see the deck they'd created. It was really . . . something. As they walked us through the deck, I was bombarded by stock images of famous actresses we had no connection to, hot-pink frilly text, and clichés about "girl power" and "boss babes." The marketing team promised that this campaign was going to be huge! My boss was thrilled, and it seemed like many other people on our team were, too. I, on the other hand, hated it. It went against everything I imagined this platform could be. It felt shallow, cliché, and patronizing, like a presentation created by men based on what they thought women wanted—not something that would resonate with women at all.

However, as I saw how excited everyone else was, I felt that I must be missing something. I mean, this big muckety-muck marketing guru was confident that this campaign would succeed. What did I know? I also felt guilty. We'd spent tons of money on this thing, and it was my idea! I couldn't tell them it was garbage, right? I convinced myself that I was probably wrong here. I didn't want to cause conflict, so I held my tongue.

We moved forward with the deck. Since I didn't feel that I could stand behind it, I told my boss that the marketing team seemed to have a handle on things and could run with it from there. And wouldn't you know, not one of the corporate sponsors they had promised came through. We invested more than $25,000 in my idea only to watch it die a quick, painful death, and my boss was *pissed*. He asked me to do a postmortem with him on why it had fallen apart. As we walked through the experience, I admitted that

I'd hated the deck and hadn't thought it would work. He replied, "Well, why didn't you say something?" I didn't know what to say. In truth, I hadn't said something because I'd convinced myself that I was wrong and hadn't felt that my opinion was as valuable as those of others in the room. My perspective didn't feel worth the potential conflict, and I didn't want to hurt anyone's feelings.

By this point in my career, I'd already seen the consequences of stifling my truth, but I hadn't realized the deeper implications of my actions: every time I withheld my truth because I doubted my value, I dishonored myself. The same is true for you.

When you tell yourself that your voice doesn't matter as much as others' voices and hold back your truth, you deprive us all of the gifts only *you* can contribute to this world—the gifts you have because of every ancestor who persevered before you, every person whose shoulders you stand on who paved the way for you, the people who gave you life, and the people who've supported your journey. All the things that had to align in the history of the universe for you to exist in this exact moment are staggering. Everything you've endured, overcome, contributed, created, learned, loved, lost, and experienced has resulted in the unique miracle that is . . . you. Whenever you doubt your truth, you don't honor all you are. *This* is why honoring your voice matters.

One of the most authentic leaders I've ever met, Alfa Demmellash, co-founder and CEO of Rising Tide Capital, says that every time she walks into a room, she asks herself, "Why am I here? What is uniquely mine to contribute? What could I say, think, or feel in this moment that is as unique as I am? What is it about me being here in this time, in this body, in this moment that could contribute and not be driven by external noise?"

Authentic leaders like Demmellash are honest, transparent, and vulnerable enough to share their truth, even in the face of potential judgment, conflict, or discomfort. Research has shown that this is a critical aspect of authentic leadership, specifically finding that leaders who have personal moral standards (read: values) and who are transparent about their actions and interactions create a more positive, appealing, and supportive organizational culture.[5] And sweet cheese and crackers, I'll be the first to say this is easier said than done. If you struggle with this, too, you're not alone. There's nothing wrong with you. This is just how we've been trained as women.

Growing up in a patriarchal society means learning from a young age that our contributions are worth *less* than men's and that we're secondary. We're trained to prioritize everyone else's comfort over our feelings and do what needs to be done to avoid conflict. At some point, we begin to feel that sharing our opinions isn't worth it, isn't welcome, or will cause more harm than good. We grow up questioning whether every action we take is okay. Then we enter the workforce, and we're interrupted, ignored, talked over, doubted, paid less, passed over for promotions, and excluded from leadership. In response to the constant trauma, we shrink, hold back, and doubt our value.

But here's the thing: your perspective is as valuable as everyone else's in the room. I don't care what their title is, where they went to school, how much experience they have, what their track record is, or how much money they make. Your truth is equally valuable. Is there any part of you that can accept that? Does it even compute? How about if I say every time you offer your ideas, even if they make others uncomfortable, you're enriching the conversation and benefiting everyone by gifting them with a different perspective to consider? How does that sit with you? Because it's all true. Let me show you what this can look like in practice.

In 2019, I was still the CEO of Conscious Company Media. VaShone Huff, founder of MSC Strategies, was hired by our company's sister company to support its major annual event called SOCAP. VaShone jokingly says, "Everybody knew me because I was one of the only Black people on the team. I was kind of SOCAP famous."

As VaShone and I got to know each other better, I told her a bit about our team's upcoming 250-person World-Changing Women's

Summit. As we discussed the program for the event, VaShone says she was thinking, "Oftentimes, my most challenging relationships in work have been with white women. I wanted to explore this more because I feel like we're actually more in the same boat as women, and it felt really important to me."

VaShone typically doesn't struggle with speaking her truth. That said, throughout her career, she'd found that the powers that be often wouldn't take her contributions seriously. "I'd bring something to the table, and they'd say, 'I'm going to think about it.' And then every time I'd see them again, they'd just keep saying, 'Oh, VaShone, I'm still thinking about it,' but they'd never follow through. That happened all the time." Despite these previous experiences of having her ideas repeatedly ignored, VaShone pitched me a concept for our event: "I think you should consider a session about the experience of women of color in the workplace and how it's different than white women's experience. You have a really powerful platform with this event and could do something important with it. We need to start having honest conversations like these so all women can rise together, not just white women." I told VaShone I loved the idea and wanted to think it over with my team. My team loved it, too, and I called VaShone the next day to say, "Let's do it! Would you consider working with us to bring it to life?" She accepted and joined the program team for the event. We spent a full day of our event digging into the conversation she'd suggested with women from around the world. *All* of us benefited from VaShone's truth.

While honoring your truth benefits those around you, it can benefit you in unexpected ways as well. In 2019, Khalila "K.O." Olukunola, founder and impact architect of ReEngineering HR, experienced a profound ripple effect of honoring her truth. She'd just given a presentation at the Women's Venture Fund when a man named George Taylor approached her. Taylor was opening a brewery to employ active rival gang members in Wilmington, NC, hoping that providing these young men with a stable income and having them work together would curb gang violence in his community.

Taylor was looking for people who'd successfully turned their lives around to come talk to his new employees about second chances. Olukunola told him about a young woman she knew who'd been kicked out of the house at age thirteen by a father who was struggling with alcoholism. To avoid homelessness, she moved in with cousins who sold drugs to support themselves and began selling them herself. Eventually, she was arrested and spent more than four years in prison. Upon her release, she got second-chance employment at Sprint, worked her way up to owning her own successful event-planning company, and was now happily married and living the life she'd once dreamed of. Taylor said, "I have to meet this woman! Can you make an introduction?" In the pause that followed, Olukunola made a decision that would change her life. See, this story was hers. But as a community leader and successful business owner, she'd hidden it from everyone in her professional life for more than a decade. She was ashamed and worried that people might not want to do business with her if they knew about her past.

Amid these concerns, Olukunola reflected on a promise she'd made to herself while incarcerated that she'd impact the lives of people who'd had experiences like hers when she was released. "In that moment, my whole journey came in front of me. Something in me said, 'Remember what you said.' I realized that this purpose was more important than my pride." She took a breath and told Taylor, "That young woman was me." Taylor was blown away by her truth and invited Olukunola to speak to his new employees. She accepted his offer, and the men were so engaged by her presentation that Taylor approached Olukunola afterward to offer her a contract to help build the culture at TRU Colors Brewery. Over time, the contract turned into a full-time role as chief culture officer for the brewery.

Her decision to finally honor her truth changed the trajectory of her life. Olukunola reflects, "Your story is what's going to get people to buy into you. You are at your most powerful place when you are in your most authentic voice." Honoring your truth, which often means being vulnerable, helps you step fully into your power. It's nearly impossible to be authentic if you're hiding things, holding back, or carrying around loads of shame. Cultivating authentic leadership means doing the work necessary to feel comfortable in your own skin—to value your experience regardless of who else is in the room and offer it freely, knowing that it benefits you and those around you.

Tips for Honoring Your Truth

1. Align Your Truth with Your Values

From time to time as I wrote this book, I'd find myself getting pretty angry about the whole patriarchy situation. During one such time, I happened to be attending a business conference chock-full of successful men. I arrived pretty much determined to single-handedly eradicate patriarchy by "calling out" any man who even breathed a whisper of patriarchal beliefs. Let's just say I got a *wee* bit feisty speaking my "truth" to several men at this event. However, after the event, I didn't feel great about my behavior.

As I reflected on *why* I didn't feel great, I realized two things: (1) I wasn't offering my truth in a way that aligned with my values, and (2) people can't hear your truth if you're calling them out in a way that intentionally shames or belittles them. Technically, I was being honest, but authentic leaders strive to deliver their truth as their highest and best self. Carter Stepanovsky, director of service delivery at Salesloft, focuses on "calling people in" instead of "calling people out" to root in their values when having tough conversations.

When it comes to honoring your truth, strive to say what needs to be said from a place of dignity and grace that aligns with your values. It will lead to better outcomes, and all parties involved will feel better.

2. Identify Your Voice and Unique Contribution

One challenge of honoring your voice is deciphering what's truly *your* voice versus the voices of others that might be holding you back.

Author and thought leader Akaya Windwood says of this dynamic, "As a Black person, the world told me I didn't know the real rules of the game. That as a person who was raised working class, I didn't understand what the people who went to Harvard and Yale understood. That as a woman, I should be nice and not stir the water, right? At the time, I thought those were my voices. Over time, I came to understand that those were the voices of oppression I inherited that actually aren't true. It took me into my thirties until I went, 'No, wait a minute, that's bullshit. That's not my voice. That's the voice that I got taught due to where I live, my communities, and the world I'm in.' It's an important developmental moment when, particularly as women, we go, 'Oh, that's not my voice. My voice sounds like this.'"

To help you find your voice, when you're entering a room or communicating with others, ask yourself the same questions Demmellash uses to find her voice:

- What is uniquely mine to contribute?
- What could I say, think, or feel in this moment that's as unique as I am?
- What is it about me being here in this time, in this body, in this moment that could contribute and not be driven by external noise?

3. Look for Red Flags

Anytime you find yourself thinking any of the following, it might be a sign that you're holding back your truth. Notice these red flags and practice holding yourself accountable for changing your behavior if needed.

- **Doubting Your Contribution:** If you notice yourself thinking anything along the lines of "I'm sure this is a stupid idea/question," "I'm sure someone has already thought of this," or "I'm sure I'm wrong," take a breath and practice leaning into your truth and believing in its value.

- **Talking *About* Someone:** Anytime you find yourself complaining *about* someone or something behind someone's back, it's a signal that you're not honoring your truth. Every time you speak your truth to someone whom you're uncomfortable sharing with, your ability to consistently honor your voice grows.
- **Comparison:** Are there certain rooms or people you tend to shut down in front of? You're likely comparing yourself to someone, convincing yourself that for some reason, your perspective isn't as valuable as theirs. Try to remember that your voice is as valuable as every other person's, regardless of who's in the room.

Authentic Leadership Practice #3: Question the Norm

When Deepa Purushothaman began her career at Deloitte in 2002, of the incoming cohort of seven hundred senior consultants, she was three to four years younger than everyone else and the only one who didn't have an MBA. Instead of defaulting to the norm and feeling that she needed to try to assimilate on account of her differences, she says, "I felt so out of place, but it turned out to be a gift. There was no way I was going to fit in, so I just didn't even try."

From the start, she wondered whether she could succeed without molding herself to what was expected. So when she saw her peers refusing to ask for help on hard assignments, Purushothaman did the unexpected and openly asked for help. Anytime she had an assignment that was outside her area of expertise, she sought out someone on the team—often a firm partner—who had deep knowledge of the issue to teach her more about it. Her work stood out as a result. She was multifaceted and had a deeper knowledge base than her peers because she'd spent so much time learning different approaches from those around her. She'd also built connections with her colleagues from whom she'd learned in person.

Purushothoman's decision to deviate from the norm came full circle years later when she was asked to present to become a partner. Because she'd spent so much time learning from the senior partners, unlike most of the other candidates, who were meeting the senior partners who'd decide their fate for the first time, Purushothaman had already built solid relationships with everyone. She crushed the final presentation and soon became one of the youngest partners in Deloitte's history.

Purushothaman's story illustrates what it looks like to question the norm. By refusing to conform to the status quo of her peers and admitting that she didn't know everything, she differentiated herself. While questioning the norm can set you apart, it can also unlock new ideas and innovation, something Melanie Dulbecco, CEO of Torani, has discovered time and again.

While the status quo dictates that there's a very specific playbook Dulbecco should use to run her multimillion-dollar flavored-syrup enterprise, she's found success doing just the opposite. As an authentic leader, Dulbecco regularly questions the way things have "always been done." This practice has led to myriad new ideas that have set her company apart. In one instance, her team was working with a big-name consulting firm to create new compensation plans. The consulting firm presented Dulbecco with their proposal based on current market rates. They told her that compensation for her hourly workers was fine and shouldn't be adjusted but that her executives were making less than the market and should be paid more. Dulbecco replied, "What if the market is immoral? What if we want to think about how to create more opportunities for our hourly people, who often don't have the same opportunities as the rest of us?"

The consultants were shocked. They ended up creating a compensation plan entirely different than that of the market. Torani pays above market rate to hourly workers, market rate to managers, and below market rate to executives and provides *everyone* with a suite of benefits, bonuses, and profit distribution. The result? The company has steadily grown by 20 percent every year for nearly thirty years.

Dulbecco is now regularly asked to present at business conferences worldwide about strategies such as this and many others that she and her team have developed simply by forging a path that deviates from the norm.

While many of us have been told to follow the rules, not rock the boat, and just do as we're told on our path toward success, conforming to the status quo without question can hold you back from great leadership. When following the crowd means stifling your truth, compromising your values, or holding your true self back, you'll never be able to fully step into your authentic power.

Tips for Questioning the Norm

1. Seek Your Own Guidance

When you're doing something that you feel you need guidance on, before looking at examples of how everyone else does it, try exploring how *you* would do it. For example, many people have told me that I need to create a website for this book. Initially, I was tempted to review a bunch of other author's websites to try to emulate them, but in the spirit of walking the talk, I paused before doing so and wrote down what felt most important to me when it came to my website before being influenced by looking at anyone else's. This isn't to say that seeking inspiration and insights from others is bad. The practice is to connect with yourself to explore how you would do something to see what comes up that's authentic to you before you look at anyone else's version.

2. Look for Red Flags

Any of the following statements might signal that you're leaning more toward assimilated leadership than toward authentic leadership for fear of doing things differently:

- "This is how things have always been done around here."
- "This is how everyone else is doing it."

- "*I should . . .*"
- "Conventional wisdom dictates . . ."

Authentic Leadership Practice #4: Cultivate Emotional Regulation

On October 25, 2023, founder and CEO of Smitten Ice Cream Robyn Sue Fisher awoke to a phone call from police at 3:00 a.m. alerting her that one of her stores had been broken into. Fisher arrived to find the entire shop destroyed and spray-painted with anti-Semitic messages and the words "FREE PALESTIEN" misspelled on the front of the shop, even though Fisher had never publicly spoken about her Jewish identity. Fisher was heartbroken.

The media quickly picked up the story, and Fisher was thrust into the spotlight as the voice of the Jewish community in the wake of the escalating conflict between Israel and Palestine that had begun earlier in the month. Soon the press began hounding Fisher for a comment. Instead of replying immediately or hiring a PR firm to issue a blanket statement, Fisher says, "I felt like I had to take personal responsibility to help create the world that I want to live in instead of succumbing to the madness. I took a long walk in the woods. I was bawling and definitely let myself just feel all of it. Then I wrote a letter to the community. I probably rewrote it like forty times, and I didn't respond to the media until I felt like I had my voice right. I just made everybody wait until I felt like I could work through the emotions and end up in a place that stayed the person I want to be."

When Fisher finally felt that her response was true to her values and her voice, she printed the entire letter on a poster and hung it on the plywood that covered the broken windows of her shop. Part of the letter said, "This is a defining moment for us as a community, as leaders, and as parents of children who are watching us and learning from our actions. We cannot choose how others treat us, but we can choose how we respond. I CHOOSE LOVE. Now more than ever."

Fisher's response went viral, picked up by publications such as the *New York Times* and making international news. Fisher says the response to her message was extraordinary: "I heard from thousands of people from around the world. People were sending artwork. I had so many kind emails, people telling their life story and expressing thanks for answering this way. I heard from people from all different communities, Black, Jewish, Asian, and several Palestinian parents who said, 'Thank you for not throwing us under the bus.' It turned into the most beautiful display of connection." Someone even set up a GoFundMe page that raised enough money to cover the expenses of rebuilding Fisher's shop.

Fisher's story exemplifies the role that emotional regulation plays for authentic leaders. Emotional regulation means being able to healthily manage and respond to your emotions. And no, this doesn't mean *suppressing* your emotions. It means being self-aware enough to recognize that you're feeling a strong emotion and grounded enough to moderate your response in the face of those feelings. Emotional regulation is a critical leadership skill. Research has shown that leaders who can regulate their emotions build psychologically safer teams, meaning employees feel safe to take risks, question leadership, make mistakes, and bring their full selves to the table.[6] Emotional regulation is also essential to authentic leadership. If you want to lead from your values, effectively question the norm, and honor your truth, you need to be grounded enough to intentionally *respond* to circumstances instead of simply reacting.

Tips for Cultivating Emotional Regulation

1. Focus on Three Key Steps

When you feel tempted to react to something while feeling strong emotions, try the following:

1. **Pause:** An incredible teacher once told one of the groups I was working with, "Anytime the emotion exceeds the

moment, pause." When you notice an outsized emotion, do what you can to step back. Take a few deep breaths. Go to the bathroom. Go for a walk. Get some fresh air. Sleep on it. Whatever you need to do to pause and make space so you don't react but instead can *respond* will serve you well.

2. **Label:** Try to label the emotion(s) you're feeling. If you identify a strong emotion like anger or sadness, it's a cue that you might be tempted to react from that emotion instead of intentionally responding from a grounded place. Notice if your body responds in different ways to different emotions or if specific circumstances trigger certain emotions for you.

3. **Process:** Ignoring and suppressing your feelings will only make them worse. When you feel big emotions, find a way to work through them. Some of the best-known strategies are talking with a friend about what you're feeling and why, physical activity, writing in a journal, meditation, and therapy.

2. Lean Into Curiosity

Co-founder of the Conscious Leadership Group Diana Chapman says that curiosity is an exceptional tool for emotional regulation. She says, "I don't think humans can change how often we get triggered. What I think we can change is how quickly we can shift out of that and get ourselves back into a more curious, open place."

Chapman recommends tapping into curiosity by trying to separate the genuine facts of the situation from the story you're telling yourself about it, especially when you feel the need to be right or defend your position. She also recommends asking yourself how the opposite of your story is at least as true as yours. She says, "It doesn't have to be more true, just at least as true, so that the mind lets go of wanting to prove itself right. The more open and curious we can get, the more possibilities we get to learn from and the more responsive we can be."

Authentic Leadership Practice #5: Seek the Right Environment

Being surrounded by people or working for organizations that don't share values similar to yours makes it *much* harder to lean into your authentic leadership and truly thrive. You might remember that not feeling aligned with your company's values is one of the six primary drivers of burnout.[7] Vicki Saunders, founder of investment platform Coralus, discovered this dynamic throughout her career, saying, "In the past, for quite some time of my life, like decades, I didn't feel like I was surrounded by people who had the same values I did and who encouraged me to do what I felt was right. Finding your people or being in a community of folks who increasingly are just like, 'You've got this,' is what allowed me to live more in my intuition and values."

I'll be real here: you truly might not be in a position to express your most authentic self at work. You may have legitimate reasons to feel that your job security is at risk if you don't mold yourself to a certain standard, or you may work under someone who doesn't permit you to be your authentic self. Your financial survival, your family's well-being, or your safety might feel threatened if you do things differently. Those are very real fears and situations. The inability to be your authentic self is already painful enough—there's zero shame here. In such cases, simply noticing what doesn't feel authentic, examining it, and knowing what you wish you could do differently still provides value. You can also take baby steps and try changing small things here and there, or you can lean into practicing your authentic leadership with your friends and family. All is not lost.

I don't highlight this possibility to discourage you but to acknowledge that committing to authentic leadership might require change. If you truly can't show up in a good way or influence positive change within your organization, you probably need to leave the organization to be your highest and best self. I don't say this lightly. I've felt trapped in toxic workplaces before and know how desperate this situation can be. That said, nothing is permanent, especially if you doggedly refuse to settle for less than you deserve.

Tips for Seeking the Right Environment

1. Reflect on Your Current Environment

Take the time to explore how your personal values overlap with your work and the people around you by reflecting on the following:

- What are the core values of the company I work for? Is there any overlap between the company values and my personal values?
- In what ways do I express my values through my work? Do I feel like there are any specific ways in which my workplace encourages me to express my personal values?
- Does my workplace hold me back in any way when it comes to expressing my values? Are there any circumstances under which I feel pressured to compromise my values at work?
- When I'm leaning into my values, which people in my life encourage me to do so?
- Is there anyone in my life whom I don't feel comfortable expressing my values in front of or who discourages me from doing so?

2. Take Steps Toward Change

If you know that your work doesn't support you in being the best version of yourself and feel it's time to move on, thought leader Akaya Windwood recommends the following:

Release Hopelessness: "I think a lot of the desperation feels like you're stuck there forever. You're never stuck forever. But in the moment, and especially as a young woman, it can feel that way. I'm sixty-seven and can look back and say, 'You weren't stuck. You just thought you were.'"

Commit to Change: "Remember that while you might need this job, it's not good for you, and you will not have this job for the rest of your life. Move into a different place of 'I don't want this job. I'm not in a moment where I can say screw it, but I *am* going to go do something.'"

Stay Open to Possibilities: Once you've committed to changing your circumstances, "start exploring what else is out there, where you can contribute next, and what's calling to you. Now is the time to get curious and creative."

Make a Timeline: "While you're still doing your work, say, 'I'm going to notice what satisfies me about it and stay in this role with a good heart for the next X amount of time.'" When you define a timeline, "it takes the desperation off because you know you're leaving."

HONESTLY, THIS STUFF ISN'T EASY. MAKING DECISIONS THAT GO against the grain, speaking your truth when no one else shares your experience, and forging your own path away from the status quo are all challenging. But so is living a life where you can't fully express yourself. One of the top five regrets of people who are dying is "I wish I'd had the courage to live a life true to myself, not the life others expected of me."[8] In the moments of tension between assimilated and authentic leadership, I invite you to think about the life you truly want to live. What do you stand for? Who do you aspire to be? Is anyone's opinion of you worth sacrificing those ideals?

At the heart of all this is the reality that the more of us who stand up and choose a better path, the harder it is for harmful business practices to continue. Every time we stand in our truth and refuse to abandon ourselves, we chip away at the harmful layers that encrust the business world. We also model to others that they can stand in *their* authenticity, too, helping to tear down patriarchal expectations for how women "should" behave inside and outside the workplace. You never know who's watching or what impact your actions might have. Slowly but surely, though, as more of us refuse to accept the status quo, we shift what's considered acceptable and how business is done. We feel more aligned, happier, and healthier as we do so, and we experience better results to boot.

Key Chapter Insights

- Many working women feel the need to change themselves to be accepted by men and fit in with the business world. Trying to assimilate by changing yourself has been linked to loss of identity and increased depression, mental illness, burnout, and chronic disease.
- Leaders who've shifted to an authentic leadership approach feel happier and less stressed while also proving to be more effective in the workplace. Authentic leadership makes employees feel a greater affinity with and commitment to their organizations, increases trust, and enhances employees' creativity and positive emotions.
- Authentic leaders strive to lead from their values, honor their truth regardless of circumstances, question the norm and do things differently, regulate their emotions so they can respond rather than react, and seek healthy environments where they feel supported as their best selves.

Chapter 4

FROM OVEREXTENDED LEADERSHIP TO OPTIMIZED LEADERSHIP

I met Michelle at an executive women's leadership retreat I was hosting at her organization. She hurried into our opening session at the last minute because she had squeezed in a workout *and* some work before we started at (checks watch) . . . 8:00 a.m. As our session got underway, I learned all sorts of things about Michelle: she was the youngest person in the history of the company to hold her role, frequently traveled for work, coached her son's softball team, and did CrossFit. She had so many balls in the air that it was hard to keep count.

Michelle could barely sit still through the first few hours of our session. This woman needed to be doing something. Constantly. However, as we got deeper into the work and Michelle stopped being so busy, she started to feel. The facade began to crumble. It turned out she was in full swan mode. To everyone on the outside, she appeared to be gracefully gliding across the water, but in fact she was frantically paddling underneath to keep herself afloat. She was exhausted. On our last day, Michelle admitted, "Everyone thinks I have this perfect life—the perfect family, a successful career—but I'm barely keeping it together. It just never ends. If I stop, though, *someone* will be disappointed. I feel like I always have to keep doing more to get ahead."

All of us nodded along. We understood—that constant feeling that we're being judged for something and found lacking. So we keep adding more to our plate. We go on autopilot, so consumed with the relentless busyness of our lives that we don't even know how we really feel anymore. This is the trap of the overextended leader.

The Traditional Playbook: The Overextended Leader

High-achieving women have a couple of things working against us. For starters, we're in the first few generations of women who've been "allowed" to work. Many of us have even been encouraged to do so. While the business world is beginning to adapt to make space for women, the patriarchal societal expectations of women haven't adapted to follow suit. Women are often still expected to take care of most things on the home front, even if they're working. Caretaking, community involvement, social activities—they all still mostly fall to women.

Journalist and creator of the Double Shift Katherine Goldstein, whose work highlights the unique challenges of the status quo of motherhood, says, "I feel like modern society and motherhood is some form of Ponzi scheme. The expectations we put on women manifest for a lot of us as guilt, which is a form of social control. You feel so overwhelmed by what's being asked of you that you don't have the bandwidth, community, or wherewithal to demand change. Guilt makes you quiet, shrink, and not want to talk about things."

The expectation for working women to be the primary caretaker at home was on display during the COVID pandemic. Women with children were significantly more likely to leave their jobs than men with children. Ultimately, nearly two million women dropped out of the workforce from 2020 to 2022.[1] This expectation for working women extends all the way to the top. Of the top 1 percent of female executives, only 22 percent have a stay-at-home partner compared to 70 percent of men who do.[2]

The second issue working against women is feeling pressured to be infallible at work to prove ourselves on account of the lingering patriarchal beliefs about our supposed inferiority. Nearly 60 percent of Americans say women have to work harder than their male counterparts to prove themselves in the workplace.[3] We face additional scrutiny from colleagues and feel pressured to participate in external résumé-building activities to set ourselves apart. Former CEO of women's network Ellevate Kristy Wallace reflects, "As a leader, it felt like I needed to check all the boxes. It's like, you need to be on a board. You need to be a thought leader. You need to do this. You need to do that. One day, I kind of stopped and realized just how unrealistic everything I was expected to take on was." We have to keep doing more even though, as you might recall, having a workload that doesn't align with your capacity is a key driver of burnout.[4]

On top of all of this is the toxically masculine narrative that leaders can't be seen as "weak," meaning they can't ask for help or show any cracks in their armor. Many of us internalize these ideas, feeling like we need to show how "tough" and self-sufficient we are by handling everything alone. We have to do it all.

Now, you might be more like Michelle, somehow managing to do it all. You show up to the business meeting having already worked out and responded to all emails before 8:00 a.m. You're crushing it at work, have a house that's so clean you could eat off the floors, hand-sewed a dragon costume for your kid's musical last night, and deadlifted your personal best last week. You hold it all together with practiced ease, seemingly floating through life on a sun-drenched cloud holding delicious gluten-free, dairy-free, sugar-free cake pops in one hand and a multimillion-dollar sales contract in the other. And you're just *fine*. Everything is *fine*. Except in the rare moments when you slow down long enough, you probably realize that you're very much not fine. As Taryn Bird, director of the Kate Spade New

York Foundation, says, "You just feel like you're going on autopilot. 'Well, she did that, so I have to do that.' Or 'My class is doing that, so I have to do that,' or 'Everybody else at the workplace is doing this, so I have to do this.' When we take a step back and are honest with ourselves about what we want, when we want it, how we want it, and what our true desires are, they're too often really out of alignment with the life that we're living."

Or maybe your journey tracks more with mine. You show up at your kid's after-school event rocking sweatpants and a hat to cover your unwashed hair, watching other parents show up with homemade treats while you forgot you were supposed to bring snacks, all while trying to covertly smell that brown spot on your jacket to determine whether it's melted chocolate or toddler poop. Compared to the people around you, you don't exactly feel . . . impressive. Yet with all you have on your already full plate, you wonder how in the fresh hell you're somehow supposed to be doing even *more*.

Whether you're the superhuman managing to do it all or the not-quite-as-superhuman just doing your best, it . . . sucks. Those in the former category are so busy they don't have a spare minute to breathe, while those in the latter group never feel good enough. Yet all of us contend with the increased stress, scrutiny, and pressure to just keep doing *more*, and it's holding us back from truly great leadership.

Every day, you wake up with a certain amount of energy in your cup. When you commit to too many things, you spread your limited energy too thin across the board to accomplish everything, and you don't give yourself time to refill your energy reserves once you're fully depleted. While our individual attention spans vary, research has shown that you can deeply focus on a task only for a certain amount of time before your performance declines, at which point your brain needs rest. Research has suggested that an estimated 42 percent of your time should go toward resting to optimize your health, performance, and resilience.[5] When you don't honor this cycle and just keep *doing*, your performance and ability to persist deteriorate. Physician-educator Parneet Pal says, "A huge principle leaders don't fully understand or appreciate is that with your body, your productivity, and your performance, there are limits. There are limits to the growth, right? So if we are constantly focused on producing and hustling and we don't take the time for regeneration, the system is going to fail."

It's also worth noting that what you consistently give your attention to is what you *actually* value. Regardless of what you say, if you regularly give your limited energy to things that fall outside what you claim to value, you can't genuinely live according to your values.

The new playbook invites you to stop compromising the quality of your life by overextending yourself and step into optimized leadership instead.

The New Playbook: The Optimized Leader

A number of years ago, one of my investors invited me to a private dinner at her home in honor of Vicki Saunders. Saunders had recently launched a venture called SheEO (now Coralus) to encourage women to invest in female-led companies. By some random stroke of luck, I was seated next to the guest of honor at dinner. I was awestruck. She was brilliant, vibrant, and engaging. So much so that when I left the dinner, I was lit up about her work and started thinking of ways to make my work more impactful as well.

In the years that followed this dinner, I invited Saunders to speak at my company's events and interviewed her for a number of articles and podcasts for Conscious Company Media. In each interaction, I felt similarly inspired. It was as if she somehow managed to always show up as her best self. I initially assumed that this was just how Saunders was built. She was one of those women who miraculously always had her shit together. But the more I got to know her, the more I realized that she was intentionally doing things behind the scenes that *enabled* her to show up in such an authentic, focused, and inspiring way. She told me that she intentionally managed her time and didn't say yes to anything that didn't light her up. She spoke about surrounding herself with values-aligned people and not forcing things when they didn't feel right. She seemed to understand exactly what she needed to do to be at her best and then, regardless of societal expectations or judgments, cut away anything extraneous that stood in the way of bringing her optimal self to the table. She didn't try to do *everything*. And by choosing to do less, she was somehow able to do more. Saunders is what I now call an optimized leader.

Optimized leaders understand that being overextended, stressed, or depleted stands in the way of being their best selves. I mean, how do you feel when you're in any of these states? When I'm stressed and overextended, I tend to feel distracted, easily frustrated, and quick to anger. If I'm exhausted or depleted, I struggle with brain fog and focus and want to be left alone. In either case, it's much harder for me to live as my highest self or perform any of the leadership practices from previous chapters. My guess is that something similar might be true for you.

Thriving as a leader (and as a person) is based on how you show up and make people *feel*. President of Kindred Organizational Consulting Kendra Coleman says, "What's small is big. It's all about the small moments; the day-to-day conversations and decisions are where we make the biggest, most significant, meaningful impact. In my experience, a lot of the disconnect that happens on the micro- and macrolevel is depleted people who aren't in tune with themselves projecting their own insecurities without realizing it in relation to the others." It's nearly impossible to consistently make others feel good when you don't feel good yourself. When you're exhausted, depleted, and overextended, you can't tune into yourself and show up with intention.

The people in your life who matter—your friends, family, colleagues, community members—don't care about how much you're *doing*; they care about the quality of your *being*. Optimized leaders prioritize this quality. By releasing things that don't serve them, finding support, and drawing healthy boundaries, they create conditions that enable them to feel that they have resources and are grounded and present enough to consistently show up as their optimal selves. The following practices can help you do the same.

Optimized Leadership Practice #1: Release What Doesn't Serve You

Last year, I hosted my family for the holidays. As I prepared for my mom, dad, brother, sister-in-law, two nieces, and mother-in-law, I wanted everything to be perfect. We're talking pine-scented candles in every room, multiple light projectors, a twenty-five-foot inflatable snowman, and a twenty-foot PVC pipe strapped to our second-story deck through which I could drop bags of freshly baked cookies down to people in the park. I might have gone a *smidge* overboard.

The day of everyone's arrival, after my eighth batch of holiday cookies, I realized that I hadn't hung our stockings yet. I was hammering nails into the wood paneling above our television in lieu of a fireplace when my husband walked into the room and asked, "Couldn't we use something less permanent to hang those?" I slowly turned my head toward him like a predator spotting prey, removed the two nails I had clenched between my front teeth, and snapped, "If you're so picky about this, then you do it!" I set the hammer down and went straight out the front door into below-freezing Colorado temperatures wearing yoga pants, a T-shirt, and slippers. And I just started walking.

When I'd made it a few blocks down the street and lost all feeling in my arms, I was struck by the questions "What actually matters here? Why am I doing all of this?" At my core, what mattered was spending meaningful time with my family and making joyful memories. But I'd become so wrapped up in everything being "perfect" that I was at my wits' end. I'd barely spent time with my kids and husband and wouldn't exactly say I was a beacon of joy.

I sheepishly returned home and apologized to my husband. I took stock of everything left on my to-do list, focusing on what needed to be done based on what truly mattered to me. Vacuuming downstairs, nope. Making cinnamon rolls by hand instead of buying them, nope. Decorating the kitchen table, nope. I removed every single thing that wasn't necessary to what truly mattered and just let things be good enough.

When my family arrived the following morning, the house wasn't spick-and-span. The food wasn't all homemade. My kids weren't bathed or dressed in perfect holiday outfits, and, let's be honest, neither was I. But by letting go of "perfect," I'd created the space to rest, relax, and feel grounded so that when my family showed up, I was at my best. I now call this practice "essentializing"—meaning intentionally prioritizing the things that truly matter in your life and releasing everything else so you can be at your best. It's like pruning a rosebush to nurture the best blooms.

To begin cultivating more optimized leadership, you need to slow down, start saying no, and release unnecessary things from your life that hold you back.

Tips for Releasing What Doesn't Serve You

1. Let Go of Unhealthy Habits or Behaviors

One consistent practice that many optimized leaders lean into is identifying unhealthy habits and behaviors and working to release them from their lives. Unhealthy behaviors include all sorts of things, but the common element is that they hold you back from being the best version of yourself.

As my awesome little holiday meltdown illustrates, perfectionism is an unhealthy behavior that holds many of us back from being our best. In my case, the need to make everything "perfect" led to unnecessary stress, exhaustion, and compromising time with my loved ones. My experience tracks with research showing that perfectionism leads to higher levels of stress and decreased psychological well-being.[6] Of perfectionism, Simple Mills CEO and founder Katlin Smith reflects, "You can't pursue perfection. You just have to continually keep moving toward better, whether it's in your personal life, with a product, or with a company. Better is better, and it's enough."

Michelle Pusateri, founder and CEO of Nana Joes Granola found that a different behavior stood in the way of her best. In college, she started bartending and says, "I got caught up in the lifestyle. The parties, staying up all night, the drinking, the drugs, everything." Pusateri went to culinary school after college and began dreaming of building a name for herself in the culinary world. She started pursuing her dream while working at hotels but continued engaging in her unhealthy lifestyle. She says, "I didn't really realize how much of a toll it took on my life, but at one point, I got myself into a little bit of trouble. That's when I knew something had to change. If I wanted this career, I'd have to look at my behaviors and grow up a little bit. From that day forward, I went to my first AA meeting and stopped drinking. I've not done a drug, smoked a cigarette, or had a drink since that moment where I knew I had to change my life." Pusateri's decision to release the unhealthy behavior ultimately resulted in a hugely successful culinary career that evolved into launching and leading her company Nana Joes Granola.

To be clear, the message here isn't "Everyone needs to stop drinking and being a perfectionist!" The practice is to identify harmful habits and behaviors that hold *you* back. These will be different for everyone. Alcohol isn't problematic for me; drinking alcohol in *excess* is. If I have more than two alcoholic drinks or drink more than one night in a row, I can feel it taking a toll on my physical and mental health. Once I noticed that this behavior wasn't healthy for me, I drew a hard line around it.

You can start identifying your own potential unhealthy habits by asking yourself the following:

1. Are there things I put into my body or activities I engage in that consistently take a toll on me, deplete my energy, or make me feel down?
2. In the last three months, at what times did I feel most stressed and depleted? What do each of these moments have in common?

3. Think of times in the last three months when you've felt at your absolute best. What are the common elements surrounding these moments? Once you've found elements that seem to help you be at your best, ask yourself what habits or behaviors get in the way of regularly having these elements in your life.

2. Essentialize Your Time

When it comes to optimizing your leadership, it's critical to be intentional about how you spend your time. How much of your precious time do you waste doing things out of obligation, for appearances' sake, or because you don't want to disappoint someone? How often do you return home from yet another activity and find yourself exhausted, wondering whether life will *ever* just slow down enough for you to catch your breath?

I'll be the first to tell you that your life isn't magically going to slow down unless you *choose* to slow it down. You're the one saying yes to everything. This is one of the key practices Vicki Saunders leans into, saying, "I'm very intentional about where my energy goes and the impact that's coming from that energy. I constantly pay attention to that equation—is the energy I'm putting into this activity creating the impact I want to have or not? It's a constant reflection at the end of every day: is this activity moving towards what I want to do or away from it?" Chief operating officer and co-managing director of Serenbe Development Garnie Nygren says, "I think many of us have a lot of noise around us, and there's a difference between being busy and being surrounded by noise. My plate can be really full, but that doesn't have to mean I have noise around me, right? I find if I'm taking care of the noise, I'm able to be much more present, intuitive, and open."

One tool to help you cut out the noise and stop saying yes to everything is the energy/impact matrix. In response to any opportunity or invitation, ask yourself, (1) Will the activity renew or deplete

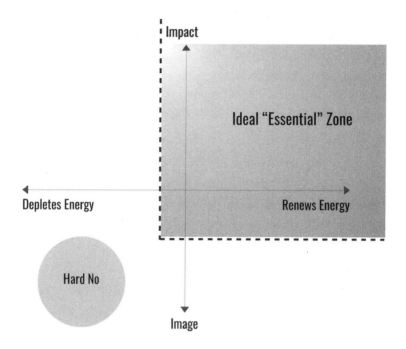

my energy? And (2) Is my desire to say yes based on image (read: concern about judgment or appearances) or impact (read: because it's meaningful or aligns with my values)?

Ideally, the most essential items—the ones you say yes to—renew your energy *and* have some sort of positive impact. If something clearly will deplete your energy and you feel that you're doing it only to maintain some sort of image, it's a clear no. Beyond those two states, the choice is yours.

There will definitely be things that don't renew your energy but are so meaningful that it doesn't matter. When my dad was going through chemotherapy, driving forty-five minutes to the cancer center to sit with him during his sessions didn't renew my energy, but it was so meaningful that it didn't even cross my mind to say no. Sitting through your child's school performance might not restore your energy, but the impact of being there for them is worth it. The more meaningful something is, the less it matters that it may be depleting.

The same is true when something truly renews your energy but isn't necessarily impactful—the more it renews your energy, the less that matters. I mean, I'm not changing anyone's life when I attend a concert to dance my face off or have a girls' dinner, but those types of activities restore so much of my energy that they're always worth it.

3. Essentialize Your Relationships

Several years ago, I had an important person in my life who was the epicenter of regular drama. My business coach at the time pointed out that we spent more time talking about this relationship than we did about my legitimate business issues. As we talked it through, I realized that I was staying in this unhealthy relationship only because I was afraid of hurting the other person's feelings. Eventually, I went through the painful process of releasing this relationship from my life. It wasn't easy, *and* I felt tremendous relief on the other side. So did my husband, who told me one night over dinner, "It's so nice to talk about something else besides drama. Welcome back. I've missed you."

Difficult as it might be, part of optimizing yourself might be releasing people from your life who aren't aligned with your values; consistently drain your energy; feel exploitative; lead to frequent unnecessary drama; or, as CEO of Roanhorse Consulting Vanessa Roanhorse says, "are relationships that don't love you back." This is another practice that Saunders puts into play, saying, "When it comes to the people you're surrounded by, relentlessly, brutally clean your closets all the time of that shit. The more you limit them, the more flow there is, the less friction."

Beyond the benefit of experiencing less friction, when you release relationships that don't serve you from your life, you create more space for the relationships that *do* serve you. And whom you surround yourself with matters. Pal says, "One of the strongest predictors of long-term behavior change is the people you surround yourself with. Surrounding yourself with people who are aligned with the way you think so you can hold each other in moments of weakness is superimportant." Real Leaders CEO Julie Van Ness adds, "Who you choose as your friends decides your future—take that concept and apply it to your business, who you work with, who you live with, and who you hang out with, and choose wisely."

When it comes to identifying relationships in your life that might not serve you, reflect on the following questions:

- Is there anyone in my life who is a constant source of stress and anxiety? Are there any relationships in my life that consistently feel like they drain my emotional gas tank but never fill it back up?
- What relationships in my life don't feel like they love me back or feel entirely one-sided?
- Are there any relationships that detract from your ability to lead?
- What types of people do you want to spend more time with? Who will support you in being the best version of yourself?

4. Audit Your Content Consumption

I got COVID in late 2023. While isolating in a hotel, I turned on *The Super Models* while seeking a "mindless" show. After watching Naomi Campbell and Cindy Crawford for an hour, I went to the bathroom and looked in the mirror. The contrast was *bleak*. The self-criticism followed suit: my weight, my skin, my hair, my body type, my age. It was all the worst. It took sixty minutes to destroy my entire sense of self-worth. This is the power of content.

Currently, there are more than five billion internet users around the globe, and we spend nearly seven hours per day online. Worldwide, more than 60 percent of the global population now uses social media, and on average, we spend more than two hours per day on social media sites.[7] Social media, television, books, podcasts, videos—we're constantly inundated with content that impacts our lives. Social media use has been proven to be addictive, is associated with depression and anxiety, and negatively impacts sleep patterns.[8] Exposure to media with little or no educational value has been shown to reduce IQ levels, decrease civic engagement, and make people more likely to engage with populist movements, while high-quality content can make people feel more inspired.[9] The information you consume influences how you think of yourself, how you think of others, your purchasing patterns, and changes in your behavior.

But here's the thing: you *choose* what content you give your attention to. Like the legend: "There are two wolves, and they are always fighting. One is darkness and despair, the other light and hope. Which one wins? The one you feed." Every piece of information you take in or put out feeds your soul, and you're the curator of that information. So feed your soul with the good stuff.

Libby Rodney, chief strategist at the Harris Poll, practices feeding her soul with the good stuff: "My favorite thing to do is only fill my LinkedIn posts with people who are doing cool, optimistic, interesting stuff or have an interesting, optimistic point of view. It's one microthing I can do to fill my brain with what's possible. To look at where change is coming from and explore what we can learn."

Rodney's intentionality tracks with that of many of the women I talked to who feel more optimized because they're mindful of their content consumption. They limit their social media usage or don't have accounts, read books that inspire them, and listen to educational or positive podcasts. Whatever it may be, they consume information with intention.

When you're perusing social media, watching a show or movie, reading or listening to a book, or listening to a podcast, ask yourself, "Does this feed my soul in a good way?" My husband and I both practice this in our lives, and it has made a huge difference. I feel less judgment in my life. I also feel more inspired, more hopeful, and less angry. When you need something "mindless," remember that this content still impacts you. Seek something relaxing that still feeds your soul in a good way instead.

Optimized Leadership Practice #2: Embrace Support

When I first wrote the proposal for this book, I submitted it to a publisher whom I had a warm connection with and felt good about my chances of getting a deal. I received an email two weeks later saying, "I'm sorry to say I don't have an offer for you." I was gutted. I'd worked on the proposal for ages and had started dreaming about writing this book. However, based on this rejection, I considered scrapping everything.

After the sting of the initial failure wore off, I decided that I wasn't ready to give up. I came up with a game plan to move forward and very much didn't want to accept that my first step had to be asking for help. I was so uncomfortable asking for help at this point that I'd literally written my entire first book proposal and submitted it to a friggin' publisher without guidance from *anyone*. You can see how well that worked out for me. Not wanting to repeat past failures, I sucked it up and reached out to a handful of authors in my network. Seeking help changed *everything*. Incredible, generous humans like Deepa Purushothaman and Jane Wurwand steered me in the right direction, without which you wouldn't be reading this book today.

All this is to say, if you're uncomfortable asking for or accepting help, you're not alone, *and* this behavior is holding you back in countless ways. Refusing help is one of the most common harmful traits I see among high-achieving women. The pressure to do everything on our own comes from both sides. Toxic masculinity tells us that asking for help and support at work is a sign of weakness. Patriarchy tells us that our role is to take care of others and that asking for anything for ourselves is selfish or a burden on others. The aversion to asking for help runs so deep that research has found that children as young as seven already fear asking for help out of concern that it makes them look weak or stupid.[10] While asking for help makes many of us uncomfortable, it's a critical practice of optimized leaders.

Asking for help changed Vanessa Roanhorse's entire life. After working in Chicago, she and her partner returned to New Mexico so they could raise their child alongside her family on the Navajo reservation, where she had been raised. Despite Roanhorse's previous groundbreaking work on climate resiliency through the Delta Institute, she struggled to find work in New Mexico without a college degree. While sleeping on the floor of her sister's home with her fourteen-month-old and partner, she decided to ask for help. She made a list of her contacts and sent an email to everyone asking for help finding her next role. Her request was answered with a contract with the city of Albuquerque through the partnership of Living Cities. This contract was the first of many over the next nine years, resulting in enough work for Roanhorse to launch her own business, Roanhorse Consulting. As founder and CEO, she currently employs ten people, many of whom live on the same Navajo reservation, where economic opportunity is hard to come by. All because she asked for help.

For the sake of becoming the highest and best version of yourself, you must embrace receiving support from others. There's nothing weak about doing so. Anytime you're tempted to see accepting help as a weakness, remember that's just toxic masculinity talking. Once you realize this, you can start seeing embracing help as a defiant act that chips away at beliefs that are harming society. Also, you're not just holding yourself back by trying to do everything on your own; you're pressuring other women to feel that they must do the same. Kristy Wallace's sister-in-law helped her see this dynamic in her life. While Wallace was pregnant with her third child, she'd strap one of her children on her back and the other on her front and carry all three kids. Some part of her felt that she needed to show everyone that pregnancy couldn't slow her down. On one such occasion, while carrying all three kids, she bent down to pick up some shopping bags and refused help from her sister-in-law. Her sister-in-law spoke up: "Kristy, every time you deny help and try to do it all, you're doing a disservice to all women." Wallace's story helped me understand another benefit of asking for help: it models to others that embracing help is okay.

To start you on your journey toward getting more support for yourself, begin with reframing what it means to ask for help.

Tips for Finding Support

1. Shift Your Mindset

Fun fact: when you accept or ask for help from someone, you improve *their* life. Research has shown that people who frequently help others report greater vitality and self-esteem. At the same time, expressing kindness correlates with increased well-being.[11]

Think about the last time someone asked you for help. How did it make you feel? My guess is that it felt pretty good. Why? We all thrive when we have a sense of purpose, and helping others gives us purpose. As Susan McPherson, author of *The Lost Art of Connecting*, says, "People feel valued when you ask them for help." This dynamic helps to explain why studies have shown that people are happier and more willing to help than anticipated.[12]

The next time you feel yourself holding back from asking for or accepting help because you feel like too much of a burden or want to be entirely self-sufficient, strive to shift your mindset. Remember, asking for help gives the other person more meaning and will likely help you deepen your relationship. This mindset shift can also help you reciprocate more often as you remember that the more you help others, the more you bolster your vitality, self-esteem, and well-being. Ann Shoket, CEO of the women's community TheLi.st, says, "One of my unwritten rules of creating community is trying to have two gives for every ask to ensure balance." The more you accept help and offer help to others, the more you model to others that it's okay for them to do the same.

2. Identify Your Major Pain Points

Many optimized leaders have taken the time to identify the biggest pain points in their lives that either consistently drain their energy or bring them over the edge so they can find support and ask for help where needed. When I did this practice, my list of pain points included the following:

- **Partner Travel:** I consistently struggle when my husband travels for work, leaving me alone with two young kids. By the time he comes home from a trip, I'm a husk of my former self. I now proactively ask for additional help anytime my partner travels. I ask my parents, mother-in-law, or friends to come over to give me a hand with my two kids. I get food and groceries delivered. Whatever I need to do, I do it.
- **Lack of Decompression Time:** I'm an ambivert. I am fully capable of extroversion, but I need to balance time spent with others with time for myself. If I spend considerable amounts of time with other people, I crash on the other side. Now, if I do things like host an in-person event, lead a retreat or workshop, or have my family stay at our house for multiple days, I block the subsequent days off as personal days to be entirely alone. If I'm attending a conference, I take breaks to go on a walk alone or slip out to find a quiet place to read. Anytime I'm required to be in large groups, I schedule the same amount of time to decompress by myself, enabling me to show up in a much better way.
- **Lack of Movement:** Another time I consistently struggle is when I haven't been able to be physically active for several days in a row. Last year, I realized that I didn't have time to work and exercise with the childcare schedule we had. Rather than just sucking it up, I asked my partner if we could agree on paying for childcare for an additional hour four days a week. I now use this extra hour on Monday through Thursday to move my body. If I'm in all-day meetings or events, I've become comfortable asking the group for at least a forty-five-minute break so I can go move my body. If it's not possible, I find time to walk

before or after the event or at least stand in the back of the room where possible to ensure that I don't sit all day. I find a way, no matter what.

Paying attention to the major pain points that regularly take you over the edge is a key step in finding needed support. To help you do so, reflect on the following:

- When was the last time you felt like you were at your wits' end? What were the circumstances? Do these circumstances typically push you toward the edge, or was this a one-time thing?
- Are there certain activities, circumstances, or people that consistently drain your energy or cause you stress? How can you spend less time on these things?
- What's the one thing in your life that, if changed, would relieve you of stress or make your life feel more easeful?

3. Release Your Need to Control Everything

When Erin Wade was CEO of Homeroom restaurant, a handful of people on her leadership team asked her to take some time off. Wade had been going through a divorce, and despite thinking she was keeping everything together, apparently she wasn't. "I basically got kicked out of my own company," she jokes. Her team asked her to do the unthinkable: take a sabbatical.

Wade reflects, "Even though I was the CEO, no one was so important that they were needed there all the time. We truly had such a strong team. They could cover it. It's such a different way to model leadership." Wade released control. She took three months off and shared her leadership responsibilities with her team. She described her time away as transformative. By letting go of the myth that she needed to do everything, she allowed her team to step up and grow together.

While not all of us can take three months off and hand over the reins to our colleagues, Wade's story illustrates the power of releasing the need to control *everything*—something many high-achieving women struggle with. When you insist on controlling everything in your life (#perfectionist), you put unnecessary stress on yourself and deny the people around you the opportunity to step up and grow.

When it comes to identifying any areas in your life that are ripe for you to release control or let someone else lead, reflect on the following:

- Are there elements of your work you're holding on to because you feel that no one else can do them like you do? When you hear yourself saying, "I'm the only one who can do it," ask yourself if that's actually true.
- Are there any tasks that you can invite someone else to take on that would help them grow while taking something off your plate?

Optimized Leadership Practice #3: Set and Commit to Boundaries

When I was running Conscious Company Media, our first editor-in-chief after me was Rachel. We were a start-up, meaning everyone on the team was asked to chip in on occasion and take on things that were outside their typical responsibilities. As CEO, I tried my best to be conscious of how much I was asking of everyone—and sometimes I fell short.

In one instance, I asked Rachel to take on yet another task outside her role. With a history of always saying yes, I was taken aback this time when Rachel said no. But Rachel didn't just say no; she nailed this particular no: "I hate having to say no to this, Meghan. I know we're a start-up, and I've been happy to do things that aren't on my job description in the past because I believe so much in what our company does. *And* it's because I believe so much in what we do that I have to protect my time right now. I'm already overextended with our next issue coming up. If I take on more, I'm worried it will impact the quality of my work and our next print issue. I need to be honest with you and hope you can understand." True story: I wasn't exactly thrilled that Rachel said no, and her approach gave me very little room to push back. However, Rachel did three things with her response that stuck with me:

1. She reminded me that what I was asking of her was not part of her job description. What she didn't say but I felt was the reminder that her job description was the agreement she and I had made about our commitment to each other. As her employer, I can ask her to do more than what we agreed to, but she has every right to say no.
2. She expressed that she understood the nature of our start-up culture and reminded me that she'd gone above and beyond in the past without asking for anything more for herself.
3. She highlighted that the important work I'd hired her to do would suffer if she said yes and that she truly cared about the company and the quality of our work.

Both at work and at home, saying no and drawing clear boundaries are hard for many of us. If you're like me and have been raised to "not talk back" and avoid conflict at all costs, saying yes often feels like the easiest way to avoid disappointing others, having difficult conversations, or not living up to other's expectations. Yet drawing healthy boundaries and saying no are critical to your ability to show up as your highest and best self. Being an intentional leader means being grounded, attentive, and present as much as possible. Being overextended works directly against your ability to show up this way. Not only does being overextended impact the quality of how you show up with others, but it also impacts the quality of your work. Every time you say yes out of obligation or when you already have too much on your plate, you're working against your ability to flourish in all aspects of your life.

Several women with whom I requested interviews for this book told me no because they needed to protect their energy to be at their best. Of course, I wanted to talk to these women, but I was thrilled that they were doing what they needed to do to protect their mental health. Setting boundaries to protect your mental and physical health is a key step toward optimized leadership and your ability to thrive.

Tips for Setting Boundaries

1. Set Yourself Up for Success

After years of working nights and weekends as CEO of my own company, resulting in full-scale burnout, I knew I needed to set healthier boundaries for myself when I returned to work after having my second child. At the outset, I told my colleagues that my workday ended at 3:00 p.m. so I could pick up my kids and that I no longer planned to work on weekends. However, I still found myself checking my work email or responding to Slack messages outside the working hours I'd set for myself. On one such occasion, when responding to a co-worker's 6:00 p.m. Slack message and grumbling about how he wasn't respecting my boundaries, I realized *I* was the problem. Because here's the thing about boundaries: no one will respect your boundaries if you don't respect them yourself. If you tell someone that you don't work on the weekends but then regularly reply to their emails on the weekend, you're sending mixed signals and can't blame them for being confused.

Once I realized that I needed to take my own boundaries seriously, I examined what was holding me back from doing so. In my case, my damn phone was the culprit. It was just a little too easy to sneak a quick peek at my work email while I was making dinner or attending a kid's soccer game. So I took my work email, Slack, and anything work-related off my phone—and haven't changed this practice to this day. I also started physically putting my computer in another room when I was done for the day and refused to open it again until the next workday began. To address my initial anxiety about missing something important during nonworking hours, I told my colleagues to text or call me if they needed me for anything actually mission-critical. Unsurprisingly, once I genuinely committed to my boundaries, others did as well.

When it comes to setting boundaries for yourself, clarify what boundaries you need, clearly communicate them to others, and commit to them by setting yourself up for success. Stop answering work-related messages outside working hours. Take work-related apps off your phone. Ask your spouse to hide your computer from you—do whatever it takes to hold yourself accountable. Every time you hold true to a boundary, you help those around you understand how you'd like to be treated and show them it's okay for them to set boundaries for themselves.

2. Shift Your Mindset

Research has shown that people often overestimate how disappointed others will be if they refuse an invitation. The lead author of the study, Julian Givi, says, "Our research shows the negative ramifications of saying no are much less severe than we expect."[13] When you say no or put boundaries around your time, remember you're making assumptions about how the other person will feel. They'll likely be far less disappointed than you imagine.

Another way to look at turning down professional opportunities is that your no means someone else gets to say yes. Instead of simply turning down requests, Roanhorse looks through her network to see if there's someone else who would be a good fit for the opportunity in her place. When she declines the request, she recommends her contact and gifts them with the opportunity instead.

Breaking long-standing patterns isn't easy. It takes courage to seek support, release things that don't serve you, draw boundaries, and admit that you can't do everything alone. But here's the thing: there's no award at the end of this whole thing for the busiest person who accomplished everything alone. Your value is not contingent on how much you *do*. You're inherently worthy as you are. Full stop. Making excuses for why you have to do everything by yourself doesn't make you more valuable; it just makes you more exhausted, disengaged, or resentful. Every time you release something that doesn't serve you, accept help, and draw a boundary, you're not just enhancing your life and leadership; you're modeling healthier behavior to women everywhere and slowly chipping away at patriarchal double standards and expectations for women to overextend themselves. To be the best leader and person possible and usher in a new way of being for the sake of everyone around you, embrace what's needed to be your optimal self.

Key Chapter Insights

- Many working women contend with patriarchal gender roles outside work, taking on more household responsibilities and emotional labor than their male partners in heterosexual households while also feeling that they have to go above and beyond in the workplace because they face more scrutiny at work than their male colleagues do.
- In addition to the gendered pressure to go above and beyond in all aspects of life, high-achieving women contend with the toxically masculine pressure to do everything on their own, meaning never asking for or accepting help to prove how strong and self-sufficient they are. Trying to take on everything results in increased levels of burnout as well as decreased performance, creativity, resilience, and quality of life.
- Optimized leaders focus on the quality of how they show up over the quantity of how much they're doing. They intentionally create conditions in their life that help

them be at their best—including finding needed support, releasing things that don't serve them, and setting clear boundaries—all of which decrease the likelihood of burnout, bolster creativity, improve performance, and increase overall happiness and well-being.

Chapter 5

FROM SACRIFICIAL LEADERSHIP TO SUSTAINED LEADERSHIP

Zahra Kassam had her first child when she was twenty-nine. Kassam had been trained as a Montessori school teacher and completed her master's in education at Harvard, so she understood the importance of early education for childhood development. When she started looking for educational toys for her baby and couldn't find any, she researched the issue and found that at that time, only 4 percent of toys in the United States were safe for children under three. Her interest was piqued and soon turned into a passion. With the help of a designer from the Rhode Island School of Design, she began tinkering with toy designs to see if they could create Montessori-based learning toys that could be certified safe for babies. After three years, they found success, and MontiKids was born from their persistence.

The company took off. We're talking about multiple investment rounds, appearing on *Shark Tank*, being invited to the White House, winning numerous awards, and making media appearances. Kassam says, "It became my mission in life for a while. I really went all in."

During the chaos, Kassam found out that she was pregnant with her second child. MontiKids had twenty employees at the time and was heading into its next investment round, which Kassam successfully closed while pregnant. When she delivered her second child in November 2017, she felt that she had to put her business's and children's needs above her own. "I was in my hospital bed at 4:00 a.m. writing investor emails. I just didn't stop. Technically, I told people, 'I'm going to take a maternity leave,' but I was working. All these things were happening, and I was putting out all sorts of fires. I had really bad postpartum depression. My milk would come in every few hours, and I would just sob. Then I would literally shake it off and go on a TV interview. I started having panic attacks, and it just got worse and worse. Even with the depression, I went to therapy a few times and then was like, 'I don't have time for this. It's not working.' There was so much pushing through and performing."

By early 2020, Kassam was in bad shape. "I was truly sick. My mental health was not okay, but I was also physically sick. I had shingles. There were several months when I literally couldn't use my wrists because I had carpal tunnel. I couldn't pick up a coffee mug and had to get my hair blow-dried because I couldn't wash my hair. Then I got a concussion. It was just one thing after another. My body was like, 'You gotta stop.' My concussion doctor was like, 'You have to slow down. The reason you're having such bad symptoms is because you're doing this company and you're mothering, and it's just too much.' I kept getting all these signals to slow down, and I needed to, but I wasn't."

Finally, when COVID hit and Kassam's oldest son's school closed, she decided to use it as an opportunity to take sick leave. They moved from their home in Oakland to a farm that Kassam's family owns in Pescadero, California. Kassam finally stopped pushing through. "I came back to myself there. I had lost connection with who I really was. It was the most healing journey—being in nature, putting my hands in the dirt, growing and eating good food, waking up with the sun, and just being by the ocean. It was incredible." As it became clear that her company needed to embark on another fundraising round, Kassam knew she couldn't sacrifice herself anymore. She decided to close MontiKids. She eventually moved to Half Moon Bay to work on the farm, where she is now committed to her family, healing, and new passion for regenerative agriculture.

When Kassam told me her story, I said I'd heard similar tales from more high-achieving women than I could count. I'd also lived it myself. So many of us sacrificed our well-being in the name of success and eventually broke down. This is the traditional-playbook approach of sacrificial leadership.

The Traditional Playbook: Sacrificial Leadership

At a CEO retreat that my company hosted last year, I asked the group—five men and five women—to reflect on the main thing standing in the way of being the leader they needed to be to take their company to the next level. When we came to the last person, she said something that broke my heart: "What's holding me back is believing I'm worthy of care." Phew. I think women around the world felt that answer in their bones.

Maybe you recognize a little of yourself in this story. Feeling unworthy of care or that caring for yourself is somehow wrong, selfish, or overly indulgent. You ignore your own needs while prioritizing everything and everyone around you. You tell yourself your needs are secondary—that they don't *really* matter. Even when you find a sliver of time to nourish your well-being, you question whether it's okay to rest, get help, take time off, or do something that makes you happy. Well, friend, a lot of that is the patriarchy talking.

As women living in patriarchal societies, we're conditioned to believe that our value comes from taking care of others—children, partners, family, friends, and community. Putting ourselves last to care for everyone else is seen as an admirable and virtuous quality in a woman. You may remember from Chapter 1 that the Matés' research found that one of the top three traits leading to chronic disease is *compulsive and self-sacrificing doing for others*. The authors say, "These personality features, found across all autoimmune conditions, are precisely the ones inculcated into women in a patriarchal culture."[1] When we add contemporary business culture to the mix, the pressure to sacrifice oneself intensifies further.

The toxically masculine, win-and-profit-at-all-cost contemporary business world tells us that we must do whatever it takes to get results. We're asked to prioritize our work above all else, stay late, work extra hours, travel more, do more with less, work on vacation, or take on another project—and then as women, we know we're being judged more harshly if we don't. Success means sacrifice.

As working women, we're conditioned to sacrifice ourselves at home and at work. The result is sacrificial leadership. Where overextended leaders feel that they have to do everything by themselves to prove their worth, sacrificial leaders put their needs last and feel that they're not worthy of care. Often these two leadership styles go hand in hand and exacerbate each other.

When you ignore your needs—sleep, exercise, health appointments, time with loved ones, rest, etc.—you will suffer. Full stop. There's no escaping the consequences. You're not the one rare superhuman who somehow doesn't need the critical, life-sustaining elements that all humans need in order to sustain their health and well-being. But some part of you thinks that maybe, just maybe, you'll be fine ignoring your needs for the long haul. You won't.

Stephanie Nadi Olson experienced the consequences of sacrificing herself for success while she built her company We Are Rosie. "I completely lost myself. It's a slippery slope where you start ignoring things. My body would wake up in full anxiety, like an adrenaline response at 2:00 a.m. or 4:00 a.m. Every day. I never slept past 4:30 a.m.; sometimes I was up till midnight working the night before. Those things become part of your normal, and you tell yourself, 'I'm doing okay,' but you don't realize you're not." Nadi Olson realized that she wasn't okay when she began having regular panic attacks, suffered from anxiety and depression, and had a herniated disc caused by the stress of looking at her computer for long hours over four years. While lying in a hospital room getting a spinal injection, she finally asked herself, "At what cost?" Soon after, she decided to replace herself as CEO.

The sacrificial leader narrative influences many of us to feel that we need to be *giving* or *producing* at all times. Taking time for yourself becomes nearly unheard-of, but your body and your soul are begging you to pay attention. You can either choose to start prioritizing yourself now or wait until the struggle becomes so intense that you don't have a choice and are forced to stop when you break.

Many of the women I've met who are now thriving either walked the same path—working so hard that they eventually burned out and could return to work only after they prioritized their well-being—or decided to prioritize their well-being from the start. In either case, they highlighted the next practice in the playbook: sustained leadership.

The New Playbook: The Sustained Leader

When I first met Susan Griffin-Black, co-founder and co-CEO of EO Products, she pretty much broke my brain. She was a speaker at one of my company's events, and I noticed that, unlike most business leaders, she didn't seem overly busy, stressed, or overwhelmed. In fact, she seemed the exact opposite—calm, grounded, warm, and thoughtful. When she took the stage, she lit up, discussing building an organization with compassion and purpose. I was in awe of her, *and* . . . a small part of me wondered if she was full of shit.

Later that year, I went to EO Products headquarters to interview Griffin-Black for a podcast. While some part of me hoped to look behind the curtain and find that she was a hot mess like the rest of us, I saw no such thing. She was entirely present during our interview, listening deeply to each question and responding with transparency and vulnerability. She spoke of prioritizing her family, giving back to her community, and how important it is to love your work. She seemed genuinely fulfilled—maybe even truly happy?

I left the interview, got into my rental car in the parking lot, and, naturally, started sobbing. I mean, I was barely holding it together leading my company. Seeing Griffin-Black seem so peaceful and content while running a half-billion-dollar enterprise made me feel like I was doing something terribly wrong. Like I'd been slogging my way up the mountain on foot only to see her casually flying by in a damn gondola. Why wasn't she struggling or running around like a chicken with her head cut off like the rest of us? As I thought about the many things I'd heard Griffin-Black discuss, something stuck out. In addition to leaning into many practices of holistic, authentic, and optimized leadership, she seemed to nurture her well-being *while* she was on the journey. I later realized that Griffin-Black is a sustained leader.

Sustained leaders prioritize the key elements that support and improve their health and well-being. As with optimized leadership, supporting your well-being *while* you're on the journey helps you be more engaged, grounded, and intentional with everyone around you—family, employees, friends, bosses, community, clients, etc. Showing up this way elevates all components of your life, enabling you to evolve into the leader who's being called for to create a better world and feel good as you're doing so.

While all of this sounds lovely, I fully admit that it's easier said than done. When I wrote the proposal for this book, I was emerging from two years of one of the darkest periods of my life. Much of that darkness served as the inspiration for this book. I didn't want anyone else to make the same mistakes and suffer the consequences. From that place, I pored over all of the interviews I'd done, like the one with Griffin-Black, to find the best-known practices of leaders who seemed to be nurturing their well-being while leading at such high levels. Every time I identified a common thread, I captured it in the proposal. I attempted to incorporate it into my life: committing to the basics, nurturing genuine connection, prioritizing joy, seeking professional help, and practicing compassion.

The proposal moved from an idea to a book deal. I co-founded two small businesses while raising two small kids. Things started to get busy again. The busier things got, the more tempted I was to prioritize everything I had to do over the practices I'd identified to sustain my well-being. At some point, I was talking with one of my besties, Hannah, about feeling pulled toward prioritizing my work above all else again. She said, "Meghan, what would the book tell you to do?" It felt so obvious—if I was writing a book about this stuff, I needed to commit to the practices. Even so, prioritizing my well-being felt indulgent—it was the first thing I was willing to let go of as I struggled with feeling that I "deserved" care. But every time I was tempted to deprioritize these practices, I forced myself to stay the course.

Gradually, I felt my life changing. I felt myself move along the spectrum from total darkness to mostly okay to mostly fine to mostly good to mostly great to mostly thriving, which is where I sit today. I say "mostly thriving" because it's disingenuous to state that I'm perfectly happy and thriving every second of every day. I still have down moments and even down days. I still flirt with self-doubt, overcoming achievement addiction, and people-pleasing. But I can unequivocally say that I'm consistently flourishing.

While moving from suffering to okay to fine to good to great to thriving, I learned that there's a *huge* difference between these states. It's not an incremental difference when you shift from constant stress and exhaustion to feeling that you have resources and are supported, rested, and healthy. It's one of the most profound shifts you can make in your life.

The following practices can help you become a sustained leader and feel these shifts in your own life.

Sustained Leadership Practice #1: Commit to the Basics

Several foundational elements are well documented as critical to your physical and mental health: sleep, a healthy diet, mindfulness, and physical activity. I imagine none of this is particularly new information, but it's worth highlighting these practices as the foundation for how you feel and show up every day. Every sustained leader I know understands how critical these practices are and strives to prioritize them in their life. Here's why:

Sleep: Contemporary research has consistently shown that typical adults need to sleep at least seven hours per night. Regularly sleeping less than seven hours is correlated with many adverse health issues: increased weight gain, obesity, diabetes, hypertension, heart disease, stroke, depression, impaired immune function, increased pain, impaired performance, increased errors, and even risk of death.[2]

Sleep also plays a critical role in your ability to learn. Per the Division of Sleep Medicine at Harvard Medical School, "Research suggests that sleep helps learning and memory in two distinct ways. First, a sleep-deprived person cannot focus attention optimally and, therefore, cannot learn efficiently. Second, sleep itself has a role in the consolidation of memory, which is essential for learning new information." Poor sleep impacts your mood, judgment, motivation, and perception of events.[3]

Nutrition: What you put into your body profoundly impacts your mental and physical health. Per physician Eva Selhub, "Your brain is always 'on.' It takes care of your thoughts and movements, your breathing and heartbeat, your senses—it works hard 24/7, even while you're asleep. This means your brain requires a constant supply of fuel. That 'fuel' comes from the foods you eat—and what's in that fuel makes all the difference. Put simply, what you eat directly affects the structure and function of your brain and, ultimately, your mood."

Eating nutrient-rich food is akin to giving your brain the highest-quality fuel, while eating unhealthier, processed foods high in refined sugars is the exact opposite. Consuming "low-quality fuel" harms the brain, promoting inflammation and worsening your body's ability to regulate insulin. Outside the brain, an estimated 95 percent of your body's serotonin, the neurotransmitter that regulates your mood, sleep, experience of pain, and appetite, is produced in your gastrointestinal tract. The function and production of neurotransmitters in your digestive tract are heavily impacted by the good bacteria that line your intestines, which are influenced by the food you eat.[4]

Given the impact of food on your brain and your body, contemporary research has shown a significant link between nutrition and mental health issues such as depression, anxiety, and ADHD. In one study, people with ADHD who were given a healthy diet rich in specific vitamins and minerals significantly improved their attentiveness, reduced their aggression, and increased their ability to function compared to the placebo group. A 2019 study found that simply increasing the intake of fruits and vegetables reduced the symptoms of those struggling with mental health issues.[5]

Mindfulness and Reflection: Just as your brain needs good fuel, it also needs to rest. Beyond sleep, mindfulness practices quiet your brain and give it the rest it needs, bolstering overall health and well-being. Simply put, mindfulness is practicing paying attention to the present moment while working to release any judgments, attachments, or reactivity about what you notice.

People can tap into mindfulness in several ways, including meditation, spiritual practices, and reflective exercises. The key is finding a way to quiet your mind, be fully present and aware, and release judgment or attachment to emotions as much as possible. Doing so has been shown to reduce anxiety, depression, insomnia, and high blood pressure while also helping people effectively manage pain and addiction. Mindfulness has even been shown to positively alter the structure and function of your brain.[6]

Physical Activity: Regular physical activity is critical to health and well-being. One of its key benefits is that it helps us address the impact of stress. Authors Emily and Amelia Nagoski found that in the face of stress, our bodies try to protect us by releasing several hormones and chemicals, including epinephrine, adrenaline, glycogen, and cortisol. This process slows digestion, shifts our immune system, and diminishes our reproductive functioning and tissue repair. These bodily changes heighten our awareness and conserve energy to protect us while we address the stressors, but they can be harmful if they build up too much in the body. We're talking about heart disease, increased blood pressure, autoimmune disorders, and much more. You *need* to flush these hormones and chemicals from your body to prevent the harmful effects of stress from wreaking havoc on your body. While breathing, affection, positive social interaction, and laughter help flush harmful elements from your body, research has shown that physical activity is the single best way to do so.[7]

In addition to flushing harmful hormones and chemicals from the body, physical activity has been shown to reduce anxiety, depression, and negative moods while also improving cognitive function and self-esteem.[8] Regular exercise also improves brain health; reduces the risk of diseases such as type 2 diabetes, heart disease and stroke, infectious diseases, and even some cancers; strengthens bones and muscles; and increases longevity.[9]

REGARDING THESE BASIC PRACTICES, PARNEET PAL SAYS, "MOST OF the suffering, both personally and in the workplace, is related to chronic lifestyle-related diseases. We all probably know somebody who suffers from things like obesity, diabetes, hypertension, stroke, neurodegenerative disorders like Alzheimer's and Parkinson's disease, or mental health disorders like anxiety and depression. The data clearly show that most of these are called lifestyle-related chronic diseases because they relate to how we eat, sleep, move, and manage our stress. Eighty to 90 percent of these diseases are completely preventable when we do those things well."

Tips for Committing to the Basics

1. Focus on the Deeper Why

Sleep, diet, mindfulness, and physical activity all too often fall into the category of things you "should do." For much of my life, the only benefit I associated with diet and exercise was weight control (#patriarchy). While I knew that getting enough sleep and mindfulness were supposed to be good for me, they felt like things I "should" do but didn't have time for. My perspective changed when I tapped into a deeper understanding of *why* I was engaging with these practices.

Sleep, diet, mindfulness, and physical activity build the foundation for your overall well-being. Your well-being is one of the most critical components of the quality of your life experience and how others experience you. Founder and CEO of Kuli Kuli Foods Lisa Curtis says, "It's a marathon, not a sprint, right? I'm a big believer in getting eight hours of sleep. I work out almost every morning, and I eat well. If you're trying to go far, you must be in a good place. If I'm not taking care of myself, I can't care for my family, employees, or business. I do a lot to ensure I'm in a good place."

Beyond the impact of your well-being on others and your ability to effect change, I've found that prioritizing these basic practices makes me feel *so much better* as I go through the day. My body feels strong and healthy, and I feel happier, energized, and inspired. I now think of getting adequate sleep, eating well, practicing mindfulness, and getting physical activity as ways to honor the life I was given by treating my body as beautifully as possible and optimizing how much I'm enjoying the experience while I'm lucky enough to be here.

Tapping into a deeper *why* like this helps me commit to and even enjoy these basic practices. I mean, trying to motivate yourself to go to the gym is much easier when you're going in service of strengthening your relationship with your partner, feeling good, and being more impactful at work rather than because you want to fit into a pair of damn jeans.

Try tapping into your own deeper why by thinking of how your well-being could support the things that matter most to you in life.

2. Remember, Something > Nothing

Remember that something is better than nothing if you're sincerely pressed for time. Meditating for five minutes daily has been shown to reduce stress.[10] Research has shown that three one-minute bursts of vigorous exercise each day and fifteen minutes each week can lead to a longer lifespan.[11] So when you can't find the time, find a way to sneak something in.

Katlin Smith, founder and CEO of Simple Mills, says that when she's genuinely too busy, she prioritizes finding two minutes to move her body, two minutes of meditation, and two minutes of reading to support these practices as consistent habits. Don't let "sneaking the basics in" become your default mode instead of prioritizing these habits in your schedule, but don't let perfect become the enemy of the good, either.

Sustained Leadership Practice #2: Nurture Genuine Connection

In 2023, the US surgeon general, Vivek H. Murthy, published a health advisory stating, "Social connection—the structure, function, and quality of our relationships with others—is a critical and underappreciated contributor to individual and population health, community safety, resilience, and prosperity." The report's key message: isolation is destroying us. Loneliness and social isolation are correlated with increased risk of heart disease, depression, respiratory illness, stroke, anxiety, and dementia—all risk factors that lead to premature death—and also lead to worse performance at work.[12] Unfortunately, one in five people worldwide felt lonely "a lot of the day yesterday."[13] Yet how many times have you prioritized your work over spending time with people you love? How often do you let everything you "have to get done" serve as an excuse for not seeing friends, scheduling a date night, or meeting new connections out in your community?

While research has established how detrimental loneliness is to our overall well-being, others have established the profound benefits of connecting with others. The longitudinal Harvard Study of Adult Development—the longest study on adult development in history—found that the key driver of living a long life is cultivating meaningful social connections. Yale researcher and professor of psychology Laurie Santos found that the single element that makes people happier than any other is social connection.[14]

Sustained leaders refuse to compromise time with their loved ones in the name of success. Griffin-Black is a prime example. In 2012, her family moved to Marin County, California, from San Francisco and her corporate office was moving to Marin as well. While looking for new office space, the CFO found a cheaper location for their headquarters in Richmond. Griffin-Black says, "He was like, 'It's only eighteen minutes to Richmond across the bridge.' I was like, 'Eighteen minutes on a bridge, when you have a sick kid on the other side, is an eternity. Forget it.' We chose to manufacture in Marin, which is more expensive, but I never missed a parent-teacher conference, a basketball game, or a school play. I never had to choose between those two things, and I don't think any parent should have to."

Tips for Nurturing Genuine Connection

1. Start Small

Santos's research revealed that even small social interactions like connecting briefly with a stranger will improve your sense of happiness. Every interaction you have builds a greater feeling of social connectedness and bolsters your overall well-being. You can start with small practices like the following:

The Compliment Game: One fun way to increase your social interactions is by seeing how many strangers you can compliment in a specific amount of time. The more detailed and heartfelt the compliment, the better. I love to do this when I'm traveling, and I can't tell you how wonderful it is to see people's faces light up when they hear something positive from a perfect stranger. You brighten their day and yours. It's nearly impossible to stay in a bad mood while playing, and you never know how much of an impact your words may have on someone else.

Ask Meaningful Questions: I was checking out at the store recently when the cashier asked the man ahead of me, "What's something you feel grateful for today?" He smiled and replied, "I just reconnected with my high school crush. We're both divorced, and I'm excited to see where this might go from here." Everyone in the checkout line heard him and started asking questions about his budding relationship. In a matter of minutes, four perfect strangers had a heartfelt conversation that left me walking out of the store smiling.

Asking people thoughtful questions, like those provided below, is a great way to have small yet meaningful interactions out in the world:

- "Who or what is inspiring you right now?"
- "What's something good that happened to you lately?"
- "What do you feel most grateful for right now?"
- What's something you're looking forward to in the next year?

2. Find Your People

"Finding your people" doesn't mean "networking" in some generic professional group; it means intentionally finding others whose passion and values align with yours. If you're passionate about the industry you're in, search for like-minded industry groups, for example, Women of Renewable Industries and Sustainable Energy. If you're not thrilled about the type of work you do or the industry you're in, look for values alignment in organizations like Women in Sustainability or Women's Earth Alliance that focus on specific issues. You can also use a platform like Meetup to search for communities that fit your interests and passion areas. Whatever it is, think about what's important to *you* and find a way to connect with people who share similar interests.

If you can't find a peer group that speaks to you, create a group to help them find you. Vanessa Roanhorse co-founded Native Women Lead to connect with other Indigenous women business leaders. Michelle Finocchi launched Moving the Needle to bring professional women together to learn how to make progress on specific social and environmental issues.

Whether you join a group or create one of your own, putting in the effort to find people who "get you" will increase your sense of connection and bolster your well-being.

3. Build Your Own Support Circle

As a young female founder of a mission-driven start-up, I felt like I was in a niche within a niche within a niche. Finding people with whom I felt that I could relate and talk shop felt nearly impossible. Yet at every conference I went to, I'd usually find at least one person who danced to the beat of a similar drum. When I found that person, I went out of my way to connect with them. In some cases, I'd lean into my vulnerability and just tell them I thought they were amazing and that I wanted stay in contact. This practice, which Jocelyn lovingly refers to as "superfriending," turned into one of my superpowers. It's how I connected with Jocelyn as well as Erin Wade, Emily Mochizuki Lutyens, Steph Speirs, Ayla Schlosser, and many others you're meeting in this book.

When I truly started feeling the pressure and loneliness of my role, I reached out to the women I'd "superfriended" to see if they wanted to co-create a support circle. I proposed that we meet virtually once per month to help each other work through challenges. Seven out of the eight women I invited said yes. For two years, we met virtually for ninety minutes every month. The profound sense of connection and support I got from that group of women still sticks with me to this day, as do all of the friendships. Is there a group of women you could do something similar with? If not, could you at least set the intention of trying to find them?

4. Host Salon Dinners

How many times do you host or attend a dinner party and find yourself engaging primarily in small talk with the few people around you? While you're technically being social, these types of conversations don't often result in the deep, meaningful connection that helps us feel less alone in the world. Salon dinners can help you deepen your connection in spaces like this. The general framework is to ask the group an engaging question that everyone is invited to answer *one at a time* while everyone else listens to the person who's speaking. As a group, you all engage in this single conversation rather than everyone splitting into small side conversations. The more meaningful the question you ask, the deeper the sense of connection. I host salon dinners with our friends and at the business retreats I organize, and they regularly result in some of the most meaningful interactions I have throughout the year.

Sustained Leadership Practice #3: Prioritize Your Joy

Last year, I did something unspeakable. I left my husband and two young children, flew to London, and took five days off to . . . wait for it . . . enjoy myself. Cue audience gasp. "You just left your family for a week? You didn't work or anything? Didn't you feel . . . guilty?" I know. I know. I can barely comprehend it myself. Let me tell you why I took this trip.

In 2022, my dad was diagnosed with both ampullary and thyroid cancers. His treatment required months of chemotherapy. I joined him for a number of the chemo sessions, trying to keep his spirits up while playing historical trivia or just holding his hand while he slept. While he rested, I looked at the faces of the other patients in the cancer center and was heartbroken to see how many of them appeared to be my age or younger. Seeing them often made me think of the indomitable Leila Janah.

Janah was a force of life. She'd founded numerous purpose-driven companies and graced the cover of our magazine in 2016. When I interviewed her for the article, she'd just returned from wingsuit flying in France, and I was blown away by her brilliance. She seemed to be sucking the marrow out of life. So when I heard in 2020 that Janah had lost her life to cancer, I was devastated. She was so young. So full of life. So joyful. It didn't make sense. Janah and I were the same age, and as I looked at the faces of the young warriors in the cancer center fighting for their lives, I wondered what I would regret if this was my last year of life. When I asked myself this question, I realized I would regret not making more time for the things that brought me true joy. At the same time, I couldn't quite articulate what even brought me joy any longer.

As I'd gotten older, progressed in my career, and become a mom, doing things for fun felt more and more like a luxury—so much so that I'd disconnected from my joy. Does this track with your experience? Has doing something joyful for yourself started to feel lavish or unrealistic? Or maybe some small part of you feels that by denying yourself joy and putting everyone else first, you're proving something? Vanessa Roanhorse's therapist calls this being "a martyr with no audience." Denying yourself joy doesn't prove anything or make you more deserving; it just makes you . . . joyless. Our societal obsession with *doing* has made too many of us lose sight of the beauty of *enjoying*.

When I realized that I'd lost touch with the beauty of enjoying, I decided to reconnect with my joy, starting with identifying what truly brings me joy at this point in my life. I wrote about memories when I felt pure joy; laughed so hard I couldn't catch my breath; or felt awestruck, inspired, or profoundly alive. I looked for patterns from these memories and saw common experiences that brought me joy: traveling and exploring, meaningful conversations in intimate groups, uninterrupted time with people I love, walking in nature, enjoying delicious food, and experiencing beauty and artistry. I'd been able to sneak some of these things in over the previous years, but not enough.

So in 2023, filled with relief from an unexpectedly good prognosis for my dad, I practiced prioritizing joy. Of everything I'd identified that brought me joy, I hadn't been able to travel for anything beyond work in a very long time. Between having a baby in 2019, COVID in 2020, having another baby in 2021, and then simply being a mom to two young kids while trying to work, taking a trip for enjoyment seemed like something I might do again in, oh, let's say . . . a decade?

My brother Jeff lived in Cardiff at the time, and we'd always dreamed of going to a Liverpool game together. I came up with the idea to head to the United Kingdom, explore London alone, go to a Liverpool game with Jeff, and then travel to Cardiff to see my brother's family. It was totally unrealistic. It was asking too much. It was perfect.

I proposed my idea to my husband. My ever-supportive, wonderful, deeply caring husband replied, "You're joking, right?" His immediate response would have completely derailed the old me: "He's right. I'm asking for too much." However, the new me—the one who prioritized my joy—stuck with it. I told him the deeper *why* behind the trip and then said the most foreign sentence I'd ever uttered, "This feels important. I'd like to try to figure out how to make it work." He got it. I also proposed that we each get one week per year dedicated to nurturing our joy, which we agreed to.

Two months later, I woke up by myself in a London hotel and didn't even know what to do with myself. I couldn't remember the last time I'd had a day where I didn't have something I needed to take care of or someone's opinion to consider, a day that wasn't already scheduled for me. I got to do whatever *I* wanted to do. It was such a foreign feeling that I felt paralyzed at first. I sat in silence and asked myself, "What's calling to you right now?" The things that consistently brought me joy were calling my name—delicious food, exploring, and finding beauty. I explored gorgeous parks while listening to music. I bought a decadent pastry to eat on a sun-drenched bench in a flower garden. I explored anything that caught my eye, ate anything that looked delicious, looked for beauty, and focused solely on what made me happy. The entire trip went like this.

When I returned home to my family, my cup was overflowing. I felt reenergized and reinspired, as if those days spent reconnecting with my joy had seeped into the cellular membrane of my body. This is the beauty of joy. It nurtures your very soul. Pal says, "When it comes to our well-being, it's really important to do things that light you up." Sustained leaders understand the power of joy and build it into their lives. They release the patriarchal guilt placed on women to deny their happiness for the sake of taking care of others and instead embrace their joy as a key component of being the best leader possible and living a worthwhile life. As author Karen Walrond says, "If we feel guilt about joy, the bad guys win. We can't let them win. Joy is how we develop resiliency. Making the effort and intention to tap into our joy, that's how we remind ourselves of our humanity, our interconnectedness, and why it all matters."[15]

Tips for Prioritizing Your Joy

1. Seek Small Daily Moments

One way to bring more joy into your life is to look for one small moment of joy each day. This practice conditions your brain to look for and pay more attention to joy. Authors Brené Brown and Karen Walrond say practicing taking a picture of something beautiful every day and journaling about one good thing that happened each day helps them regularly tap into joy.[16] Executive Coach Mary Meduna-Gross practices savoring a daily moment, like enjoying every detail of her morning coffee, from the way it smells and tastes to the warmth on her hands and the sounds she can hear around her. Whatever the medium, build a habit of looking for small daily moments of joy to help you bring more joy into your life.

2. Schedule It

I know, there's something about "scheduling joy" that feels . . . off. But it's often necessary. Start now by taking time to put joyful activities on your calendar. Once they're on your calendar, treat them with the same reverence that you would any other commitment.

Restaurateur Erin Wade loves surfing. She says, "Even though I was so pro-work-life balance for everyone else, I didn't do it for myself. I was setting such a shitty example. I started putting surfing on my calendar and told everyone, 'Unless there's an emergency, on these mornings, I'm in the ocean, and I'll be back in the afternoon.'" Wade unashamedly scheduled her joy, modeling to her team that they should do so as well. Entrepreneur Emily Mochizuki Lutyens and her partner, Cesar, schedule weekly time for their joy. Every Tuesday night, Cesar stays home with their young daughter so Emily can nurture her joy. Every Thursday, Emily and Cesar swap so Cesar can do the same. Every Friday, they have a date night to be joyful together. One leader I work with takes off a full day on the last Friday of every month to go on a three-hour hike, have lunch at a restaurant they love, and then spend the afternoon alone doing whatever they want.

What's something you could schedule regularly to nurture your joy? And no, I'm not talking about something you kind of enjoy that's actually an excuse to check something off your to-do list. I'm talking about something for which the sole purpose is joy. Quiet time to read a book? Coffee with your bestie? Dance lessons? Whatever it is, schedule it.

3. Plan Your Dream Joy Experience

When entrepreneur Maryam Sharifzadeh discovered how joyful she felt visiting Playa Xinalani in Mexico, she dreamed of visiting this beautiful place every year. Instead of writing her dream off as "unrealistic," she tapped into her creativity and found a way to make it work. Sharifzadeh launched a weeklong annual yoga retreat in Playa Xinalani to enable her to visit every year, after which she stays for a week by herself to connect with her joy.

What's a dream experience that would bring you deep joy? Is it a trip? Multiple days of uninterrupted time with friends? A class or certification? Instead of thinking about all the reasons you can't do it, start asking yourself, "How can I make this work?" It's not a luxury; it's a necessity. And you're worthy of experiencing joy. Period.

Sustained Leadership Practice #4: Seek Professional Help

Of all the leaders I've interviewed, there's one thing people cite more than anything else as the most important thing they've ever done for their well-being: professional therapy. Author and thought leader Akaya Windwood says, "Therapy literally saved my life." Vanessa Roanhorse says, "It's allowed me to unpack all the stuff I needed to understand better to be the person I want to be. All the incredible tools that got me here no longer serve me because a lot of them were grounded in trauma that I am finally working through."

Perhaps you've already experienced the power of working with a professional counselor, therapist, or psychiatrist, in which case feel free to jump to the next section. However, if something is holding you back from seeking professional help, I offer my story (#vulnerability) in case it's helpful in any way.

When I resigned from my role as CEO of Conscious Company Media in March 2020, I wasn't expecting COVID. With the lockdown, our nanny could no longer watch our nine-month-old son, Jack. Since I'd just resigned and hadn't yet launched the new company I'd been planning, it made sense for me to become Jack's full-time caretaker instead of my husband, Scott, who was already gainfully employed.

As days of social isolation with no outlet for my passion for entrepreneurism turned into weeks and weeks turned into months, I started to slip away. I felt a constant low-level terror that my son would injure himself. I frequently snapped at Scott. I felt impatient and frustrated with anyone around me. I wasn't happy, but I was still functioning. I was just *fine*.

One evening, Scott asked if I'd consider going to therapy, and I was taken aback. We'd discussed going to therapy before when I'd been navigating the stress of running my company—especially after my panic attack. However, each time I considered it, I'd tell myself I didn't have time to find someone to work with or convince myself I didn't actually *need* it. I was running an entire company. Wouldn't I need to go to therapy only if I wasn't able to work, couldn't get out of bed, had harmful thoughts, or something like that? I started pulling out my old excuses, but something was different this time: Jack. I realized I wasn't even close to being the mom I wanted to be for him.

My friend recommended her therapist, Lynn. During our first session, Lynn said she felt that I was clinically depressed. Seriously? That seemed a little extreme. I pushed back against her diagnosis, and Lynn gently helped me understand that my vision of what depression looks like didn't reflect how it often shows up in real life. She suggested that I experiment with taking a low dose of an antidepressant over the coming month. I was embarrassed. I felt like taking an antidepressant meant something was "wrong" with me. Lynn asked if I would judge someone who's diabetic for taking insulin.

"Of course not!" I said.

"It's the same thing," she replied. "Your brain chemistry isn't functioning properly, and you likely need medication to help."

I started taking Lexapro and within a week noticed a huge difference. I felt calmer and more peaceful and started enjoying spending time with my son.

I continued seeing Lynn as we worked through some of the pressing issues first and expanded to deeper ones over time. At times, I felt frustrated with the pace of healing. I expected that some light switch would flip at some point, and I'd magically be healed.

However, healing is a gradual progression. Instead of a light switch, it's more like a dimmer switch that slowly turns on. It takes time to untangle all the crap that has collected over years and years of life. But the first time I responded to a situation in a new, healthy way rather than falling back on my old harmful patterns, I understood how profound the work of healing is.

I had such a positive experience with therapy that I felt open to seeing a psychiatrist at the recommendation of my friends Teuta and Jess, both of whom had recently been diagnosed with ADHD. Knowing me and hearing about behavior patterns that we all shared, they gave me the contact information for their doctor to see if I was neurodivergent as well. It turns out, I went thirty-seven years of my life without knowing I have ADHD. My diagnosis explained so many things I struggled with—organization, forgetfulness, abandoning projects halfway through. Again, I began taking proper medication, and my entire life changed.

I'd resisted getting professional help with my mental health for so long, convincing myself that I was okay or that it was too much of a hassle. These excuses held me back from receiving critical diagnoses and healing. I uncovered limiting patterns and beliefs I didn't even know I had and cultivated greater self-awareness. I addressed many of my toxic traits like people-pleasing, withholding truth, and martyring myself. Getting professional help has been one of the most consequential and profound actions I've ever taken. If you're holding back from getting help, I can't encourage you strongly enough to prioritize finding a way to work with a professional. It will transform your entire life.

Tips for Seeking Professional Help

1. Shift Your Mindset

If the perceived stigma or judgment of going to therapy is holding you back from seeking help, I've gotten past my concerns by thinking of therapy as having a personal trainer for my brain. While many people go to the gym, your biceps don't dictate the quality of your life—your brain does. For me, training my brain to respond healthily to people and situations is one of the most important things I can do to improve the quality of my life and the lives of those around me. So why wouldn't I get a personal trainer for my brain to help me do so?

2. Make the Time

Beyond stigma, lack of time might be standing in the way of your working with a professional. Adding yet another thing to your already jam-packed calendar might seem daunting. That said, depending on the cadence, we're talking about one to four hours per *month*. Honestly, I'm guessing most of us spend at least four hours per month or more scrolling through social media or watching television.

Prioritizing your mental health and well-being is worth setting your phone down, shifting a few things around, or saying no to yet another obligation every once in a while. These will likely be the most impactful hours of your entire month, so make the space.

3. Examine Your Financial Reality

The cost of therapy can also be a significant barrier to getting help. I still remember my roommate in college going to therapy and dreaming that someday I might be able to afford it as I waited tables and barely made rent each month. It truly wasn't accessible to me at the time. In my late twenties and early thirties, therapy still didn't feel financially realistic. That said, in 2020, COVID drastically reduced my nonessential spending. We weren't grabbing drinks with friends, going shopping, or going out for dinner any longer. Within a few months, I felt like I had enough money to start seeing a therapist twice per month and realized that I could've afforded therapy much earlier if I'd reprioritized what I spent my money on.

If finances are preventing you from finding help, there are a few potential solutions. To begin, explore whether your health insurance covers therapy and if so, which providers. Next, you can start saving for a mental health fund by setting aside small amounts each pay cycle to afford help within the next six to twelve months.

If one-on-one sessions aren't financially realistic right now, you can also explore community healing spaces or try cultivating a group of peers with whom you can regularly be open and vulnerable. Akaya Windwood says, "With my younger brown women, I'm finding that if I can create the conditions by which they can be brave together, healing happens. I'm experimenting with the conditions that I can help create so that there is space to be very brave. In that brave space, amazing things happen. Among those amazing things, healing happens."

Sustained Leadership Practice #5: Cultivate Compassion

When I asked Pal about her top recommendations for sustaining well-being, there was one answer I wasn't expecting: compassion. After she told me about her daily compassion practice, I thought about the role compassion plays in high-achieving women's lives. Many of us are overly critical of ourselves. We're weighed down with guilt about all the things we "should" be doing. We feel judged for not living up to unrealistic gendered societal expectations. In professional situations, we're judged more harshly by others and conditioned to judge others. We often judge ourselves based on extremely high expectations for our performance. There's so much *judgment* in our lives. It's exhausting.

Practicing compassion invites you to meet this judgment with kindness. In contrast to empathy—trying to sense or understand someone's feelings—compassion means acting on that understanding with an authentic desire to help. Compassion, kindness, and giving to others are linked to a longer life; reduced risk of cardiovascular disease and high blood pressure; better cognitive function as we age; greater happiness, well-being, resilience, and resistance to burnout; decreased symptoms of depression; and better relationships.

Research has shown that being compassionate for a mere forty seconds can measurably lower your sense of anxiety.[17] All of this is to say, bringing more compassion, both for others and for yourself, into your life results in a greater quality of life.

Tips for Cultivating Compassion

1. Practice Gratitude

Gratitude is a gateway to compassion. The more you practice gratitude, the easier it is to meet others from a place of kindness and ease. Robert Emmons, who studies gratitude, says two core elements of gratitude are focusing on the good things in your life and focusing on the people who've played a role in the good things in your life. Of the latter, Emmons says, "I see it as a relationship-strengthening emotion because it requires us to see how we've been supported and affirmed by other people." The more we focus on the people involved in the good things in our lives, the more inspired we are to be compassionate and pay it forward.

In addition to cultivating greater compassion, research has shown that gratitude can bolster your immune system, lower your blood pressure, make you feel less lonely, and enhance other positive emotions.

The simplest practice for tapping into gratitude is keeping a gratitude journal where you write down what you're grateful for every day. Emmons found that this practice enhanced people's well-being in as little as three weeks.[18]

2. Compassion Practices

If you find yourself wrapped up in judgment about someone else, Pal recommends a daily five-to-ten-minute compassion practice.

> 1. Sit quietly and think of someone you love. For one full minute, focus on them. Think of their face, their smile,

and their laugh, and send them the following intentions for at least a full minute:
   a. May you have happiness.
   b. May you be free from suffering.
   c. May you experience joy and ease.
2. Now, think of someone in your life whom you're struggling with. Maybe someone you've had a conflict with or with whom you're not seeing eye to eye. Picture them and send them the same intentions for at least a full minute:
   a. May you have happiness.
   b. May you be free from suffering.
   c. May you experience joy and ease.
3. Now, think of yourself. Think of something you're struggling with based on your own actions or decisions. Something you feel guilty about, shame around, judgment, or any sense of negativity that has caused you to think less of yourself. Sit quietly and repeat the following intentions for at least a full minute:
   a. May I be happy.
   b. May I be free from suffering.
   c. May I have joy and ease.

EVERY DAY, YOU MODEL TO THE PEOPLE AROUND YOU HOW THEY should treat you and how they should treat themselves. When you constantly put yourself last or disregard your own needs, you signal to others that it's okay for them to put you last as well. This behavior doesn't impact just you. When you choose to model to others the harmful belief that sacrificing yourself is okay, it's a disservice to women everywhere. On the other hand, when you start believing you're worthy of care and begin prioritizing your well-being, you show others that this is how you should be treated while permitting them to feel worthy of care themselves. Moreover, every aspect of your life will improve. Your relationships. Your health. Your performance. Your energy.

Shifting toward sustained leadership and taking care of your well-being *while* you're on the journey is one of the most life-altering choices you can make. Additionally, shifting toward sustained leadership will help you lean into the three other new-playbook leadership practices—being holistic, authentic, and optimized—and vice versa. All of the new-playbook leadership practices work together and complement one another. The more you lean into one, the easier it will be to practice the others and the more your leadership and life will evolve toward greatness. Whether you'll rise to meet the opportunity is up to you.

Key Chapter Insights

- Between patriarchal expectations of women and high-pressure business cultures, many working women become sacrificial leaders who disregard their own needs in service of taking care of others and achieving "success." Consistent self-sacrifice leads to increased instances of chronic disease, heart disease, elevated blood pressure, burnout, mental health crises, and decreased performance.
- Sustained leaders prioritize their well-being, regularly engaging with practices that result in significantly improved physical and mental health, decreased instances of burnout, enhanced resilience, and increased levels of overall happiness.
- Being the most effective leader possible means focusing on the foundational elements of well-being, including adequate sleep, nutrition, mindfulness, and physical exercise; cultivating connection with others; prioritizing joy; seeking professional help; and practicing compassion.

Part II

Reimagining the Workplace

Chapter 6

FROM HARMFUL WORKPLACES TO BENEFICIAL WORKPLACES

CAT PEREZ HAD JUST LANDED A DREAM JOB AT AN UP-AND-coming start-up. Shortly after starting, she noticed some concerning behavior from her new CEO. He micromanaged women but not men and doubted women's work product, even when they were in senior leadership positions, yet quickly accepted work from any men on the team. He excluded the Hispanic women data analysts on their team from company events, and Perez even overheard him making disgusting remarks about how attractive a job applicant was before she'd even left the building. She says, "It was a horrible environment. It was supermisogynistic. I realized this was the leader who was driving the company outcomes."

Perez wasn't happy, but the final straw came when multiple women on the team told management about being sexually harassed and degraded by a specific client. In response, the CEO said he needed to prioritize the high-paying client, and he ignored his employees' complaints. Perez resigned shortly afterward. She wasn't surprised to see many of her co-workers follow suit. Ultimately, the

CEO stepped down for unspecified reasons. Perez is one of countless employees in the global workforce who work or have worked in traditional-playbook harmful workplaces.

The Traditional Playbook: Harmful Workplaces

In August 2023, twenty-one-year-old Moritz Erhardt was found unresponsive by his roommates. In the three days leading up to his untimely death, Erhardt had worked more than seventy-two hours straight as an intern for Bank of America Merrill Lynch. As one of hundreds of interns at the company, he worked extra hours to try to set himself apart in the highly competitive financial industry. Upon examining Erhardt's body, the coroner highlighted stress and fatigue in his cause-of-death report.[1] Erhardt was the victim of a high-stress, overly demanding business culture—a dynamic too many of us are familiar with. Cultures like this are just one example of how contemporary workplaces harm employees.

Under the cover of maximizing shareholder value, business leaders feel pressured to get results no matter the cost. This toxically masculine "win at all costs" ethos results in business leaders making decisions that threaten the economic, physical, and/or psychological safety of their workers. These decisions destroy people's lives.

When it comes to workers' physical safety, traditional-playbook leaders are pressured to do things like cut corners on safety measures, ignore employee complaints, or overwork their teams. Worldwide, roughly 3 million workers die annually from work-related injuries or diseases, and as many as 400 million are hurt on the job.[2] An estimated one in ten—roughly 280 million—global workers have experienced physical violence at work.[3] And when it comes to overworking employees, working long hours has been proven to increase the risk of cardiovascular disease, chronic fatigue, stress, depression, anxiety, hypertension, alcohol use, and occupational injury.[4]

Shareholder supremacy incentivizes business leaders to threaten employees' economic security as well as their physical safety. Leaders feel pressured to reduce costs at every turn—cutting employee wages, sending jobs offshore, laying off employees, and consolidating roles. Since the adoption of shareholder supremacy, while workers have increased the amount of income generated in an average hour of work by nearly 60 percent, wages have increased by less than 15 percent.[5] Currently, an estimated one in seven people worldwide struggle to meet their basic needs every day, and this struggle is detrimental to their health.[6] Recently, the American Medical Association's Council on Medical Service issued a statement saying, "There is widespread consensus that populations with low incomes have worse health outcomes."[7] Low wages and the ensuing financial stress have been directly linked to increased obesity, anxiety, depression, low birth weight, and hypertension and even lead to faster memory decline later in life.[8] Similarly, job loss has been shown to be detrimental to individual mental and physical health, leading to increased stress, loss of identity, and interpersonal conflicts at home.[9]

In addition to threats to workers' physical and economic safety, far too many employees feel psychologically unsafe in the workplace. In the name of "getting results," leaders lean into toxically masculine and patriarchal behaviors like using fear, control, anger, and dominance to manage employees. These managers see women and other marginalized populations as inferior and don't believe the truth of those employees' experiences; punish employees for mistakes; demand loyalty and obedience; and excuse toxic, violent, or noninclusive behaviors from "high performers" in the name of winning. Often these behaviors have an outsized impact on women and people with other marginalized identities, leaving them in a constant low-level state of fear and stress. This psychological harm often causes workers to leave their jobs and can have long-lasting consequences for their self-esteem and overall well-being.

Unfortunately, workplaces that cause harm—economic, physical, or psychological—erode people's mental and physical health. A better way exists. In the new playbook, leaders aspire to create beneficial workplaces—environments where people are not just free from harm but where going to work actually *enriches* their lives.

The New Playbook: Beneficial Workplaces

When Susan Griffin-Black and her ex-husband founded EO Products, she says, "We started the company with this idea of building a company we would want to work for in the most human way. People work their whole lives to retire and finally live. We were like, 'Can we live like we're already retired and build a life *while* we're working? What would it take to build a company other people want to work for?'" This ethos—building a company where people can enjoy their lives while they're working—has helped turn EO Products into a beneficial workplace.

Leaders of beneficial workplaces refuse to compromise anyone's well-being in the name of profit. They strive to build companies that are economically, physically, and psychologically safe, but they don't stop there. These leaders also seek to *advance* their employees' lives in some way. As for Griffin-Black, benefiting employees centers around employee happiness and finding joy at work. It can also look like building a company that improves employees' mental health or helps them develop as people and meet their potential. The key element is that each day, employees leave feeling their lives are better as a result of going to work.

Can you imagine what the world would look like if more businesses did this? In a world where more than 40 percent of employees experience "a lot of stress" every week and nearly 80 percent have experienced work-related stress in the last month, how much would change if most of the global workforce went to work every day and returned home feeling *better* than when they left?[10] If most people felt that their work *improved* their lives instead of being a key source of stress? This world is possible. The following best-known practices, including finding solutions to feedback, modeling healthy workplace practices, bolstering everyone's economic well-being, normalizing and supporting mental health, and helping employees develop, can help you create this world by building a more beneficial workplace with your own company.

Beneficial Leadership Practice #1:
Take Feedback Seriously & Find Solutions

In 2017, co-founder and CEO of Homeroom restaurant Erin Wade received an email from fifteen of her team members requesting a meeting. Wade knew the request was serious and quickly set up a meeting to hear more. On the day of the meeting, multiple employees told Wade they were being sexually harassed by customers.

Wade was honored that her team trusted her enough to bring the issue to her attention instead of sweeping it under the rug. After their initial discussion, she invited anyone who wanted to join to co-create a solution with her. She scheduled working sessions with her team, dedicating as much time as needed to find a solution. She was just as busy as any other business leader out there, yet her team's safety came first.

Through open dialogue and some trial and error, the Homeroom team created a new system, which Wade says was 100 percent her employees' idea. She just facilitated the conversation. If a customer gave an employee a bad vibe or if they had any hesitation about serving a table, they'd tell their manager they had a "yellow," and the employee could ask the manager for whatever they needed, like watching the table or taking it over for them. If an employee experienced an ambiguous interaction that gave them a bad vibe, like a comment that wasn't overtly sexual but still made them uncomfortable, they could report an "orange." At that point, the manager was *required* to take over the table. If the customer did something overtly sexual, like saying something inappropriate or trying to touch a staff member, the employee would report a "red," and the manager would ask the guest to leave. No questions asked. Wade says the system was effective because "women didn't have to relive stories of what was happening to them or have someone make a judgment call as to whether or not it was worth acting upon." The system automatically validated the employee's experience.

Once the new system was implemented, Wade says the company went from nearly everyone having a "red" story to almost no one having one. Wade wrote an op-ed in the *Washington Post* about the system after seeing a *New York Times* story about a local chef who'd been harassing his employees. The op-ed went viral. Wade was then invited to testify about it in front of the Equal Employment Opportunity Commission, the part of the US government that oversees discrimination and harassment suits, which then recommended Homeroom's system as its national standard. Wade says, "It felt amazing to have something start as a problem, have these amazing collaborative systems create an incredible solution, and then use my voice as a mouthpiece to help spread that solution in a huge way."

Compare Wade's story to Cat Perez's experience. In both cases, employees came to the CEO detailing sexual harassment from customers. Wade took the issue seriously and found a much-needed solution. Perez's CEO ignored his employees' concerns to retain a profitable client and kept his employees in a harmful situation. When leaders don't listen to and believe their employees, they create unsafe workplaces that perpetuate harm. With nearly one in five workers experiencing bullying at work, one in four reporting having been verbally abused at work in the previous year, and 15 percent experiencing direct discrimination and harassment, workplace harassment has become a key source of work-related stress that is often downplayed or ignored.[11] Business leaders who want to create beneficial workplaces can't ignore these issues; they must take feedback seriously and prioritize finding solutions to protect everyone and create psychologically and physically safe organizations.

Finding ways to solicit feedback and ensuring that your team genuinely feels supported when they share their experience with you will help you cultivate a more beneficial workplace for all.

Tips for Taking Feedback Seriously and Finding Solutions

1. Provide Feedback Mechanisms

One of the ways Wade built a culture where employees felt safe bringing problems to the surface was by making feedback a regular part of their experience. Every time employees left for the day, they were asked to fill out an optional survey: How would you rate your day? Do you have any suggestions? Is there anything you want to note for company leadership? Wade often received hundreds of weekly responses, providing her with a wealth of data to use as CEO. She looked for key trends and potential issues that helped her with decision-making and took the time to follow up on key issues with her employees.

Kari Warberg Block, CEO of Earthwise, has her team supervisors collect employee feedback throughout the month and flag key issues to discuss at monthly "coffee with Kari" meetings where employees are invited to sit down and discuss their observations directly. Employees are encouraged to ask Warberg Block questions, voice their opinions, provide differing ideas, and talk through anything as a group.

Tara Milburn, CEO of Ethical Swag, uses a company-wide Slack channel dedicated to company improvement where employees can voice ideas about process improvements, current challenges, or general feedback. While some smaller issues are addressed quickly based on team-member agreement, others serve to start larger team-wide discussions that Milburn flags for further attention.

Indigo Ink co-founder Liz Richardson hosts a daily all-staff meeting with her team of fifteen as part of the feedback cycle. Beyond discussing what everyone's currently working on, they build time into every meeting for anyone to voice feedback that is then discussed as a team. She says it takes about three months for new employees to feel safe enough to voice their concerns and highlights repetition and curiosity as critical elements that enable her team to openly discuss feedback.

Employees need to have clear mechanisms to voice their opinions to company leadership to ensure their safety. What types of feedback mechanisms do you have at your organization? Do employees feel confident that their feedback is taken seriously and that they won't be punished for mentioning challenging issues? How often do you receive feedback from team members, and what could you do to increase the frequency? Whether it's a daily survey, weekly Slack check-in, regularly scheduled meetings, or something else entirely, regularly soliciting team-member feedback will go a long way toward cultivating a beneficial organization.

2. Listen to Understand

When it comes to listening to feedback, Griffin-Black says, "Any really good leader needs to understand the intention behind listening, which is, ultimately, to lessen suffering." If someone has taken time to bring an issue to your attention, it means they're struggling. The best way to begin lessening anyone's suffering is to ensure that they feel heard and understood. To that end, as a leader, your first priority isn't to identify solutions; it's to genuinely listen. Listening to understand means being curious and receptive, asking thoughtful questions, regulating your emotions, and gathering as much information as possible. Once you've done so, you can work toward finding genuine solutions to lessen that individual's suffering.

3. Invite People to Co-create Solutions

One of the quickest ways to deteriorate psychological safety in the workplace is by ignoring or not believing employee feedback. Wade says, "At so many organizations, people are so disenfranchised. You can mention the problem, but then someone else is either going to fix it for you or they're not going to address it at all." It's incumbent on you as a leader to prioritize finding solutions. Inviting your team to co-create solutions with you is one of the best ways to do so. Whether or not your employees accept your invitation, giving them the *option* of working on the solution gives them a greater sense of agency and helps them see that you're taking it seriously. Either way, ensuring that you close the loop and communicate what steps were taken to address your employees' concerns is a critical step in the process.

4. Establish Clear Guidelines

When it comes to harassment; bullying; or verbal, psychological, or physical abuse, work with your HR team or an HR professional to establish clear guidelines for everyone on your team to address and report any employee violations. Hannah Drain Taylor, co-CEO of fractional HR company Talent to Team, says one of the most important messages her company has relayed to its leadership team is to treat all team-member complaints seriously. They've identified specific issues that are automatically elevated to company executives for full investigation and provided managers with guidance on how to handle others.

While there are HR issues that are clearly black-and-white, like multiple members of a team reporting sexual harassment or finding child porn on someone's computer, other issues can fall into gray areas. In these instances, take the issue seriously by investigating it from as many angles as possible. Speak directly with all parties involved, talk to any witnesses, and seek to find documentation when possible. The more information you can aggregate, the better your response is likely to be.

Beneficial Leadership Practice #2: Normalize Healthy Workplace Practices

When employees feel pressured to work too many hours, feel they can't take breaks, are forced to work overtime, or have excessive workloads, they're at higher risk of physically injuring themselves on the job and burning out. The risk of workplace injury has been shown to be 1.62 times higher for employees who have had inadequate rest than for those who are well rested.[12] Even so, only one-third of employees feel that their workplace culture encourages breaks, and only 40 percent feel that their employer respects their time off.[13] Overly demanding workplaces that push workers too hard in the name of success are putting employees directly in harm's way.

Sufficient rest doesn't just reduce stress and the risk of physical injury; it's been shown to *improve* performance as well. In addition to the findings mentioned in Chapter 5 showing that sufficient rest improves individual performance, creativity, and ability to persist, the Kate Spade New York Foundation's research on workplace mental health found that taking one week off for every six weeks worked bolstered the resilience and mental health of employees across the board.[14] Stephanie Nadi Olson, founder of We Are Rosie, implemented a company-wide policy *requiring* everyone to take a week off every quarter to give them time to rest and rejuvenate.

Leaders of beneficial workplaces like Nadi Olson understand the importance of taking time off for themselves and for their teams. They build rest into their company cultures and model it themselves. Steph Speirs, co-founder of Solstice Energy, says, "We think of a high-performing work culture as the same process of building muscle in your body. You have to strain the muscle to build muscle, but you also need rest. If you don't rest your muscles, you don't actually grow the muscle fibers to make the muscle stronger. So we give people six weeks off a year for PTO, not counting if you use PTO for doctor's appointments or silly things like that, and have a policy around personal time where you can take up to four hours a day for personal time throughout the nine-to-five hours for whatever you want to do, as long as you get your work done."

Impact capital executive Diane Henry says, "I firmly believe that when you're solving hard problems, you need a certain amount of white space for your mind to make the connections it needs to make to advance the next right idea, make the right next decision, or whatever it is. There's neuroscience that backs me up in this. This is especially true the harder and gnarlier the problems are. That white space is essential when we're talking about our values, our judgment, our outlook, and our ability to dwell in possibility and not dwell in fear—all the things we need as leaders."

Tips for Modeling Healthy Workplace Behavior

1. Model Healthy Work Habits

While over 70 percent of executives think their employees feel that they promote a healthy work-life balance and encourage paid time off, only 53 percent of workers feel encouraged to use their PTO, and even fewer feel supported in taking time off for mental health needs, including therapy (46 percent).[15] Roughly half of employees say they take less paid time off than their employer offers.[16] When it comes to creating healthy company cultures where employees feel supported in resting and taking time off, your team looks to you to set the tone. To create a beneficial workplace, it's critical that you model healthy workplace practices yourself, including using your PTO and taking time off.

Take breaks, and don't hide the fact that you're doing so. Be open with your team about the fact that you're going to a therapy appointment, taking a walk, or reading a book on the roof for half an hour. Try to avoid eating lunch at your desk every day. Strive to communicate with your colleagues during work hours only. This means not sending or replying to anything work-related outside working hours unless it's mission-critical. Every time someone on your team sees that you sent an email at 2:30 a.m. on a Saturday, they feel pressured to do the same. It's not okay. If you must work during nonwork hours, schedule your emails to send when working hours begin. When it comes to PTO, use it and don't "half work" while you're out of the office. Let switching off completely be the standard, and don't apologize for doing so. The better you are at openly taking breaks, enjoying downtime, putting boundaries around nonwork time, and genuinely taking PTO, the healthier your workplace will be and the more your performance and life will improve.

2. Reconsider Your Definition of "Full-Time"

In 2019, Emily Mochizuki Lutyens resigned from her role as CEO of Legworks to address a major health issue triggered by stress. After months of health care and rehabilitation, Lutyens felt ready to work again but also worried about what reentering the workforce would mean for her health condition. She accepted a leadership role at a mission-driven organization based in Denver that, shortly after she started, announced that it was going to pilot a four-day work week. The company's CEO brought in an analyst for ninety days to monitor how the change impacted the organization's performance. The result? While working 20 percent less for the same amount of pay, the team maintained 100 percent productivity as before. Of the change, Lutyens said, "I'm definitely happier, and I think that I'm just living my life better," and the CEO said, "It's changed everything. It reduced workplace stress, reduced burnout. So our team was able to continue to produce at the same level of quality and quantity of output, and every Friday was off."[17]

While many organizations still cling to the idea that full-time work means at least eight-hour workdays and forty-hour work weeks, in truth, your organization would likely benefit from everyone working *less*. Shorter work weeks, including four-day work weeks, fewer daily working hours, and having two afternoons off every work week, have been proven to increase work performance by bolstering productivity and creativity; to improve mental and physical health by significantly reducing stress and sleep problems and decreasing the likelihood of burnout by an astounding 67 percent; and to increase life satisfaction.[18]

When it comes to your organization, what would it look like to redefine "full-time" work? Doing so will not just improve company performance but also improve your team members' lives and your own.

Beneficial Leadership Practice #3: Bolster Everyone's Economic Well-Being

Some of the most common causes of work-related stress are low wages, job loss, and unemployment. New-playbook leaders strive to relieve their team of this stress by bolstering their team's economic well-being. Stephanie Gripne, founder and CEO of the Impact Finance Center, is one such leader. She says, "We're trying to re-create the middle class that's been lost, and it's not that hard. It's my commitment to do those things." To live up to this commitment, Gripne identified three critical issues her employees face that often serve as the on-ramp to the middle class: refinancing debt, increasing wages, and getting anyone into homeownership who wants it.

Step one: Gripne surveyed her employees to see if anyone had debt they needed to refinance and on what terms. She then approached her company's investor network to find investors who wanted to step up and refinance her team's debt.

Step two: Gripne is pioneering a "thriving wage." Her working definition currently includes "having enough money so you can have a down payment and be able to buy a house, pay off your student loans, save for retirement, eat vegetables every day of the month, go out to dinner twice a week, and go on a vacation." Calculating these needs in her hometown of Denver, Colorado, Gripne found that employees needed to make around $65 per hour, as opposed to the living-wage standard of $25 per hour for a single adult without children or the state minimum wage of $14.42. Her organization now uses "thriving wage" calculations to establish employee compensation for everyone on the team.

Step three: The company assists employees in taking their first step toward homeownership, including securing financing when needed. In one case, Gripne personally co-signed a loan for an employee's house because the employee's father had a mental illness. She says, "I think the answer is creating an organization that I would want to work for. I think of it like creating community infrastructure that people can come in and use that is work with dignity and high impact and an escalator to get to that middle-class dream."

Can you imagine what it would be like if other business leaders had a similar mindset? If leaders used their connections, investors, and business growth to bolster their employees' financial standing instead of increasing their own wealth or that of a small group of shareholders? And yes, it costs more money to do this. But do you know what else costs money? Employee turnover, not hiring the best talent, and decreased productivity and engagement on account of employees being stressed about barely making ends meet. Yet only one of these cases improves the lives of everyone.

When was the last time that you thought about the economic security of *everyone* on your team? Are you sure that everyone is able to make ends meet? Is there anyone on your team who might be experiencing significant financial hardship, and is there anything you can do about it? Exploring questions like these is a key step toward creating a truly beneficial workplace.

Tips for Bolstering Everyone's Economic Well-Being

1. Pay a Living Wage

Companies can ensure that employees can meet their basic needs by using MIT's Living Wage Calculator, developed by Amy Glasmeier and Tracey Farrigan. A living wage is what an employee needs to make to meet the minimum standard of living in their community, accounting for the cost of "food, childcare, health care, housing, transportation, and other basic needs like clothing, personal care items, and broadband, among others."[19]

Major companies like Accenture, led by CEO Julie Sweet, are "real living wage" certified and have adopted living wage policies for their suppliers as well. Accenture requires all UK suppliers to provide employees with a living wage and strongly encourages anyone in its global supplier network to follow suit. Companies that encourage living wage policies understand that bolstering economic security for employees and suppliers leads to increased employee retention, and suppliers have been shown to be more reliable and to produce better-quality products as a result.[20]

At a minimum, your company should seek to pay workers and suppliers a living wage. And if your company is increasingly profitable, follow in Gripne's footsteps and push yourself to go beyond a living wage toward a thriving wage.

2. Examine Your Compensation Structures

Per the Economic Policy Institute, CEO pay increased by more than 1,000 percent between 1978 and 2023, while the average worker's pay increased by only 24 percent during that time. Last year, CEOs were paid 290 times as much as a typical worker, compared to a CEO-worker pay ratio of twenty-one to one in 1965.[21] Even in the face of this glaring disparity, many companies simply align their compensation tiers with "market rates." More business leaders need to follow in Dulbecco's footsteps from Chapter 3 and ask themselves, "What if the market is immoral?"

Some companies have begun publicly committing to capping high-level executive pay. Executives at Dr. Bronner's, including its CEO, have their salary capped at five times the wages of the lowest-paid employees, who make $28 per hour. If your compensation structure has huge gaps between tiers, especially between executives and hourly or entry-level workers, explore a more equitable compensation structure and find the courage to put it into action.

Beneficial Leadership Practice #4: Normalize and Support Workplace Mental Health

In her role as president and CEO of the Texoma Health Foundation, Michelle Lemming was given the mandate to improve community mental health outcomes in four rural counties near the Texas-Oklahoma border. Based on her childhood experience with mental health, she knew that her work was cut out for her. Lemming grew up with a bipolar mother and spent part of her childhood as her mother's sole caregiver—a role she still has to this day. As she contended with the realities of her mother's condition, Lemming knew one thing for certain: "Even though I didn't even really know what was happening to my mother, I knew it was absolutely not okay to talk about it with anyone."

Despite roughly *one billion* people around the world contending with mental health issues, the toxically masculine beliefs that showing emotions and asking for help are signs of weakness has stigmatized many mental health discussions.[22] This stigma often extends to the workplace as well. At present, nearly 60 percent of workers aren't comfortable discussing mental health at work, even though 92 percent of employees say it's important to them to work for an organization that provides support for mental health.[23]

Lemming realized that oftentimes, the behavior we learn at work informs how we behave at home. If her organization ever wanted to normalize mental health discussions in its community, Lemming felt she must start with the organization itself. She had everyone on staff go through Laurel Mellin's Emotional Brain Training program. Employees were trained to rate their mental state on a scale from one to five. One represents the feeling of thriving, being in a flow state, and feeling entirely present and engaged. Conversely, a therapist working with the organization described five as "If you're not throwing something, you really would like to throw something. If you're not yelling, you'd like to yell. If you're not just breaking down, you want to break down."

After the training, Lemming started asking everyone on her team about their number each morning. If someone checked in as a one, the team wouldn't distract them or give them mundane tasks so they could get their best work done. If someone checked in as a four or five, the team would try to give them easier tasks and make sure they felt supported in taking time to do whatever they needed, whether it was attending therapy, taking a walk, or taking a mental well-being day. Lemming noticed that paying attention to her number each day helped her be honest with herself about her own well-being as well.

As women struggle with higher incidences of mental health issues than men, workplace stigma about mental health disproportionately impacts women. Taryn Bird, director of the Kate Spade New York Foundation, which focuses on mental health, says, "Women are twice as likely to experience trauma than men, twice as likely to live with anxiety, depression, post-traumatic stress disorder, and complex post-traumatic stress disorder. Just by being a woman and a girl, you are exposed to a higher degree of emotional abuse, sexual abuse, workplace discrimination, and racial discrimination."

Bird and her team came face-to-face with the importance of supporting women's mental health with one of their first social-impact programs establishing a factory in Rwanda to employ local women. "We were going through a lot of the professional and vocational training with these women. Eighty to 90 percent of them had either a connection to or were a survivor of the 1994 genocide. These trainers were coming in, they were delivering training, but it was going in one ear and out the other because there was a high level of post-traumatic stress disorder living in the bodies of the workforce. We decided to put the more traditional empowerment program that was focused solely on economics, like savings and financial planning, on the back burner. We brought in a counselor, and then we brought in a yoga for trauma program. We were essentially doing an intervention that was improving the voice, choice, and power and then the collective operations of the business."

As Bird's experience illustrates, when employees contend with mental health issues in unsupportive workplaces, they can't perform nearly as well as they could if they were in more supportive environments. Finding ways to support your team's mental health is a profound way you can both mitigate harm and improve your employees' lives. It allows employees to feel supported at work instead of feeling that they need to hide. Imagine the impact of workplaces being places where people begin to *heal* instead of being places that *cause* mental health issues. Creating a beneficial workplace that bolsters employees' well-being is possible.

Tips for Normalizing and Supporting Mental Health at Work

1. Check In Regularly

In their work on what they deemed "deliberately developmental organizations (DDO)," researchers Robert Kegan, Lisa Lahey, Andy Fleming, Matthew Miller, and Inna Markus discovered that including personal check-ins at the beginning of team meetings was a common practice of high-performing companies. Speaking about Decurion, a DDO company, they say, "These check-ins at the start of each meeting foster a critical way of closing gaps, reducing the possibility that members will be disconnected, operate on autopilot, or forget that at Decurion, people are 'ends rather than means.'" One Decurion leader told them, "'Full humanity is not just welcome but required here.'"[24]

Including personal check-ins at the beginning of team meetings is a simple yet powerful tool for supporting workplace mental health. The question can be as simple as "How are you *actually* doing today?" During these check-ins, give your team members enough space to answer the question and encourage everyone, including yourself, to bring their full humanity to the space. One of the best ways to encourage your team to do so is by stepping into your vulnerability. Let your team see the real you, including your challenges and struggles. This will model to others that they're safe to do the same.

2. Take Mental Health and Well-Being Seriously

Maryam Sharifzadeh, founder and CEO of Zen as a Service (ZaaS) and Office Yoga, says, "Well-being is the missing piece at many organizations. You have departments for finance, engineering, marketing, and sales, but rarely well-being. When there's a dedicated well-being committee or department, that's when we really start to see a little bit more holistic functions happening within companies."

When it comes to your organization, how seriously do you take mental health? What steps could you take to support everyone's well-being more intentionally? Could you seek professional training, provide paid mental health days, have mental health professionals available to employees as part of their benefits or people on-site who've received mental health training? The more seriously you take bolstering your team's mental health, the more beneficial your workplace will become.

Beneficial Leadership Practice #5: Nurture Continued Learning and Growth

Last year while touring a Barry-Wehmiller (BW) facility, I met Ken, who told our group about one of the most important moments of his life. More than a decade before, his son had moved home following a difficult personal situation. At the time, Ken worked for a BW manufacturing plant in Green Bay, Wisconsin. Each night, he'd return home from work to find his son struggling with his new reality. So Ken would give him all sorts of suggestions for what he "should" do moving forward. His son didn't want to hear it and began pulling away.

While Ken navigated his increasingly fraught relationship with his son, his company announced that its Listening Like a Leader training was coming to Green Bay. He decided to join. He says, "The training made me realize I'd never actually listened to the people in my life." Ken returned home after the training, sat down with his son, asked him about his day, and then practiced truly listening.

At first, Ken's son didn't believe his father had changed. Yet after a few weeks of Ken practicing his newly acquired listening skills, their relationship began to transform. Through their continued nightly conversations, his son eventually decided to join the military as his next step, a move that launched him on an entirely new career path. Ken credits his company's training program with saving his relationship with his son. The training was so impactful that Ken trained to become one of the professors who now teaches the programs to other BW employees.

Ken's story illustrates another way companies can *improve* their employees' lives: continued learning and development. As growth and mastery are one of our top three intrinsic motivators, in addition to purpose and autonomy, giving your employees opportunities to learn and grow is one of the best ways to enrich their lives. Roughly 94 percent of workers say they'd stay at their company longer if it invested in helping them learn, and learning opportunities have been identified as the top driver of a great work culture.[25] Stanford psychologist Carol Dweck, who coined the term "growth mindset," found that when entire companies focus on continued learning and embrace a growth mindset, their employees report feeling far more empowered and committed.[26] These practices also help companies attract incredible talent. Co-founder of the Conscious Leadership Group Diana Chapman worked with software company Asana for years to help its co-founders build a growth-oriented culture. She says, "We onboarded the first 2,500 Asana employees, and many of them said they turned down double the pay that Google was going to give them to come to Asana because of the culture. In the future, any company that's especially toxic won't make it unless they're attracting people who want to play a toxic game. But over time, less and less people want to do that. People are ready to be happy."

Torani CEO Melanie Dulbecco says focusing on their employees' growth is the key to driving the entire organization's growth. In the thirty-two years she's been CEO, she's overseen an average growth rate of 20 percent every year, meaning the company consistently doubles in size every three and a half to four years. Dulbecco says, "Yes, our growth has been tremendous, but that's the lagging indicator. That's what catches the interest of investment bankers, financial types, and business leaders. I always think about what the *leading* indicators are. The leading indicators have everything to do with the growth and development of our people."

By continually helping your team learn and develop, you'll enrich their lives and build a more resilient, beneficial company in the process.

Tips for Nurturing Continued Learning and Growth

1. Provide Consistent, Meaningful Feedback

Providing your team with regular, meaningful feedback is a great tool for helping them grow. A whopping 80 percent of employees who received meaningful feedback in the previous week say they're fully engaged in their work. Per Gallup's research, "Meaningful feedback doesn't hinder performance—it *fuels it*. The operative word here is *meaningful*."[27] The key elements of meaningful feedback include the following:

- Make your feedback frequent and timely.
- Ensure that your comments are focused and specific.
- Focus your feedback on the future.
- Be conversational by practicing active listening and ensuring that feedback goes both ways.

If you're uncomfortable having these types of conversations with others, think of yourself as a coach who's helping someone reach their potential rather than a manager or co-worker who's being "critical."

2. Rethink "Professional Development"

Often when we think about "professional development," we think of things like executive presence, public speaking, or negotiation. I'm not knocking these programs, but material that truly improves employees' lives focuses more on life skills, bolstering well-being, or addressing key sources of stress. Take the Listening Like a Leader program. It helps employees build more meaningful relationships at home and at work. Learning how to listen also helps employees navigate conflict and communicate more effectively, which reduces one of the key work-related stressors: co-worker conflict.

When you're thinking about your organization's professional development offerings, consider widening your scope to include deeper issues that bolster people's lives: listening, communication, conflict resolution, stress reduction, mindfulness, emotional regulation, gratitude, positive habit building, and growth mindset. The more your topic helps your team personally develop in ways that benefit their work *and* their life, the more enriching and beneficial it will be to everyone.

CHANGING FROM HARMFUL, EXTRACTIVE WORKPLACE PRACTICES to beneficial ones that improve and enrich people's lives profoundly affects how work impacts people's lives. When people come home feeling resourced and supported instead of depleted and used, the ripple effect impacts their family, friends, community, and every other person they interact with. Additionally, beneficial workplaces help address gender discrimination and objectification in the workplace, which continue to prevent women from thriving. Creating a beneficial workplace both strengthens your organization and creates a better future for everyone.

Key Chapter Insights

- Company leaders who feel pressured to prioritize profits over employee safety build harmful workplaces that compromise people's economic, physical, and psychological well-being. This leads to increased levels of employee stress, fear, anxiety, physical injury, and burnout, all of which hurt organizational performance in the long run.
- Leaders of beneficial workplaces prioritize their employees' economic, physical, and psychological safety, which creates a virtuous cycle: they help employees thrive, and, in turn, employees help the company thrive. Beneficial

workplaces experience increased employee engagement, satisfaction, and retention; recruit top talent; have more creative and innovative teams; and experience greater physical and mental health across the board.
- Beneficial workplace leaders ensure that employees feel as safe as possible while striving to improve their lives by taking feedback seriously and finding solutions, modeling healthy workplace practices, bolstering everyone's economic well-being, normalizing and supporting mental health, and nurturing meaningful personal and professional growth.

Chapter 7

FROM DISENFRANCHISED WORKPLACES TO DIGNIFIED WORKPLACES

My first "real" job after college was in the fundraising department at a large environmental nonprofit. During my onboarding, the office manager detailed company protocol telling me where to sit, when to show up and leave, how much time I had for lunch, and what benefits and payroll looked like. As I returned to my desk, I realized an interesting "feature" of our office. We worked in a two-story office, and the four of us with "assistant" or "associate" in our title worked downstairs. Everyone above the associate level worked upstairs. I was so excited about my new job that I didn't give the office layout a second thought, but within the first month, I thought about it quite a bit.

For those of us relegated to the basement, there was a bit of an us-versus-them dynamic. Some days, it felt like no one even remembered we were down there. My boss (the incredible Whitney) was great about including me in conversations and decisions, but my three downstairs co-workers dealt with entirely different circumstances. Often the only time they engaged with their "superiors" was when they were summoned upstairs to receive instructions. They'd return to the basement and gather to vent their daily frustrations—gossiping about co-workers, lamenting company decisions, complaining about their latest task, criticizing a colleague's work.

As a bright-eyed and bushy-tailed new employee, I was constantly distracted by my co-workers' conversations and had no clue how to handle the situation. For a twenty-three-year-old conflict-avoidant people-pleaser, the idea of just *asking* them to stop was entirely out of the question—so should I join in? Should I put on headphones and blatantly tune them out? Should I tell someone upstairs? The environment was so toxic that I felt like something was wrong with *me* because I liked my job. After a few months of being steeped in this negative environment, I started dreading going to work. Fortunately, right as this happened, the organization announced that we'd be moving offices. When we moved to a traditional, single-story floor plan where I was seated in the office next to my boss, I felt more engaged and focused. In truth, I loved my job.

For the longest time, I thought there was something wrong with my three basement co-workers. I felt that they had nothing to complain about—like they were simply *looking* for things to be angry about. But during the journey, I realized that their behavior was symptomatic of a much larger problem. While my boss included me in decision-making, sought my opinion, and made me feel seen and cared for, my co-workers were experiencing the impacts of working in a traditional-playbook disenfranchised workplace.

The Traditional Playbook: The Disenfranchised Workplace

I recently co-led a CEO retreat at a machine manufacturing plant in Phillips, Wisconsin, population 1,530. During our tour, we met Tom, who'd worked at this plant for twenty-nine years. From 1995 to 2008, a different company had owned the facility. Tom described working there, saying, "I was just a number that did what I was told. I clocked in when I was supposed to, listened for the bell for lunch, and listened for the bell that told me I could leave. The leadership of the company essentially told us, 'We know better than you. If we want your opinion, we'll give it to you.' I complained to others but never felt I could *do* anything about it." Tom was describing what it feels like to work at a disenfranchised workplace.

Like so many in the global workforce, Tom didn't feel trusted, respected, listened to, or valued at work. His organization used the hierarchical, rigid, command-and-control model, which originated in the military and was popularized in the 1950s and 1960s by those returning from World War II and entering the business world.[1]

Under the command-and-control model, leaders make decisions from the top that are then dictated to those below them to be obeyed without question. Maybe you've experienced or are currently experiencing how it feels to work in this type of culture as someone who's not in a leadership role. People make decisions for you. You're told what to do, where to do it, when to do it, and whom to do it with. No one asks for your opinions or feedback. You're not entrusted with company information. No one explains why decisions are being made. Working in this type of culture feels pretty awful. There's a clear reason why. Hierarchical command-and-control leadership overlooks one of the most fundamental elements of the human experience: dignity.

Dignity is a core human need, included as a pillar of the Universal Declaration of Human Rights. Individual dignity requires feeling acknowledged, safe, autonomous, trusted, and accepted for who you are. Every time one of these elements is violated, it chips away at your humanity.

Unfortunately, the profit-at-all-cost mentality has led many business leaders to implement practices that degrade employees' dignity in the name of short-term gain. Employees have decisions made for them, which strips them of their autonomy. Employees aren't trusted with company information or to manage themselves, making them feel disrespected. Employees aren't considered valuable enough to be included in decision-making, which makes them feel inferior to others and strips them of autonomy. On top of this, cutthroat, abusive corporate cultures make employees feel unsafe and unaccepted for who they are, and employees are often overworked and unacknowledged for their contributions. Research has now proven that workers who experience abuse, mismanagement, and overwork and who lack autonomy experience less dignity.[2]

Currently, an estimated seven out of ten US workers feel that their opinion doesn't count in the workplace.[3] These employees experience "autonomy frustration," which has proven to lead to increased depressive symptoms and psychological disorders.[4] Furthermore, lacking autonomy and control is one of the six major drivers of employee burnout. When employees lack dignity, they respond in all sorts of ways—anger, frustration, disengagement, depression, anxiety, and much more. *This* is why my three co-workers at my first real job behaved the way they did. They weren't entitled assholes; they were humans doing their best in the face of being stripped of their dignity for the majority of their waking hours.

Circling back to Wisconsin, Tom's manufacturing plant had been bought by a new company, Barry-Wehmiller, in 2008. The team began noticing changes immediately. Instead of everyone on the factory floor wearing color-coded hard hats to delineate hierarchy, everyone was given the same color hat. The leadership team invited many factory employees to participate in creating "guiding principles of leadership," including elements like facilitating communication, recognition, and trust. Managers were trained in concepts like listening, being of service to others, and encouraging employee growth. They were encouraged to do away with traditional ideas about supervisors wielding power over others. One of the employees there at that time, Jeff, told us, "I grew up in a law enforcement family. I always thought leadership was about telling people what to do. They made it clear to us that a leader's job is to grow and support the people around you as a team and that strict hierarchy doesn't allow for harmonious teamwork. It changed my entire life."

The before and after of this particular organization illustrate the profound impact of transitioning from a disenfranchised to a dignified workplace. Take Tom, for example. Tom started thriving at work. He said it was the first time in his life that he felt like his voice mattered. Once he felt valued, he said he became inspired to stop complaining about everything and start doing something about it. Ultimately, he worked his way up into a leadership role, which he holds to this day. When I asked him about the impact of working at a dignified workplace, Tom told us, "It changed my whole life, even outside of work. It helped my marriage. It made me a better community member. I learned how to respect other people's opinions that differed from mine without getting combative. I felt happy for the first time in a long time." *This* is the power of a dignified workplace.

The New Playbook: The Dignified Workplace

When Gayle Jennings-O'Byrne co-founded Wocstar Capital and Wocstar Fund, she had to craft an employee benefits package for her new team. Jennings-O'Byrne assumed that her new employees would want some variation of the standard stuff she'd had throughout her career: good health care, dental insurance, annual PTO, decent pay, etc. So, she created a standard benefits package based on these assumptions and began hiring.

As the company's budget and team grew, Jennings-O'Byrne thought her employees would want to use their additional budget to uplevel the team's health insurance options for the next year. She was about to do what she'd seen other leaders do throughout her career and make this decision *for* her team when she had a revolutionary idea: she decided to ask her team what *they* would want instead.

Jennings-O'Byrne brought the benefits discussion to the annual all-team off-site meeting. She transparently explained the health and dental insurance upgrades they could afford and then asked everyone which direction they'd like to take. It was a good thing she did.

The team didn't want to use the enhanced budget on health and dental insurance upgrades. She explains, "They said, 'We'd rather have a travel fund match or funds for education or new technology. If we save X amount, then Wocstar will match it dollar for dollar, and that will be our money to go travel.' It was beautiful because it made me learn more about their values and what mattered most to them."

Jennings-O'Byrne respected her employees' opinions enough to customize her workplace to the *actual* needs of her team rather than assuming she knew best and forcing her employees to adapt to her decisions as the leader. In doing so, she showed her employees that they were valued and respected, which helped build a more dignified workplace for all.

Futurist and chief strategy officer at the Harris Poll Libby Rodney sees customizable workplaces like Jennings-O'Byrne's that adapt policy based on employees' needs as one of the key shifts workplaces will need to make in the next decade to remain competitive. And no, we're not talking about providing great snacks or a gaming room in the office. Rodney describes customizable organizations as "lifestyle concierges." Rodney says, "Everyone is motivated by highly different things, but we make the mistake of thinking we're motivated by the same reasons. The more leaders are armed with what motivates people individually and as a team, the more a company can come together in service of those needs."

Dignified workplaces benefit employees, leaders, and businesses alike. Everyone feels better working in a dignified workplace. Team members feel valued, cared for, and respected. Leaders feel greater inherent satisfaction, self-esteem, and vitality. Businesses experience greater employee retention, engagement, and satisfaction; are able to recruit top talent; and experience greater creativity from their team.

Rodney's research tracked with Jennings-O'Byrne's experience that top talent is seeking workplaces where they have a voice.

Additionally, leaders who strive to meet an employee's needs show employees that they care. As we learned in Chapter 2, feeling cared for at work has become the top driver of employee engagement, resulting in decreased levels of burnout and increased feelings of thriving *outside* work as well.

Other key benefits of customizable, dignified workplaces are cultivating a greater sense of inclusion and addressing some of the specific barriers women contend with, such as male-centered workplaces and obstacles for working parents. Dignified workplaces listen to their employees' needs, enabling employers to meet those needs when possible. As inconvenient as it may be for some employers to hear, there's no one-size-fits-all solution for diversity, equity, and inclusion (DEI). We all have individual needs, so DEI needs to be increasingly *individualized*.

There are many ways to cultivate a more dignified workplace. The best place to start is focusing on respecting everyone, striving to understand everyone's experience, and giving people more autonomy. The following practices can help you start on your journey.

Dignified Leadership Practice #1: Respect and Value Everyone

One of the things I first noticed about Kathy Bolhous, CEO of CNG, was how she listened to *everyone* on her team regardless of their title. We were hosting a workshop for her company. Anytime a team member offered an opinion, she would ask a question to get them to go deeper and was genuinely curious about the answer. I was so used to being in rooms where the senior leader half listened (if that) or dominated the conversation that seeing a leader who valued everyone's perspective was unique.

I later found out that Bolhous regularly visits the company's numerous manufacturing facilities around the country and takes the time to engage with any one of her more than 2,000 employees, from hourly line workers to VPs. She even hosts an internal company podcast where she interviews hourly workers about their personal journeys. When I asked her why she spends so much time meeting with her employees, she told me, "I'm just genuinely curious about everyone I meet."

Even as the CEO of a multibillion-dollar company, Bolhous believes she has something to learn from *everyone* she meets. This mindset allows her to gain new perspectives, making her a more nuanced, informed, and well-rounded leader. It also makes her entire organization stronger. Her employees feel seen and valued as individuals and connected to company leadership, all of which increase their sense of dignity. This may have something to do with why Bolhous's company has been one of the top-performing firms in its industry for years.

Unlike those who follow the traditional playbook, Bolhous doesn't equate hierarchy with value. In traditional business culture, we stratify people by titles to indicate the level of value they bring to the company. The higher up you are, the higher your perceived value. This assumed difference in value comes with all sorts of privileges: those at the top get to make the decisions, are paid more, are rarely questioned, have access to company information, and dictate to those below them. The higher a leader rises, the more acceptable it is to not engage with people at "lower levels." For example, I worked for an organization where I met the CEO once in the *five years* I was an employee.

If you start to internalize these beliefs, you might begin to feel that certain groups who are "below" you, like hourly workers, entry-level workers, or younger workers, aren't worth your time or don't have anything valuable to contribute. Conversely, those at the bottom might feel like they have nothing of value to share with those "above" them because no one asks for their opinions, which diminishes their sense of dignity. But here's the thing: oftentimes looking at something from a different perspective will help you find a solution or an idea you've never thought of before. You also might find unexpected talents or insights from people who've been pigeonholed or overlooked. When I finally started including my entire team in decision-making at my first company, I discovered that our graphic designer, Cia, was an expense-cutting ninja—something I hadn't discovered for three years before that because I'd never thought to bring her to the decision-making table.

One of the easiest ways to bring more dignity to your work, regardless of your title, is to examine your beliefs about hierarchy and value. When it comes to your leadership, do you feel that you value *everyone* regardless of title? Do you treat people differently based on their role or choose to engage only with people at certain levels? Is there someone in your office or on your team whom you haven't taken the time to get to know because they're "below" you? The more effort you make to release limiting beliefs about how much value someone brings to the table based on titles and genuinely value everyone's perspective, the more your experience as a leader will evolve.

Tips for Respecting and Valuing Everyone

1. Question Your Assumptions and Hiring Protocols

Last year, I met an incredible woman named Erica. Not only was she a top-performing project manager at her company, but her boss told me that, outside her day job, Erica had recently pulled together a major golf tournament in a matter of months for the company's foundation, raising tens of thousands of dollars with this first-time event. Erica told me how much she loved her job and looked forward to going to work every day (#dreamemployee).

Despite the tremendous value Erica brings to the table, my guess is that many companies would overlook her in their talent pool. Why? Well, I met Erica at the Perryville Women's Prison, where she'd been incarcerated for nine years. Erica is just one of the many women I met through Televerde, a for-profit company that employs incarcerated women after providing them with job and leadership training. Each woman I met at the prison blew me away, and when we left the Perryville complex, I was struck by how much potential was being overlooked behind the walls of the facility.

Respecting and valuing everyone's contribution truly means *everyone*. If your company values potential employees based solely on credentials or excludes certain groups, you overlook huge swaths of talent—people who, often due to systemic issues, lack access to opportunity. For example, if your hiring process screens for criminal histories or requires college degrees, you're excluding substantial populations from your applicant pool and continuing to block access to much-needed opportunities for them. At present, nearly eighty million Americans have a criminal record, and roughly 60 percent of Americans don't have a college degree.[5]

Michelle Cirocco, executive director of the Televerde Foundation, who was formerly incarcerated herself, recommends that companies "ban the box," meaning eliminating the checkbox on employment applications asking about applicants' criminal history. You can discuss an applicant's history with them later in the hiring process, but when you require applicants to "check the box," these applications are often automatically screened out or second-chance applicants will choose to not even apply. With only 3 percent of HR professionals actively recruiting people with criminal backgrounds and 75 percent of people who are formerly incarcerated remaining unemployed a full year after their release, second-chance employers that offer equal job opportunities to those with criminal records are addressing a major societal need. Doing so has proven to be good for business as well. More than 80 percent of managers of second-chance employees have reported that these employees bring value to their company as high as or *higher* than that contributed by employees without criminal records.[6]

Regarding educational requirements, beyond removing college-degree requirements from job postings, Yscaira Jimenez, co-founder of LaborX, says too many companies use "pedigree-based hiring or referral-based hiring instead of skills-based hiring. There are forty thousand training programs in this country, but employers are not actively sourcing from them." She encourages hiring managers to work directly with skills-based programs, boot camps, and community colleges to establish pipelines for overlooked talent pools.

2. Look for the Girl in the Corner

Last year, I attended a women's thought leaders' event. As we mingled at the pre-event happy hour, I noticed I was the youngest attendee there and felt like I was struggling to connect with many of the other women. I started feeling insecure and told myself everyone was judging me based on my age.

When the event began, we were asked to stand up and introduce ourselves. When we got to the last attendee, the event facilitator said, "And last but not least, Debra." I realized that even though the other event staff had introduced themselves, we hadn't included Maddie, a young staff member I'd met the previous night who was sitting in the corner filming the event. We were all about to overlook her. But why? My guess is we were judging her as too young to be at the "same level" as the rest of us, meaning she wasn't "valuable" enough to be included in the group. In a split-second decision, I called out, "Actually, there's one more after Debra. We haven't heard from Maddie yet." Maddie looked at me with a smile that split my damn heart open and joyfully introduced herself to the room after Debra.

Later that day, I sought Maddie out, and we instantly clicked. She told me about her aspirations and recent move to Chicago. She even ended up helping me rethink my entire social media strategy. It was my favorite conversation of the whole event and left me wondering how many wonderful people I'd missed out on based on flawed assumptions about their "value." I'd learned tons from Maddie, made a meaningful connection, and laughed my face off. Maddie felt included, valued, and seen. Both of our experiences were improved.

As I was leaving the event, Maddie pulled me aside and said, "I'll never be able to tell you how much it meant to me that you included me in those introductions. For the rest of my career, I promise I'll always look for the girl in the corner and invite her to the table." It was one of the most meaningful moments of my career.

Next time you're in a meeting, attending an event, or at a conference, look for the "girl in the corner." Who's being left out because of assumptions about their value? Who's someone you might typically overlook whom you can invite to the table and learn from? Doing so will benefit everyone.

3. Practice Active Listening

How many times have you been talking in a meeting only to look up and see someone on your team on their phone or computer, not paying attention? Or how about saying something only to hear someone else say *the exact same thing* later? Not being listened to sucks. And let's be honest, how many times have you done the same thing to someone else?

Giving someone your full attention is a gift. It makes the person you're talking to feel more engaged, respected, and acknowledged. Being present with those around you and actively listening to their contributions bolsters their sense of dignity and improves performance. Describing what it's like to work with Eileen Fisher, Antoinette Klatzky says, "Eileen listens to what each person at the table is bringing and looks for what she really wants to happen. She invites people to bring their gifts forward and recognize what they have to contribute, which makes them more motivated, excited, and interested in the work."

Active listening is about attentively seeking to understand what someone's trying to say rather than waiting for them to finish what they're saying so you can respond with your own opinion. Griffin-Black, who is a master of active listening, says, "I listen to hear at different levels. What is this person saying? What do they need, and how can I best respond and support what they need? And I'm really careful to let moments of silence be. If I really listen to every single person, then whatever I say will be more contributory than just thinking about what I'm going to say."

A key tenet of active listening is helping people explore what they're trying to say through thoughtful questions. Active listening will help you read between the lines, gather more data to make more informed decisions, and lead more effectively. Practice active listening through the following activities:

1. Be present and engaged by maintaining eye contact, providing visual cues like nodding your head, and avoiding distraction.
2. Ask open-ended questions (not yes-or-no questions) such as "Can you tell me more about that?" "How did that impact you?" "What lessons did you learn?"
3. Avoid autobiographical listening, or waiting to speak only to tell the person how something they said relates to your life. Keep the focus on what they're talking about.
4. Hold back from expressing your opinions or judgments.
5. Reflect on what you heard them say by restating ideas to ensure clarity or by providing a summary. Examples: "What I think I just heard you say was . . ." "Some of the themes I heard were . . ."

4. Express Individual Gratitude

As Hannah Drain Taylor closed out the year, rather than just handing out end-of-year bonuses to show "appreciation," she and Talent to Team co-CEO Amy Giggey reviewed each team member's achievements. They looked through customer feedback and testimonials to find specific examples to support their highlights and asked department heads to share things they appreciated about every member of their department. Then they hosted a virtual all-team meeting and went through every employee, detailing each person's big wins and attributes appreciated by their team. As this happened, other team members piled on their appreciation in the chat box. Drain Taylor reflected, "To watch each person feel so seen and appreciated by the people they work with every day was extraordinary. Truly, it might have been the best meeting of my entire career." *After* this exercise, they announced end-of-year bonuses as the icing on the cake.

Part of respecting and valuing everyone's contributions is ensuring that they know how much you value them. Feeling appreciated and acknowledged feeds your soul. It cultivates greater internal validation beyond financial success—so much so that research has shown that when an employee receives recognition, they're 84 percent more likely to be thriving and 40 percent less stressed. Recognition can increase employees' sense of belonging at work by a factor of ten.[7] Yet many workers go through the day without feeling valued. We get so wrapped up in our to-do list, our stress, and our next goal that we forget to recognize the people around us. I would venture to guess that on any given day, most people you work with—co-workers, vendors, partners, customers—don't feel particularly appreciated. You can change that. Anyone, regardless of title, can acknowledge the people they work with.

When you acknowledge others, don't fall into the trap of throwing out disingenuous compliments. This actually might cause more harm than good. People can tell when someone's being insincere. Instead, focus on genuine, specific, and detailed comments. Telling someone they "did a great job last week" is fine. Saying, "In the presentation last week, I could tell how much time you spent finding applicable data to support your point and thought it blended perfectly with the design and flow of information" will mean much more to the recipient.

5. Ensure Pay Equity

When we're talking about valuing people, we can't overlook the importance of ensuring pay equity. Susan Alban, operating partner and chief people officer at early-stage venture firm Renegade Partners, works with companies in the firm's portfolio on their culture strategy. She says, "Fair pay is pretty low on Maslow's hierarchy of needs in a relationship between the employee and employer. If you can't look at all your employees and say, 'I have conviction you are paid fairly and appropriately relative to your peers,' I just don't think it's very interesting to work on much else. All your other DEI or ERG [employee resource group] stuff rings hollow to me if you're not paying people fairly. What you're paid is one representation of your value, so you better get it right."

Alban says the most important aspect of ensuring pay equity is structure and consistency, with a focus on objective, measurable criteria. For example, many companies use "bands" to delineate the pay structure for different roles in an organization and don't allow people to negotiate their starting salary because they want to ensure that everyone is paid the same for the same role. Alban says, "It has to be fully transparent to everyone, everywhere, all the time, for every level and every single job."

Dignified Leadership Practice #2: Understand and Use Your Privilege to Support Others

Over the last decade, Megan McDonald worked her way up to the role of VP and director of operations at a Colorado-based excavation company. Essentially, she's the number two to the president and manages the day-to-day operations for multiple construction sites.

As a woman in the heavily male-dominated construction industry, McDonald has had far too many experiences of being stripped of her dignity. Being yelled at and verbally abused by male developers and contractors. Having her decisions, qualifications, and competence questioned because she's a woman.

Perhaps the sheer volume of these instances stress-testing her sense of self-worth has enabled McDonald to recognize when something similar is happening to others. And she sees some of her workers being stripped of their dignity far more than others—her hourly Hispanic workers. She watches contractors arrive on-site who won't speak to or make eye contact with her Hispanic employees. She has strangers stop by job sites yelling, "Go back home!" or "Show me your papers!" at her employees. She has new employees provide intimate descriptions of their health conditions to request time off for a medical appointment because they've worked for other companies that either didn't allow workers to miss any work or deemed some medical needs not significant enough to warrant approved time off. All of these experiences—being ignored, disrespected, unacknowledged, harassed, and mistrusted—chip away at human dignity.

As McDonald watched her employees have their dignity tested, she realized that her position gave her power to advocate for her workers. As she ascended the organizational chart, she paid attention to how she could bring more dignity to those "below" her. She regularly speaks to employees one-on-one to solicit feedback and see if they need anything. Many employees tell her they've never had a manager ask them about their needs before. She frequently advocates for raising hourly rates and providing employee bonuses when the company is doing well. She surveys her employees to understand whether they have preferences for their hours and the job sites they work on and attempts to build those needs into their variable schedules. When one of her employees had to take four weeks off to be with his child in the hospital but didn't have any PTO, she encouraged the company owner to continue paying that employee for the full month off (which he did). McDonald says, "It just feels important to me that everyone I work with feels respected and supported. I know what it feels like to not feel that way, so it feels like part of my role is making things better for others when I can."

McDonald exemplifies some of the ways that all of us can work to understand what privileges we have and what power that gives us to bolster the dignity of everyone on our team.

Tips for Using Your Privilege to Support Others

1. Analyze Your Personal Power

The term "privilege" can feel a bit uncomfortable, but understanding your privilege and the power it affords you will help you bring more dignity to your leadership.

When it comes to privilege, meaning the advantages one person has over another, there are two primary elements to explore: your identity and your position.

Starting with identity, based on several factors, including race, sexual orientation, gender, ability, religious beliefs, ethnicity, and socioeconomic status, each of us has an identity that informs how we experience the world and see others. In any culture, there's a dominant cultural identity that holds most of the power. Most often, the dominant identity is white, male, cisgender, heteronormative, able-bodied, and economically advantaged. The more your identity aligns with the dominant cultural identity, the more advantages, rights, and benefits (read: power) you tend to have over other groups. For example, as a woman, I have less power than men. Yet I'm also white, cisgender, straight, able-bodied, agnostic, and relatively economically advantaged, all of which align with the dominant identity and typically afford me more power in any given room. The more your identity *doesn't* align with the dominant identity, the more likely it is that you experience the world differently and have less access to power.

Any woman living in a patriarchal culture who knows what it feels like to have less power than men can begin to understand how those with other identities that are different from the dominant group—people of color, transgender people, queer people, people with disabilities—have different experiences of the world. Jocelyn Macdougall says, "I see this with white women a lot. When they're able to be open and honest about how they've experienced the violence of patriarchy—whether it's physical or emotional violence or the more mundane violence that we might characterize as microaggressions, like not being listened to in the workplace, being talked over, or having our suggestions stolen by men, all of the death by a thousand cuts of patriarchy—there's often a moment where folks are like 'I understand what that violence feels like, and now I also recognize that I might be an agent of that same type of violence from a different angle.' That's a powerful insight to think, 'I don't want to visit that kind of pain and discomfort on others the way that it has been visited on me.' It's a matter of waking up and realizing what's going on and then trying to make different choices and learning how to spot when you might be at risk of being an agent of those kinds of systems of harm."

Just as your identity shapes your privilege, your job title also impacts how much power you have in any given room. In most organizations, if you're someone's boss, you have power over them. The same is true if you're a company founder, executive, or board member or are in any other leadership position.

Being aware of the power you have, whether as a result of your identity or your role, as well as the power dynamics of others will help you cultivate a more nuanced and dignified leadership approach. Per Macdougall, "Having a power analysis is critical to how I show up. It allows me to locate myself in the context of any room. I look for how I might have greater or less access to power based on my positionality to others in the room and what ways I can leverage the power I have to open up conversations about shifting power and redistributing it in more equitable ways."

Ayla Schlosser, co-founder and former CEO of leadership program Resonate, says a simple practice to examine your power is paying attention to the following: "In which ways, on which topics, or in which spaces do people turn to you or wait for you to speak first? Anytime what you're doing is accepted as the standard or your opinion is the default, that's probably a scenario in which you are holding power, whether intentionally or not. That's a good indicator of an opportunity for further investigation as to why your truth is accepted or your opinion is sought out first."

Exploring your identity and position while also working to understand the experiences of others will help you create a more dignified, equitable workplace. Start by educating yourself. Follow social media accounts, watch TED Talks, listen to podcasts, and read books by people with different identities than yours. Engage with different types of people and ask them about their experience of the world. While you're doing this work, reflect on the following questions:

- How does my identity and/or position impact the power dynamics in the room?
- Who in the room may have less power than others?
- Am I making any assumptions based on someone else's identity or position?

2. Seek to Understand the Experiences and Preferences of Others

In their role as director of service delivery at Salesloft, Carter Stepanovsky was traveling to Mexico City for a big meeting. When they landed in Guadalajara, they received an email from the company's director of DEI asking for a call. Stepanovsky says, "I called her right away, and she says, 'Hey, I just wanted to let you know that I've let everyone in this leadership meeting know your pronouns. What more do you need from us? How are you feeling about this trip and this meeting?' I almost teared up. No one has ever done that. I've always felt the burden of constantly coming out, and this small gesture by an ally who's incredibly competent meant so much."

The moral of this story: take time to understand everyone's personal preferences when it comes to allyship and advocacy. Stepanovsky says, "I love when people advocate for me, correct pronouns for me, and speak for me in a way that reduces my burden and makes me feel less vulnerable. But I encourage people to *ask* first. It's important to have someone's input and consent because everyone will have a different preference. For those in a position to create change, advocate, or act as an ally, do it in partnership with the marginalized communities you're acting on behalf of. Yes, it's more work because it's more conversations, questions, research, and discovery, but that's the only way to do it."

When it comes to understanding others' experiences and preferences, consider the following practices:

- **Honor the Individual:** While marginalized communities have collective experiences and trauma, this does not equate with having collective preferences for how they prefer to be supported. Every person is unique. As Stepanovsky says, "What I as a trans, nonbinary human want will be different than what the next trans, nonbinary human will want. This has to be on a human-by-human basis."
- **Intention Matters:** Asking someone about their experience and preferences when advocating for them can feel vulnerable. You might not know where to start or fear you will say something wrong. The best thing to do is to remember that intention matters. In Stepanovsky's experience, "If someone comes to me driven by curiosity or even love, you can ask anything. I may not answer, but I will be open to hearing any question based on someone's intent. I try to model it myself. I'll say to others, 'I feel a little nervous to ask you this, and I'm asking because I want to understand and support you,' and then I'll ask my question. Having awareness and language around your intention goes a long way." One of the best places to start is by being genuine with the person you're speaking to about your intentions and telling them, "I'd love to understand what allyship looks like to you."
- **It's Role Agnostic:** Understanding how best to advocate for someone with different privilege than your own isn't something only senior leaders need to do. It's a practice for everyone at an organization, regardless of role. Per Stepanovsky, "It's got to be bidirectional. It's got to be bottom-up, top-down, even sometimes from the sides." The more people lean into this practice and normalize the

behavior, the safer, more inclusive, and more dignified our workplaces will become.

Dignified Leadership Practice #3: Give People More Voice and Choice

More than sixteen years ago, a young man named Clemente applied to work in one of Torani's manufacturing plants. Clemente was a Sudanese refugee, one of a group of young men known as the "Lost Boys of Sudan" who'd survived a tragic exodus from Sudan during the country's brutal civil war. As Torani's CEO, Melanie Dulbecco got to know Clemente; she watched him get married, have children, and put down roots in their community, but she says he was always fairly quiet in his manufacturing role. However, when Torani rolled out a new program called "contribution management," Clemente found his voice.

Dulbecco and her team realized that traditional employee performance reviews don't give employees a voice or a choice in their own careers. Using the old playbook, managers simply *tell* employees what to work on moving forward. Dulbecco wanted something better, something that gave her team more autonomy.

The Torani team created "contribution management," which invites employees to set their *own* goals for personal and career development for the year in place of performance reviews. Managers are then trained to support their employees in achieving each individual's self-identified goals. When the Torani team went through contribution management with Clemente, he expressed that he wanted to become line lead at his facility. He worked with his manager to identify exactly how he would need to develop to reach his goal, and they created a game plan for him to work toward it. Today, Clemente is a line lead and an integral member of the Torani team.

Dignified workplaces like Torani that give employees more voice and choice provide a sense of autonomy satisfaction, a "feeling of psychological freedom and experience of integrity of one's actions, thoughts, and feelings." The importance of giving employees more autonomy can't be understated. Even something as small as being able to personalize one's workspace results in employees feeling "more comfortable in the space, more collaborative with others, and more enthusiastic about their work."[8] On a larger scale, autonomy satisfaction has been shown to be "essential for humans' growth and strongly associated with individuals' level of well-being, such as life satisfaction, and vitality."[9]

Tips for Giving People More Voice and Choice

1. One-on-One Meetings

A few years ago, Darn Good Yarn founder and CEO Nicole Snow sat down for a meeting with one of her employees. She asked the employee about her challenges and dreams, and the employee told Snow she was struggling to get out of debt by the end of the year. Snow offered to create a personal budget for her and asked if she'd be interested in additional commission-based sales work. Her employee responded enthusiastically and, it turns out, excelled at the commission-based work. By the end of the year, she'd smashed her savings goal. In this case, as the result of a single meeting and Snow's genuine desire to support her team, the employee got out of debt, the company increased its revenue, and the employee felt genuinely cared for, which has been proven to drive engagement and retention.

Snow's story illustrates the power of listening to your team. Even if you think you're doing this well, you might be overestimating yourself. One study found that 85 percent of employers believe they actively listen to their workers' needs, but only 51 percent of employees agree.[10]

I schedule a quarterly meeting with everyone on my team. I strive to be entirely present, listen deeply, ask clarifying questions, take notes, and keep the conversation focused on the team member as much as possible. My sole intention for these sessions is to understand my employees' needs so we can adapt as an organization, when possible, and make them feel supported. Here are five questions I use for these sessions that you can use with your team:

1. How are things going right now?
2. Is anything holding you back from loving your work?
3. Do you have any frustrations with how the company operates or suggestions for improvement?
4. Do you have any feedback for me to help me grow as a leader?
5. Where do you see yourself in the future, and is there anything I can do to help you get there?

2. Intentional Onboarding

Liz Allen is part of the 20 percent of the US population who is immunodiverse. She contends with a complex chronic illness that can require up to twenty hours per week of treatment. As a lawyer, Allen had much to contribute to the business world but kept coming up against workplace policies that prevented her from managing her illness while working—workplaces that forced her to sit at a desk in an office, which didn't account for days when she couldn't physically get out of bed but still could have worked from home, or workplaces with strict hours requirements and limited PTO that didn't enable her to attend the numerous medical appointments she needed.

Allen never felt comfortable advocating for her needs. She worried she'd be viewed as high maintenance or feared her colleagues would think she was getting preferential treatment. Plus, no one ever *asked* her. No one took the time to understand her needs or respected her enough to adapt their workplace policies to support her. Allen didn't feel accepted in the business world, which degraded her sense of dignity.

As Allen's career progressed, she began advocating for herself more and more. The more she spoke up to employers about her own needs, the more she realized that many other people also struggled with rigid workplace policies that didn't take *their* needs into account either. The issue was so pervasive that she began speaking publicly as a disability advocate about how workplaces can support everyone.

One of Allen's recommendations for employers is to survey employees about their individual needs as part of the onboarding process. In addition to basic information like contact information and emergency contact, add questions that will help you understand new employees' specific needs. Do they have dietary restrictions, need accommodations for their work setup, or have any individual circumstances you should be aware of? What are their pronouns? Is there anything you need to know to support them in doing their highest and best work? Collecting information like this and then taking the time to connect with your new employee to talk it over when they join the team will go a long way toward welcoming them in a supportive way.

Also, take the time to review your employee onboarding materials to ensure that *everyone* is included in the options on any form you provide. Stepanovsky says, "Fifteen years ago, my wife couldn't be on my health insurance because our insurance was based out of a state that didn't recognize same-sex partnerships. My career has gone from *that* to joining an organization that has drop-down options for same-sex couples, making me feel validated as a human. Like I exist in the world just like everybody else. Having drop-down options in a form that includes everyone's experience might seem small, but that's an example of a gesture in onboarding that can have a big difference."

3. Involve People in Decisions About Their Career

It's critical to give employees a voice and a choice about decisions that directly impact their lives. As for Jennings-O'Byrne, this could include talking to employees directly about their opinions on benefits packages, company policies, and compensation plans, or as

Dulbecco models, this could include decisions about professional and personal growth.

In addition to its contribution management system, Torani has found other ways to give employees more choice in their careers. The company's skills-block program allows hourly workers to learn certain skills related to safety, quality, and process in their first six months to add a dollar to their hourly wage. In the second six months, workers can learn another set of skills to add two dollars to their hourly wage. Through the contribution management system, managers help workers understand what additional skills are needed for different career pathways within the company.

Torani also has a program called "career mixology." If an employee is interested in exploring something new, they can change departments or roles within the company. At the heart of all of these programs is a keen understanding of how much it means to have autonomy over your career and life. Dulbecco says, "It's all about giving them a choice about what they want to learn. We say, 'Here are different career pathways you might be interested in. Maybe you want to go deep in leadership. Maybe you want to veer off towards quality assurance. Maybe you're interested in how we mix and blend products.' We look at all those things and say, 'Here are the different pathways, and here are skills that you can learn and build. You have a choice. What would you like to learn?' And then we support that."

How much autonomy do the people on your team currently have about decisions that impact their lives? Do they have options to express their opinions or feedback about company policies or their career development? The more voice and choice you can give them about their careers, the more dignified your workplace will become.

4. Provide as Much Flexibility as Possible

As Jennings-O'Byrne gave her employees more voice and choice in company decisions, they also advocated for increased flexibility. In response, the company gave everyone unlimited vacation and implemented a flexible work policy. Jennings-O'Byrne says, "They're adults and know what their deliverables are. It's not about butts in seats or clocking in and out. I already thought the concept of two weeks of vacation was archaic. I just need to know their deliverables get done. If they deliver on what they said and their work product is great, if they can get it done by Wednesday, what do I care what they do Thursday and Friday? If they want to work all day Saturday because their husband is away with the kids, so be it. Corporate culture, performance, and productivity are about human dignity and leveraging people's strengths, intellect, and creativity in a way that honors the individual, not simply establishing processes and procedures."

Giving employees more flexibility in the workplace is another key element of dignified workplaces. Flexible policies include remote or hybrid workplaces, flexible working hours, and increased or unlimited paid time off. Businesses are increasingly understanding the value of giving team members more autonomy over how they work.

One model gaining traction is the Results-Only Work Environment (ROWE), developed by Jody Thompson and Cali Ressler. ROWEs advocate for full autonomy at work. As long as employees meet expectations, how, when, and where they work is their choice. Employees of ROWE companies have proven to be more productive and less stressed while also reporting getting more sleep, working out more, and spending more time with their families outside work.[11] These findings track with the findings of research on flexible workplace policies that greater autonomy leads to improved employee productivity, mental health, physical health, job satisfaction, and happiness.[12] Speaking of working in a flexible environment, Antoinette Klatzky, VP of programs and partnerships at the Eileen Fisher Foundation, says, "There's just a lot more understanding, leeway, and connection. The focus of the work has been on how we relate to each other, how we connect to each other, and what the work product is, not on the time you come in or leave the office. It allows me to be much freer in my creative expression and contributions in the workplace."

Flexible work also allows companies to recruit workers who can work only part-time, are homebound, are in a caretaking role, or are contending with disabilities without excluding these populations from the workforce. Nearly 40 percent of women with young children say they would have had to leave their company or reduce their hours without flexible workplace policies. This research also highlighted that women face fewer microaggressions and have greater psychological safety when working in hybrid or remote environments. Currently, when women consider new work, they rank flexibility as the second most important thing after health-care benefits.[13]

At its core, giving employees flexibility shows respect. You're giving team members the benefit of the doubt, trusting that they won't take advantage of their freedom, as opposed to the traditional-playbook model that encourages managers to assume the worst of employees. How flexible is your workplace? Have you spoken to your team recently about what type of flexibility they might appreciate? Are there opportunities to give people more flexibility about how, where, and when they work?

Bringing more dignity into the workplace is one of the most fundamental changes any leader can strive for to make business better for everyone. If you respect everyone's value, use your privilege to support others, and give people more autonomy, your employees will experience greater dignity and well-being. These practices also address barriers for working parents, gender discrimination, and male-centered workplaces, which are some of the key barriers for working women. Dignified workplaces recenter dignity as a core element of the human experience, building a world where more people feel acknowledged, seen, and valued. That new world begins with you.

Key Chapter Insights

- Traditional hierarchical, command-and-control, profit-at-all-cost business norms make employees feel disenfranchised and create cultures of abuse, mismanagement, and overwork, all of which lead to increased levels of depressive symptoms, psychological disorders, and burnout for workers.
- Dignified workplaces that focus on showing employees respect, building trust, and bolstering autonomy lead to better company performance through increased employee engagement, satisfaction, and loyalty; decreased burnout; and greater productivity.
- Dignified leaders focus on valuing everyone's perspective, expressing gratitude, understanding their privilege and power, and giving people more voice and choice.

Chapter 8

FROM INDIVIDUALISTIC WORKPLACES TO UNIFIED WORKPLACES

When we sold Conscious Company Media in 2017, the other two executives left while I stayed as CEO. As the sole remaining "leader," I felt like everyone was relying on me. So I needed to be the strong, confident, infallible leader who had every answer. Part of this facade meant making company decisions without my employees' input. Part of me felt that asking them for their opinion meant I couldn't hack it on my own—and leaders can't show "weakness," right?

With this mindset, when I got pregnant with my first child, I was determined to show everyone that pregnancy wouldn't slow me down. I could still carry everything . . . including a fetus. And let me tell you, I. Showed. Up. I worked full-time, produced and hosted two large in-person events, keynoted conferences, worked extra hours, traveled until I was thirty-four weeks pregnant, and hit all of our company's goals. I was just a somewhat larger version of the cool, calm, confident leader who could do it all.

Behind the scenes, I was struggling to hold it together. Insomnia. Round-ligament pain. Leg cramps. Heartburn. Nausea. You name it. But I felt like I couldn't tell anyone. I kept up this ruse until I was a month from giving birth. As I attempted to draft a plan for my maternity leave, my walls began to crack. In truth, I was terrified—of becoming a mom, of leaving my company, of making the wrong decisions for my team. Our company was at a critical inflection point. We could put our resources toward several different revenue opportunities, but I couldn't think straight and didn't know what to tell people to focus on. Knowing I couldn't hold it all by myself any longer, I decided to ask my team for help.

I scheduled a two-day all-team meeting. Waddling into the room while my cankles tested the structural integrity of my flip-flop straps, I sat down and opened up to my team: "I need your help. I'm trying to plan for maternity leave, but I'm exhausted and overwhelmed. I don't know why I'm trying to do all of this alone given how brilliant you all are. I want to talk about our options for the rest of the year as a team and make a game plan together." I opened our books, giving everyone a fully transparent look at our financial status. I walked through our expenses and projected revenue and then detailed our current and potential product lines, making sure everyone was clear on how they connected to our company's larger purpose. Once we were all on the same page, I said, "What do you think we should do?"

While everyone seemed a little taken aback at first, the conversation slowly took off. My team questioned expenses and tweaked some of our product lines. They proposed new concepts and threw out bold ideas. Our membership manager, Kate, and events manager, Nina, started thinking about new ways we could weave upcoming content into our events. Our magazine's editor-in-chief, Vanessa, connected dots for our membership community that we'd never seen before. I'd pigeonholed all of these people and not included them in company decisions before this, meaning I'd never allowed any of them to show me what they could contribute to our team beyond their defined role. By trying to do it all myself, I'd limited the collective genius of our team.

At the end of two days, we coalesced around a co-created strategy that we all felt ownership of. My team understood *why* we'd made the decisions we did. I was able to leave for maternity leave feeling that the team was crystal clear on what to do in my absence. I no longer felt as if the weight of the entire company was on my shoulders. My feeling shifted from "I have to do it all" to "We're in this together."

What I experienced through all of this is the difference between individualistic workplaces and unified ones.

The Traditional Playbook: The Individualistic Workplace

My husband recently had lunch with his friend Matt, a fellow lawyer. While they were trading stories about their firms, Matt said that at the end of the year, he and his fellow partners have to make individual presentations to the senior partners about why they deserve more profit distributions than the other partners. After hearing from everyone, the senior partners then send checks of varying sizes to each partner with zero transparency as to *why* they do so. Matt is forced to compete against his colleagues in an opaque process that doesn't feel fair—an experience that exemplifies an individualistic workplace.

Individualistic workplaces center on individual performance and gain. They're yet another example of the influence of toxic masculinity on business. Toxically masculine beliefs about individualism include feeling that depending on others is shameful or "weak," winning is everything, everyone should be out for themselves, winners take all, and personal achievement—measured by wealth and power—is the definition of success. Individual business leaders are lionized as heroes who take credit for and reap the rewards of a team's performance; business leaders judge success by how much money they make; colleagues are pitted against each other for increased compensation or opportunities for advancement; a select few "superior" individuals make decisions on behalf of entire organizations; and employees are judged based entirely on individual performance.

Individualistic workplaces encourage employees to think solely about themselves. It's a "me-first" mentality. You must prove yourself by working harder and achieving more to set yourself apart from your colleagues. You cover your ass, get your work done, and look out for yourself.

While high achievers can succeed in workplaces centered on individual performance, this success comes at a great cost. Humans are a social species. We crave connection. As previously discussed, having meaningful social connections is the top predictor of longevity and happiness, and one of the top drivers of employee burnout is feeling a lack of community. Yet we insist on building workplaces that isolate people, discourage meaningful connections, and pit people against each other. It's no wonder so many people are struggling at work. We're lonely and suffering as a result.

Currently, one in five global workers say they experience daily loneliness.[1] Moreover, in her research, Ann Shoket, CEO of women's networking group TheLi.st, found that more than 50 percent of women feel lonely *because* of their job. The key factors of workplace loneliness include social isolation, being overworked, lack of communication, and unsupportive working environments—all of which occur in cutthroat individualistic workplaces where everyone's out for themselves. Research has shown that loneliness at work is a significant stressor that negatively impacts individual health, engagement, and job performance, ultimately leading employees to physically and psychologically withdraw from their work.[2] Shoket says, "We're alone in our roles as high-achieving, high-performing women and underrepresented leaders because we're the pioneers in what it looks like. Loneliness comes from feeling isolated, disconnected, unsupported, and unable to show up as yourself at work. That's even more true for women of color, who, on top of the loneliness, feel a lack of respect at work as they rise through the ranks. The world is not made for ambitious women."

In addition to employee loneliness, individualistic workplaces diminish a critical differentiating factor: collaboration. Humans like to work together, and we produce much better results when we do. Co-founder of Beneficial State Bank Kat Taylor says, "I know there are all these heroes out there like Elon Musk and Mark Zuckerberg, but we're moving beyond single-hero history to movement history. Working together is not only enriching, but you yield a better solution set." To that end, 86 percent of leaders say a lack of collaboration is the top reason for workplace failures, and collaborative workplaces have *five times* better financial performance than traditional ones.[3] Leaders like Taylor are ushering in a new playbook for workplace environments by building unified workplaces.

The New Playbook: The Unified Workplace

True story: when Erin Wade first told me how she ran Homeroom restaurant, I kinda thought she was joking. *Everyone* on her more than one-hundred-person team—I'm talking dishwashers, line cooks, executives, servers, you name it—was involved in making company decisions. Every week, Wade hosted an optional, paid meeting that was open to the entire staff. At these meetings, she detailed the company's current status with transparent financial statements and then talked through any major company decisions with everyone in attendance. The staff would discuss each topic, and the discussion informed final company decisions.

When Wade detailed her model during an interview for our magazine, I was still rocking the traditional individualistic leadership style. Her approach sounded . . . insane? I mean, wouldn't it just be easier to make those decisions yourself or with your leadership team? What do you do when people disagree? Don't you have enough on your plate without having to manage all of those opinions and personalities? While I secretly questioned Wade's sanity at the time, it turns out she was actually an exemplary practitioner of building a unified workplace.

Leaders of unified workplaces build equitable, connected, collaborative work environments where everyone works together toward shared goals. If you've ever played team sports, you understand the ethos. Instead of "me first," employees of unified workplaces have a "rising tide lifts all boats" mentality.

Unlike traditional-playbook workplaces, which value individual performance, transactional relationships, and individual gain, unified workplaces value collaboration, team growth, connection, and group success.

Unified workplaces make employees feel that they're valued members of a team rather than interchangeable cogs in a machine. Being a valued member of a team feels good. In Wade's experience, "The feedback I got is the fact that those meetings existed, the fact that people knew if they showed up and there was something they cared about, there was a place they could come and have their voice heard and someone would care, really meant the world. It communicated that everyone's voice really mattered." As thought leader Akaya Windwood puts it, "If everybody understood that they're an integral part of a web of humans who care about them, so much in the world would change."

Additionally, unified cultures take pressure off the individual. Instead of forcing employees to compete against each other based on individual performance, collaborative cultures emphasize employees supporting each other to reach their end goal together. Melanie Dulbecco says of Torani's unified workplace, "The whole idea of our culture is that we never go places alone."

Moving from "I'm carrying it all by myself" to "We're carrying this together" is a profound shift. Workplaces built around teamwork and collaboration have proven to reduce employee turnover by as much as 50 percent and increase employee satisfaction by nearly 20 percent.[4] The sense of community built by team-oriented company cultures helps prevent burnout and bolsters a sense of belonging. When I finally got out of my own way and stopped trying to carry everything on my own, I felt tremendous relief and a much deeper connection with my team. Additionally, when people feel that they're working on the same team toward shared goals, they're more likely to distribute work more evenly, which addresses another key driver of burnout: excessive workload. All of these factors lead to increased levels of innovation, which is why team-oriented, collaborative companies have been shown to be roughly 30 percent more innovative than traditional firms.[5]

Unified workplaces focus on cultivating connections between team members, working together toward shared goals, and collaborative processes to create more cohesive, integrated workplaces. The following practices will help you build a more unified workplace and realize the tremendous benefits of doing so.

Unified Leadership Practice #1: Cultivate Genuine Connection

Last year, Alfa Demmellash brought her entire Rising Tide Capital team together for an in-person retreat. Demmellash kicked things off with an Ethiopian coffee ceremony, an honored social custom from her home country rooted in deepening connection. She also brought in inspiring pieces of art and delicious food. She says, "It was so astounding to watch them experience that entire day. I could tell they were thinking I'd have a coffee ceremony for them for an hour, and then we'd get that beautiful deck fired up and work on our agenda. That expectation went for an entire day."

Demmellash structured the first day of the staff retreat to *not* focus on transacting, checking things off a to-do list, and being productive. Instead, she invited her team to slow down and *connect* with each other. Her organization is a unified workplace, and a key element of employees' sense of unity is feeling connected to each other. Why? Well, the relationships you have with your co-workers matter. A lot.

Many of us spend a significant portion of our waking lives interacting with the people we work with. Regardless of any notion of separating the "personal" and "professional," the quality of your relationships impacts your life. Psychologists describe co-worker relationships as "weak ties" as opposed to "strong ties," like your relationships with family and close friends. But don't let the name fool you. When it comes to life satisfaction, research has shown that weak ties are *just as important* as strong ties. Moreover, having a sense of community at work helps decrease employee burnout, increase well-being, and improve productivity.[6]

Beyond the impact of connection on the individual, deepening connection deepens trust, and trust is at the heart of great teamwork. Unified workplaces are built on teamwork. Employees of unified workplaces trust their co-workers and are invested in each other's success. Everyone feels like they're working together as part of something bigger than themselves. Much of this ethos and the success of unified workplaces come down to the quality of connections between people.

Tips for Cultivating Genuine Connection

1. Get Creative

Too often, workplace socialization revolves around small talk over food or drinks. When it comes to nurturing genuine connection, instead of yet another company happy hour, try planning activities centered around learning, play, creativity, or inspiration. When I've hosted connective events, we've brought in art facilitators, poets, and musicians. Liz Richardson of Indigo Ink hosts a weekly lunch-and-learn with her entire staff to eat and learn about new ideas together. The key is thinking outside the box to get people out of their heads to help them connect as *people*, not just colleagues.

2. Shift from Transactional to Relational

Truth be told, I spent a good chunk of my career focused on transactional relationships. I was an achievement-addicted high performer. My laser focus on individual performance led me to try to *extract* things from others—to constantly look for ways to *benefit* from knowing someone. Yet, as Akaya Windwood and Rajasvini Bhansali wrote in their book *Leading with Joy*, "Joyless, obligatory, and solely transactional leadership has gotten us into the current fixes we are in."[7]

When you focus solely on transacting with others, you come from a place of scarcity and individualism. Transaction asks, "What can I get?" On the other hand, when you're relational, you come from a place of abundance and focus on mutual benefit. You ask, "What can I give?" A relational mindset means listening to understand, seeking to build long-term connections, and releasing expectations of return. When you're relational, you're genuinely thrilled for the other person's success, knowing their success doesn't detract from *your* ability to succeed. Shifting your interactions from "What's in it for me?" to "How can I support what you're up to in the world?" is a profound change that will help you feel more connected with others and increase the sense of unity within your team when practiced with co-workers.

One practice that helps me move into a relational mindset rooted in abundance is imagining anything I do for someone else as planting a positive seed in the world. I never know what will sprout from this seed and have no expectations for it—when it will come, what it should be, how big it will be, or even whom it should benefit. All I know is that someday, it will sprout something beautiful. Sometimes I see seeds come back to me where someone will reciprocate a favor in kind or reach out to me years after we've connected about an opportunity. Sometimes I see seeds leading to a new partnership or initiative between people I know. Other times, I have no clue how a seed has sprouted or whether it has yet to do so. I just trust that something positive will happen as a result of planting these seeds. Abundance begets abundance.

Unified Leadership Practice #2: Create Shared Goals

Twenty-two years after launching her namesake brand, Eileen Fisher rolled out an employee stock ownership plan (ESOP) in 2006. The plan gave her more than six hundred employees stock in the company that they could cash out either when they left or upon retirement. To date, roughly 40 percent of her multimillion-dollar company is owned by more than 1,200 full- and part-time employees.

By sharing ownership with her team, Fisher shifted the focus away from individual performance to team performance. Her team was incentivized to work together toward a set of shared goals. They won as a team. They lost as a team. Everyone's goals positively related to everyone else's, meaning they saw their fellow team members' success as contributing to their own success. This made employees *want* to support each other's growth, hold one another accountable, and cheer on one another's success. They built power together as a team instead of following the traditional playbook, which encourages workers to try to build power over one another.

Fisher reinforced the ethos of working together by adding a profit-sharing bonus program and creating a clear company purpose and values as a team that everyone could stand behind. Each of these decisions helped unify the team to work together toward something larger than themselves. In doing so, Fisher built greater cohesion and long-term value for the entire company as research has shown that companies with shared goals, as opposed to individual or competitive goals, create better atmospheres of initiative and innovation. Shared goals have been proven to motivate team members to persist more in overcoming obstacles, take greater initiative to innovate, find solutions to conflicts, display more of their talents, and take more responsibility, all of which improve individual and company performance.[8] Having shared team goals is a key practice of unified organizations.

At your organization, how much of a role does individual performance play? Is anything currently inspiring your team to work *together*? How can you incentivize teamwork and collaboration around shared goals rather than individual goals? Taking the time to think through questions like these will start you on your journey toward a more unified, cohesive workplace.

Tips for Creating Shared Goals

1. Focus on Shared Success

Like Fisher, Melanie Dulbecco uses employee ownership to create a sense of shared success. She says, "We talk about how we build the value in the company together. Then people get their annual statements, and everyone in the company is an owner in the creation of that wealth."

While employee ownership and profit sharing are great ways to cultivate a sense of shared success, they're not the only ways. You can do things like practice transparent open-book management to set annual team goals, co-create team goals that align with bonus structures rather than individual performance metrics, or find ways to reward effective collaborative efforts. The more you think about how you can inspire a vision of shared success for your team to buy into, the more unified your team will become.

2. Create a Shared Purpose

Beyond shared success, you can cultivate a greater sense of unity around a sense of purpose. Depending on your role, you can craft a meaningful internal team goal or an organization-wide vision that inspires the hearts and minds of the entire team. Almost 90 percent of business leaders surveyed said having a shared purpose leads to greater employee satisfaction.[9]

Katlin Smith of Simple Mills crafted an organization-wide purpose to unify her team. Four years ago, the multimillion-dollar food company made the internal commitment that 100 percent of its future innovation would further regenerative agriculture. Smith uses team-based experiences to help her employees connect with the company's larger purpose. Last year, everyone went together to a regenerative farm in California for a staff retreat. Smith says, "They got to walk the land. They got to do soil experiments and see the difference in water infiltration rates for healthy soil versus unhealthy soil. We also brought out a microbiome expert from Stanford to talk to them about how the food they eat impacts their microbiome. It was amazing to see the degree to which it resonated." Each member of the Simple Mills team has a greater shared *why* behind the work they do every day. Having a sense of purpose in their work unifies the team, giving them something to rally behind.

When you think about your team or company, do you have a clear, compelling purpose that truly engages people's souls? How often do you talk about this purpose, track your progress, or help your team see the impacts of working toward it? Is it something you're excited to get out of bed for? If not, it's worth thinking through what you could do to reimagine your purpose to help inspire your entire team.

3. Lean Into Shared Values

Codifying and leaning into team values is another way to help bring your team together with shared goals. Creating core values was one of the first things Dulbecco did when she took the CEO role at Torani more than thirty years ago. "When I started as CEO, I'd just read the book *Built to Last*. They'd done all this research and found the surprising results that clear articulation and communication of core values over time is what makes great enduring companies. When I joined Torani, it was already over sixty-five years old. So I sat down with the second- and third-generation family members—I was the first non–family member to be brought in to run the company—and we talked about our history and what each of us cared about deeply. We found the common threads in there, articulated four core values, and said, 'We're going to use these to communicate. We're going to use these to hire. We're going to use these in the way we build the company."

Torani's core values are care deeply for people, grow baby grow (meaning growing people to grow the business), community outreach, and being aware of impact. Once the values were established, Dulbecco set about the task of baking them into the company culture. She says many leaders fall flat when it comes to values because "their vision, purpose, and values are only surface deep and not strongly embedded in the culture." Dulbecco personally meets with all new hires during their onboarding and does a deep dive into the company's history, purpose, and core values. After reviewing everything, Dulbecco says, "Then I say to each person, 'Not only did we choose for you to be here, but you also chose to be here. There are things about the way we do things around here that you might have noticed that feel different than other places. What stands out to you as something that you like and a reason that you chose to be here?' I find their answer always relates to our core values. Always."

The Torani team also embeds its values in the organization by consistently including them in internal and external communications, documenting the ways in which the team embodies the values, and combining market research with the company's purpose and values to determine compensation structures. These last two practices are worth highlighting. If your company claims to live by its purpose and values but still defines success based only on money and ties compensation to individual performance and productivity, this means the values are only surface deep.

One quick practice I use with my team regarding our core values is a weekly high/low values check-in. At the end of our weekly team call, I ask everyone to share either a "high"—a time in the last week they really leaned into one of our values—or a "low"—a time in the last week when they fell a bit short of one of the values or felt they could have done better. It's not about judgment. It's all about centering the values and consistently communicating their importance.

Unified Leadership Practice #3: Collaborative Decision-Making

While having a sense of shared goals cultivates a greater sense of unity in the workplace, collaborative decision-making will take your team even further. Collaboration doesn't mean select company leaders talking through decisions *in front of* a group; collaboration means making decisions and co-creating solutions *with* a group. It's the collective wisdom of the group that makes collaboration sing.

Unified workplaces lean into collaboration because it's one of the best ways to make people feel like they're part of a team. Collaboration has been shown to improve team dynamics and reduce burnout and work-related stress for employees. Building on this, employees at collaborative workplaces are 22 percent more likely to believe that their employer cares about their morale. Collaboration also bolsters performance by generating better ideas, improving employee communication, and making employees up to 50 percent more effective at completing tasks.[10]

How effectively does your team collaborate? In team meetings, do you help each other talk through ideas and stress-test one another's work or do you simply provide updates on what you're working on? Are most decisions made unilaterally or by one small team? Are there any opportunities to broaden conversations to get the opinions of more people about major decisions? Examining ways to build more collaboration into your role will not only strengthen your decision-making but help build a greater sense of community for everyone involved.

Tips for Collaborative Decision-Making

1. Prioritize Psychological Safety

Collaboration will not work without psychological safety. Full stop. This means everyone should feel safe asking questions, challenging ideas, providing perspectives, and making mistakes without fear of being punished, ostracized, embarrassed, or even losing their role. The following are some of the key pillars that promote psychological safety:

- **Trust:** Your team needs to feel trusted, and they need to trust you if they're going to give you their best. Some of the best ways to build trust with your team are to be open and transparent (see next tip), express vulnerability as a leader, genuinely listen to everyone, and ensure that you're accountable to your team when you say you're going to do something.

- **Clear Communication:** In collaborative, psychologically safe cultures, leaders prioritize communicating openly, clearly, and often with employees. In the absence of information, people tend to jump to conclusions, make assumptions, or feel uncertain. Research has shown that roughly 40 percent of workers say poor communication reduces their trust in leadership and their team and affects their stress levels.[11] Prioritizing regular communication, including company information, key updates, and clarity on decisions, is key to supporting psychological safety for everyone.

- **Avoid "Punishment":** If people on your team fear *any* negative repercussions from putting themselves out there and providing their honest opinion, they will not feel psychologically safe. Yes, team members need to be held accountable. No, accountability does not equate with punishment or discipline.

- **Encourage and Respect Diverse Opinions:** The beauty of collaboration is in the collective wisdom of the group. True collective wisdom can come only from everyone honoring and offering their truth, even when it's vastly different from that of others at the table. Psychologically safe leaders encourage others to offer diverse opinions by focusing on responding with curiosity rather than becoming defensive. At Homeroom, Wade says, if someone or a handful of people on her team strongly resisted a decision, it simply meant the team probably wasn't fully considering something. Instead of avoiding conflict and disagreement, the Homeroom team worked through it, continuing to talk through issues until everyone felt heard and clearly understood the factors that contributed to the final decision. Wade says it was rare for the team not to have total agreement at some point if they continued to genuinely engage in open dialogue with care and curiosity.

2. BE TRANSPARENT

At any time of day, employees of Maryland-based Indigo Ink can log on to their company dashboard and see fully transparent, up-to-date company financial information. Company co-founder Liz Richardson built the website that way. Richardson personally trains every employee on how to read company financial statements and encourages her team to ask questions if something looks amiss.

Richardson leads a unified culture and knows that effective collaboration requires transparency. You can't ask people for their opinion but give them only a portion of the relevant information. Moreover, when business leaders follow the traditional playbook and hold information "close to the vest," the not-so-subtle message they send is that the employees can't be trusted. If your team doesn't feel like you trust them, they won't collaborate effectively. Why should they? If you don't trust them with company information, why should they trust you with their contributions and ideas?

Wade began each of her weekly all-staff meetings by openly reviewing company financials and transparently discussing key company decisions with everyone on her staff.

Kathy Bolhous, CEO of plastics manufacturer CNG, hosts quarterly meetings where she shares company financial projections with more than two thousand employees.

Dulbecco practices open-book management, giving everyone on staff access to the company finances. She says, "To build strategies together, we share everything with people in the company, including financials, so we can all move forward together."

Being transparent with your team about as much as possible—financial information, how decisions have been made, key challenges the company is facing—is one of the quickest ways to build engagement with your people and make them feel part of a trusted team.

How open are you with your team? Do you transparently share information and discuss challenges, or do you withhold certain issues and information from certain groups of people? Can you genuinely say everyone on your team feels like you trust them? The more you share with your team, the more respected, trusted, and unified they will feel.

3. Provide Clear Structure

When Wade brought her whole team together to discuss company decisions, she created a framework called "collective success." Through the lens of the company's larger purpose of demonstrating that it was possible to create a healthy, supportive, joyful, and profitable food-service company, the entire team was instructed to consider the possible impact of major decisions on employees, customers, and the sustainable profitability of the company. Everyone on the team was asked questions such as "How do you think this decision would affect you?" and "What concerns do you have?" Then the group openly discussed how they imagined the decision might impact customers or what issues might come up from their community. Finally, the team examined the potential financial implications for the company using transparent financials. Wade says, "The goal was to make decisions that, in the long term, would allow the business to thrive. We balanced profitability with impact on different groups."

Collaboration is not synonymous with consensus-based decisions—great collaboration requires consistent structure so that everyone understands what's important and *why* decisions are made. Collaborative decision-making also doesn't mean *every* decision should be collaborative. In most cases, collaborative workplaces work best when collaboration focuses on significant company decisions, and then each department collaborates on larger department-specific decisions. If you attempt a more collaborative decision-making process, consider the structure and types of decisions that should be collaborative before getting started.

4. Ensure Fairness

Unfairness is one of the quickest ways to sink healthy team dynamics and collaborative efforts. Recall that unfairness is one of the six primary reasons employees burn out.[12] On the other hand, employees who feel that they work at fair workplaces perform better, feel more positively about their work, and are better teammates.[13] Better teammates mean better collaboration.

Research has shown that the best way to ensure fairness is to seek employee feedback regularly.[14] Ask your team members about your performance as a leader and how they think other employees might perceive how fair your actions are. The more often you seek feedback, the more likely you'll be to factor fairness into your decision-making.

Also, take time to self-audit how fairly you feel your team is being treated. Does everyone on your team have a fair distribution of work? Does anyone on the team receive preferential treatment or have access to more opportunities or resources than any of their peers? Is anyone on your team, including yourself, using weaponized incompetence while others pick up the slack?

UNIFIED WORKPLACES BUILT AROUND GENUINE CONNECTION, shared goals, and collaboration don't just improve a company's performance; they improve people's quality of life. Can you imagine how much would change if most people went to work every day and felt part of a true team? If co-workers didn't compete with each other but instead became each other's biggest fans and advocates? Moving from individualistic to unified workplaces can bring about these changes and improve work for everyone. Moreover, unified workplace practices reinforce beneficial and dignified workplace practices and vice versa. All of the new-playbook workplace practices complement each other. The more you can build into your organization, the more you, your team, and your company will truly flourish.

Key Chapter Insights

- Traditional-playbook workplaces focus on individual performance, creating high-stress environments where everyone is out for themselves. This leads to higher levels of burnout; decreased collaboration, employee engagement, and job satisfaction; and increased work-related loneliness.
- Unified workplaces built around teamwork and community decrease employee burnout, bolster innovation, increase employee retention and engagement, and foster a greater sense of belonging and inclusion for everyone.
- Unified workplaces focus on cultivating meaningful co-worker connections, creating shared goals, and collaborative decision-making across the board.

Part III

Redefining Success

Chapter 9

FROM SOCIAL SUCCESS TO SOUL SUCCESS

When I sold my first company, Conscious Company Media, in 2017, I didn't "cash out." I did an equity exchange with our parent company for the deal to go through. Given that the parent company has no intentions for upcoming liquidity events, my husband and I walked away with nothing to add to our bank account and probably never will receive any payout, not to mention the thousands of dollars of investment in the company that we never recouped. Since I didn't have the fairy-tale exit typically associated with selling a business, I told myself I hadn't been "successful."

Adding insult to injury, the parent company shut down Conscious Company Media during COVID. Even though I'd resigned earlier that year, it felt as if my company had failed and I had nothing to show for the six years I'd put into building it. Between not making money on the sale of the business and my company closing down, my sense of self-worth quickly deteriorated. I started catastrophizing, saying things to my husband like "My career is over!" and comparing myself to a child TV star who'd peaked too soon.

I started looking for ways to rebuild my confidence the only way I knew how: achievement. I launched my own website, started blogging, created online courses, and hosted virtual meetups for women leaders. It wasn't enough. I wasn't receiving standing ovations from hundreds of people. No one was inviting me to speak or be interviewed any longer. I wasn't a CEO. I couldn't achieve at the same level I'd become so accustomed to and felt entirely lost and worthless.

My therapist, Lynn, helped me untangle this whole situation. My sense of self-worth had become inextricably linked with extrinsic motivation. I *needed* to achieve and receive external validation: awards, applause, status, title, role, salary, and influence. No part of me believed I was inherently worthy just as I am, and especially not in the absence of accomplishment. I'd heard similar sentiments from many high-achieving women, and maybe the same is true for you. This is the trap of social success.

The Traditional Playbook: Social Success

Alfa Demmellash immigrated to the United States from Ethiopia as a child. When she was about to graduate from Harvard, her family had certain "ideas" about how her success might impact their future. "My parents definitely had expectations. You know, not only is the family liberated because Alfa's graduating from Harvard, but she'll do investment banking. It'll be like, 'You get a car. You get a car. Everyone gets a car!'" So, following graduation, when Demmellash told her parents she wanted to investigate pockets of economic poverty in their community, they were slightly disappointed. "They were like, 'To do what? You can't possibly be trying to get *into* the neighborhoods all of us are trying to escape from!'"

Demmellash buckled under the family pressure and accepted a job at Bear Stearns. "All of a sudden, I was all dressed up, putting on makeup and heels, walking through these doors into this giant black building, and not coming out until the sun was down. Every part of my being knew I was in the wrong place. I was spending more time in the bathroom than at the cubicle, having a conversation in the mirror with myself, saying, 'What happened? What went so awfully wrong that you're choosing to self-incarcerate in this way?' I was opting away from the people and the communities where I knew life, where I knew what was real and what deeply, at a heart level, moved me. I was like, 'Who forced you?' I couldn't answer that question other than I just wanted to prove to my parents that I wasn't being foolish or disregarding the role of money."

Demmellash had given in to the pressure of social success: abandoning what her soul called her to do in the name of practicality, trying to convince herself she'd somehow find happiness doing work she didn't enjoy if she received enough external validation. How many people have done the same? It's not terribly surprising. Many of us have been conditioned to achieve and define success based on the same script from a young age. Do well in school, win awards, compete with others, and set ourselves apart from our peers to get into the best schools to study something that will set us up for a "successful" career. We're told to get a stable, financially secure, prestigious job; climb the ladder as high as we can for forty years; gain as much influence, wealth, and notoriety as we can along the way; and retire around age sixty-five. Then, and only then, are we allowed to finally relax, pursue our passions, and do what makes us happy. This definition of success is somehow supposed to work for *everyone*.

When you consider the concept of "success," you're defining how you measure the value of your days. Ultimately, the definition of success that you aspire to reflects what truly matters to you—it's how you'll determine whether you spent your life wisely at the end of your days.

In the traditional playbook, we're conditioned to value our success based on extrinsic validation: meeting our parents' expectations, making more money than others, winning awards, impressing others with our position or accomplishments, and gaining power and influence. It's all about appearances. Many of these markers of extrinsic validation align with toxically masculine beliefs that a person's worth is defined by money, power, and influence and that winning/

achieving is always the goal. We're always seeking more, and there's a clear reason why: extrinsic motivation is addicting.

When neuroscientist Brian Knutson researched the impact of anticipating a reward (extrinsic motivation) on the brain, he discovered that the burst of dopamine that surges to the brain when someone anticipates a reward is the same physiological response that those with substance disorders experience when they have access to the substance they're addicted to.[1] Achievement addiction follows the same pattern as drug addiction. Once you achieve what you've been striving for, you feel a brief thrill but soon begin wondering what's next. You *need* your next achievement fix—one that's even larger than the last one. You tell yourself that you'll be happy once you reach the *next* thing. But there's never a stopping point. This is why you're not truly happy even though you landed that big job, got that promotion you wanted, received your pay raise, hit your sales goal, won the award, etc. You're forced to stay on the hamster wheel for the long haul in a perpetual cycle that never leads to lasting contentment.

While many of us have been told that pursuing extrinsic validation is the recipe for success, research has shown that it's not only addictive but it doesn't lead to genuine, long-lasting happiness. Psychologists Edward Deci and Richard Ryan's research explored the quality of life of students who defined their success based on extrinsic factors—money, fame, status—while in school. After college, those with extrinsic aspirations reported the *same* level of satisfaction with their lives as they had when they were in college and *increased* levels of anxiety and depression, even when they were hitting their goals.[2]

Call me bonkers, but basing your sense of self-worth and success on a never-ending, addictive cycle rooted in toxic masculinity that never makes you happy doesn't seem super . . . healthy? Yet it's what we've normalized and what many of us have relied on. And while staying within the parameters of social success may feel safe, it rarely leads to doing work that feels true to who you are. In the grand scheme of things, doing work that feels true to yourself is critical to a well-lived life. Recall that "I wish I'd had the courage to live a life true to myself, not the life others expected of me" is one of the top five regrets of those who are dying.

Fortunately, Demmellash found the courage to live a life that felt true to herself. After three days at Bear Stearns, she says, "I walked out. It was so egregious at a soul level that I was willing to do anything else. I knew my path would have to be defined differently. My soul has always said, 'Go to the places that are supposed to be escaped from and find the people there and remind them of home.'" Demmellash followed her soul's guidance, co-founding Rising Tide Capital in 2004. For twenty years, she's let her soul define her success, impacting the lives of thousands of underrepresented entrepreneurs as a result.

How you define success shapes your entire life: it informs what type of work you choose, the goals you set, the sacrifices you make, and what you prioritize. It serves as the compass that guides your decisions about how you spend your one precious life. Every woman I met who inspired me to write this book—the women who were genuinely content, healthy, and thriving while having a massive impact through their careers—left social success behind and redefined success on the basis of their soul. Taking the time to define your vision of soul success is one of the most important things you can do to improve your work and life.

The New Playbook: Soul Success

Erin Wade had followed the social success script perfectly. Princeton for undergrad. Berkeley for law school. Major law-firm job. Huge salary. She'd done everything she was "supposed" to do to achieve success. All she had to do now was work herself to the bone for the next forty years, not rock the boat, and bask in the glow of her well-earned success, right? Yeah, not so much. Wade wasn't as much *basking* as she was *deteriorating*. She started questioning what she was doing with her life.

Wade found herself reviewing stacks of legal briefs in her business suit despite actually wanting to do something much different with her career. You see, Wade loved food. She'd been the restaurant critic for her college newspaper, volunteered in restaurants to learn how to cook, and worked in restaurants after college. Even though food was Wade's passion, she couldn't afford basic living expenses while working in the food service industry in New York. After much deliberation, she did what we're all supposed to do someday—she let go of her dreams to do something "practical."

Wade decided to become a lawyer, going to law school for the same reason many people do: "I was smart and didn't know what else to do." After graduating from Berkeley, she landed an associate position at a prominent San Francisco law firm. She spent her days defending the world's largest companies, billing clients in six-minute increments, and was often asked to stay in the office until midnight. Wade says, "It truly was a demoralizing way to live."

Being a lawyer wasn't Wade's calling, and it showed. She was the last person to raise her hand when the partners asked people to "volunteer" to work late again or stay on the weekends. Eventually, the partners called Wade into their office and told her, "You know, this is a recession. We could hire anyone we want to make this much money. When we say jump, you say, 'How high?' Not 'I don't want to jump.'" They fired Wade on the spot.

Having never "failed so spectacularly," Wade was forced to think about her next steps. She says, "I'd never let go of that love of restaurants. And I honestly thought I'd be a lawyer for a decade, make enough money, and then open one someday. But I was like, 'What am I doing? I don't have kids. I don't have a house. I don't have anything to lose here. Why not take a risk and open a restaurant that I'd dreamed of opening?'" It was one thing to *imagine* switching careers; it was quite another to actually do it.

The fear set in as Wade considered abandoning her career as a lawyer to open a restaurant. She started thinking about how it could fail and how people might judge her. She worried that the restaurant might not succeed. She feared people would think she was erratic. I mean, she'd worked for only eighteen months as a lawyer, which was half the amount of time it had taken her to get the damn law degree! She felt embarrassed to switch careers so quickly after spending so much time in school. She talked to one of her friends about her concerns. "She asked me, 'What's the worst that could happen if the restaurant fails?' I was like, 'Well, I guess I'd just be a lawyer again.' She said, 'So then, why would you literally settle for your worst-case scenario?' I realized I'd been questioning whether I should stick with my worst-case scenario largely because I felt there was a sunk cost, and it would be embarrassing. At the end of the day, though, it's so cliché, but you only live once."

In 2011, Wade opened Homeroom restaurant in Oakland. The mac-and-cheese restaurant quickly became a Bay Area favorite, and Wade got to live out her dream. She eventually sold Homeroom in 2020 and now sits on multiple company boards, has opened other restaurants, became a guest lecturer at a prestigious food institute in Copenhagen, wrote a best-selling mac-and-cheese cookbook, published a business book, and much more. This all happened because she stopped caring about appearances and redefined success based on what brought her to life.

Wade's journey parallels the experiences of other flourishing leaders I've met: at some point, in the face of fear, conventional wisdom, potential failure, uncertainty, doubt, and judgment, they found the courage to build careers true to who they are and what they love.

Diana Propper de Callejon turned down a lucrative position at McKinsey—something she once coveted—because she realized that her passion was helping companies identify business and investment opportunities that solved environmental and social problems. Twanna Harris left a significant role in the corporate world to follow her truth and launch a first-of-its-kind social impact entertainment lab, connecting influencers with social causes. Stephanie Nadi Olson left her career at a major advertising company to launch her firm, which pioneered an entirely new model of agency that gave autonomy back to freelance workers. All of these women pursued their soul success.

Soul success is defined by how much you're flourishing. It's rooted in quality of life, intrinsic motivation, and inherent satisfaction. Some of the most powerful intrinsic motivators are having a purpose, pursuing a passion or mastery, and having autonomy over your life.[3] *These* are the elements that lead to true happiness and track with the key elements of soul success. Remember the research that found that students with extrinsic motivations had similar levels of life satisfaction and increased levels of depression and anxiety later in life? Well, that same research also found that after graduating, college students who defined their success on the basis of intrinsic aspirations had much *higher* levels of satisfaction and well-being than when they were in college and *lower* rates of anxiety and depression. In Deci's words, "Even though our culture puts a strong emphasis on attaining wealth and fame, pursuing these goals does not contribute to having a satisfying life. The things that make your life happy are growing as an individual, having loving relationships, and contributing to your community."[4]

Understanding the difference between extrinsic and intrinsic motivation explains why someone can be wealthy, high-achieving, and powerful and still feel dissatisfied with life. Social success based on extrinsic motivation leads to shallow, fleeting happiness. Soul success rooted in intrinsic motivation results in deep, long-lasting contentment. At its core, soul success is about crafting a personal definition of success that centers on finding meaning, pursuing your passions, and having time for what matters most to you in this life. It's about pursuing significance, building a life you love, and measuring the *quality* of your days.

The following practices can help you define soul success in your own life.

Soul Success Practice #1: Seek More Purpose and Meaning

Elaine Dinos was doing everything right. Working at a major global consulting firm in her thirties, she found that "the metrics for success were all based on external validation—how much productivity, compensation, how hard you're working, how late you're staying. Feeling rewarded for my productivity felt good. So I just kept giving everything to my employer, and I got rewarded for that. I got promoted. I got more money. I climbed the ranks." Dinos was rewarded by becoming a partner.

She had the fancy title and the compensation to go with it, and had direct access to C-suite leaders and high-profile CEOs. Despite the perks, Dinos says, "I got a lot of ego gratification, but it was a superficial version of happiness. Compensation, my title, who I knew—it was a very thin house of cards. It was filling a void created by a lack of self-worth, a lack of believing in myself, a lack of believing that I'm enough. I wasn't joyful. I wasn't whole."

During this time, Dinos's sister encouraged her to take some time away from her busy career to attend a retreat. At the retreat, Dinos began to reflect on her work. "I remember being on a hike and thinking, 'What do I actually *do* in my work?' It seems silly that I hadn't really thought about it, but I was like, 'I'm helping executives make more money. I'm helping businesses grow. Oh gosh, I'm growing consumerism. What am I doing?'" In answer to these questions, when Dinos returned to work, she started experimenting to find more meaning in her role. She sought work with some of the impact-focused clients her company had, like TOMS shoes and Interface. "If they were an impact-driven company and one of our firm's clients, I found my way onto the team. I realized how much satisfaction and joy I began to develop by aligning my values with the companies I was working with. It felt so good working with companies that were doing something good for the world, and it felt good being in their offices, seeing how engaged their team was in their work."

Dinos continued following this thread. In 2016, she wrote a white paper for her firm on what was happening inside these purpose-driven companies, exploring why they were successful. "We uncovered how much the culture and what was happening inside the companies led to their success." This paper inspired Dinos to pioneer the firm's first purpose-focused community. With "zero budget, zero permission, and zero resources," Dinos launched an internal newsletter about purpose in business. More than two hundred of her colleagues joined her community. Soon after, the CEO started quoting her report, and her work began appearing in corporate social responsibility reports. Ultimately, Dinos launched a new service line for the firm, bringing in clients who wanted to learn more about purpose.

In 2018, Dinos resigned to launch Kindred Lane. She now works with companies to align their corporate strategy with their values and purpose and do the inner work needed to bring this alignment to life. Reflecting on her journey, Dinos says, "When I think about the metrics for success I used to use for my career, they weren't aligned with what was feeding my soul. They weren't aligned with my values or success as I defined it personally." By being more intentional about aligning her vision of success with finding more meaning and purpose in her work, she changed the trajectory of her entire career and her life. Dinos says she finally realized that "I am enough, just as I am, regardless of the metrics of revenue or productivity of my company or anything else."

As Dinos experienced, having a sense of purpose is one of our primary intrinsic motivations. Research has shown that having a sense of purpose leads to increased happiness, greater longevity, better sleep, better mental and physical health, less stress, and better cognitive function.[5] It follows that employees who work for purpose-driven organizations are more engaged and satisfied with their work.[6] Simply put, we thrive when we have meaning in our lives.

With nearly 70 percent of employees feeling that their sense of purpose in *life* is tied to their work, aligning your work with a purpose that genuinely inspires you may be one of the most significant levers you can pull to move you from surviving to thriving.[7] The key is *deciding* to prioritize purpose over traditional markers of success. This might mean taking a "step down" the corporate ladder, starting something new, working at a smaller company with less "prestige," or making less money so you can bring more purpose to your work.

Former Patagonia CEO Rose Marcario has made significant career leaps to prioritize purpose in her work. In 2008, Marcario was the CFO of a publicly traded software company, one of the few women at that time to hold such a title. Despite the prestige, Marcario found herself drawn toward the emerging movement of leaders discussing how business could be a force for good. Ultimately, she followed her interest, taking on the COO role at Patagonia, a much smaller, privately held outdoor apparel company. Marcario became CEO years later.

In 2020, despite her success in what was now a high-profile role, Marcario felt pulled toward a new purpose: regenerative agriculture and restoring the planet. Again, she followed her soul. She resigned from Patagonia and became a founding partner of ReGen Ventures, a venture fund focused on investing in early-stage companies that restore the environment. Marcario says, "Life is fluid, and we grow and evolve in our thinking and capacity. Check in with yourself regularly. Don't get trapped in form and titles. Don't let someone else's dream overtake your dream. Focus on your personal gifts, what you are good at, and what you can contribute. Enter everything with a light heart and a sense of curiosity. And when it's time to change, go for it. You'll regret sitting back."

When it comes to your definition of success, how much do you think about purpose or the impact you want to have? Do you consider purpose when making significant decisions, setting goals, or thinking about your future? Instead of aiming to be the most accomplished, influential, or wealthiest, what if we started equating success with creating impact? If we stopped celebrating people for how much money or influence they have and instead celebrated each other for how much impact we make? The entire world would change for the better. That change starts with you.

Tips for Seeking More Purpose in Your Work

1. Some Purpose Is Better Than No Purpose

Just as with physical activity, having some sense of purpose and meaning in your life makes a massive difference over having none. To this end, you can start small.

Do something in service of someone else—highlight your peer's work to someone on your leadership team, publicly acknowledge a colleague's recent accomplishment, or make a meaningful introduction for someone. Depending on what you're interested in, there's likely a resource for how to become an advocate for that change, either within your organization or as an individual leader. Groups like Moving the Needle, which educates business leaders on how to make changes on specific social and environmental issues, meet regularly to discuss how to make progress on specific issues. Or you could try finding a like-minded group or volunteer opportunity that can help you bring more purpose into your life without making drastic changes.

2. Identify Issues You Care About

While making any positive impact through your work can lead to greater intrinsic validation, making an impact that truly lights you up will go even further.

Serial entrepreneur Yscaira Jimenez has consistently worked on issues that light her up by focusing on one question: "What problems do I see around me that I want to solve?" When Jimenez felt frustrated about the lack of venues in the Bronx for many of her artist friends to display and sell their art, she opened a café with a stage and a small shop centered around artists. When she watched her brother struggle to find work and hit the "paper ceiling" as one of the estimated seventy million people without a bachelor's degree in the United States, she launched her company, LaborX, to help companies connect with this talent pool. You can follow Jimenez's lead and explore specific problems that frustrate you most to narrow in on a meaningful purpose.

Another approach to identifying a purpose you care about is thinking about the type of world you want to create in the long term and how you could contribute to that vision. For Kendra Coleman, president of Kindred Organizational Consulting, her personal purpose "is creating more love in the world." Entrepreneur Ayla Schlosser's personal purpose is to "support individuals, build communities, and influence systems to create a world where everyone can achieve their full potential." To help you examine your purpose, ask yourself, at the end of your days, what would you feel proudest of contributing to, what do you want to be remembered for, or what do you want to bring more of to the world?

Once you've identified a purpose you genuinely care about, explore options for working on it. Are there organizations working on the issue that you could apply to or volunteer opportunities in your community? Is there a course or certification that could help you learn more about the problem and find additional opportunities? Is there a thought leader you could reach out to for advice? The more you explore, the more likely you are to find a way to work on the issue you care about.

3. GET CREATIVE

As in Dinos's story, another way to engage with purpose is to think about ways to bring more meaning to your current circumstances. Lily Chang, former chief portfolio services officer at private equity firm Leonard Green, advocated for creating an event for women leaders, resulting in the firm's Women's Executive Forum, which she ran for ten years.

After building two enterprises focused on impact investing, Morgan Simon started writing in her spare time about how to make the field more oriented toward social justice. It changed her entire career. Simon says, "I'd been doing a bunch of curmudgeonly writing about everything that impact investing was doing wrong, and the right people started reading it." One of those people was her future business partner, Aner Ben-Ami. This connection led to Simon becoming a founding partner of the Candide Group, where she works with families and foundations who want their money working for social justice. As of the time of writing, the company has supported over 150 companies and funds across areas like climate justice and worker ownership, with over $285 million put to work.

What creative ways could you use to bring more purpose to your current role or engage with on the side? Could you start a podcast, video series, newsletter, or blog that helps people understand and engage with the issue? Or start a book club, employee resource group, or monthly lunch-and-learn sessions? Thinking outside the box may help you find more meaning without feeling like you need to change your entire life.

Soul Success Practice #2: Pursue What You're Passionate About

While working on an ambulance in college, All Good Body Care founder and CEO Caroline Duell saw how effectively Western medicine fixed people but felt that we needed a better understanding of how to *heal* them. She found ways to explore her budding interest in healing at school, ultimately convincing the university to let her design a major in holistic healing.

Still passionate about healing after graduation, Duell found additional programs to explore other healing modalities. She moved to a farm in Marin County, California, while studying neuromuscular reprogramming and long-term holistic body care. The farm's owner encouraged Duell to plant an herb garden, which she designed based on the herbs' healing properties. The garden produced an overabundance of healing herbs, so Duell created a skin salve from the excess herbs to sell at the farmers market in her spare time. She called the salve All Good Goop.

Duell sold her salve as a hobby for five years. Sharing her passion for healing with others made her happy. Unfortunately, when she and her partner moved four hours south to Morro Bay, she was forced to stop selling her salve. Shortly after the move, though, she started getting calls from former customers telling her the salve was the only thing that helped with their child's eczema or the only thing they'd found that helped treat their burns from chemo treatments. After hearing about the tangible benefits of her passion project, Duell felt that she wasn't ready to let it go just yet. She started making mason jars of the salve to bring to customers in Marin. On one of these trips north, she stopped by a local store owned by a friend to see if he'd be interested in selling her salve. Her friend grabbed her by the shoulders and said, "Do you understand what's happening here? You're starting a business!" Duell says this was the jolt she needed to believe that she could turn her passion into something more. Eighteen years later, All Good Body Care has become a sustainable body care industry leader.

Duell tapped into a critical intrinsic motivator by pursuing her passion: mastery. Author Daniel Pink identified mastery, defined as "the urge to get better and better at something that matters," as one of our three most critical intrinsic motivators.[8] Like purpose, mastery gives us a deep sense of inherent satisfaction. When we're evolving and working on something that genuinely matters to us, we feel engaged with and inspired by our work. This is why some people experience a "flow state" at work, where they become so energized, focused, and engaged in what they're doing that they lose a sense of time and feel a deep sense of joy and satisfaction. If you've ever experienced working in a flow state, you're most likely working on something you're passionate about.

By allowing her passion to guide her, Duell gets to wake up each day and do work that brings her to life. How many of us are lucky enough to say the same? On the other hand, how many of us have settled, slogging through a job we don't enjoy or even hate because we felt pressured to choose work that aligns with societal ideas of success? Or how many of us abandoned something we loved long ago because someone told us it wouldn't be possible? Finding soul success means letting go of external pressure and limiting beliefs about what's possible. As Jane Wurwand, co-founder of Dermalogica, says, "If we're each unique, then we are here for a reason. The reason can't be the same for everyone. And if we're here for a reason, we must be fully equipped to fulfill it. Otherwise, that wouldn't make sense. The path to finding your reason for being here must be as authentic as possible to your truth. Otherwise, you'll end up living a life that someone else wanted for you instead of the life you're meant to live. When you find yourself saying, 'I don't know if I'm brave enough to be this person,' you are. That's why you were made this person. So go for it. You must because if you don't, you'll miss the turning point that will bring you to living your fullest life."

Your passion might be a particular topic, solving a specific problem, pursuing something that brings you joy, or something else entirely. The critical element is feeling engaged in and inspired by what you're doing. Whatever your passion is, it's valid, and you are fully equipped to pursue it. Centering your passion as a core pillar of your definition of success is critical to feeling genuinely fulfilled and doing work you love.

Tips for Pursuing Your Passion

1. Embrace Failure

Our uber-achievement-focused culture might have you feeling that you're supposed to win at all times, be infallible, and never fail. I. Get. It. I used to be so uncomfortable with failure that I'd avoid anything I thought I *might* fail at, shying away from anything new or challenging. But here's the truth I've learned throughout my career: failure is a gift.

When I followed my passion and built my first company, *so* many things didn't go according to plan. My first crowdfunding campaign—failed. Year-one sales strategy—failed. Our second hire—failed. None of these failures felt great, but they were hugely valuable. Inevitably, we'd gain insights or have a specific experience that was key to something succeeding in the future. I even created a handy-dandy acronym with my team to remind us of this: EFWO, which stands for Everything Fucking Works Out.

EFWO was our reminder that anything perceived as failure was happening *for* us, not *to* us, whether or not we understood *how* at the time. The speaker cancels the day before our big event—EFWO! Maybe this opens up a spot to invite someone at the last minute who will bring the exact thing we need for this event. Major advertiser pulls out for the next year—EFWO! Maybe this is the encouragement we need to explore revamping our sales strategy or pivoting our revenue model. Even when things happened that were so unexpected and awful that I couldn't see their gift at the time, I tried to remain confident that I would see their value *someday*.

Shifting your mindset to embrace failure instead of fearing it will help you find the courage to pursue your passions. To help you get started, ask yourself the following when you perceive something as a failure:

- If this was happening *for* me, what could that mean?
- What opportunities does this open up?
- What can I learn from this?
- How could this be a good thing?
- In what way could this make me better?

2. Figure It Out as You Go

Now, you might be one of those people who feel that you need to have tons of experience, know more, have better connections, or have a more precise game plan before you can do what you want.

Here's a little secret that co-founder and CEO of EcoEnclose Saloni Doshi shared with me: "Nobody knows what the fuck they're doing! All these people you think about as the world's biggest leaders or all the people you admire in some capacity, you might assume that they have it all figured out. The biggest realization I've had yet is that they don't."

All this is to say, you don't need to have *everything* figured out to follow your dreams. There's no perfect time, age, scenario, or experience level. You can figure it out along the way. I mean, I started a print magazine at age twenty-nine with five months of publishing experience. We just kept putting one foot after the other and trying to take the best next step. You can do the same thing, and your intuition is one of the best tools for helping you do so. Serenbe Development COO and co–managing director Garnie Nygren says, "I'm here because I've followed the journey and walked through the doors that have opened for me. When it feels natural or like something's pushing me to the right, I go right instead of fighting it." We Are Rosie founder Stephanie Nadi Olson says something similar about building her company from scratch: "I decided to just do the next thing that felt really good. What is the next step for this business that gets me excited? I just kept choosing ease, relief, and the frictionless path, and the road kept unfolding in front of me."

Even when a step seems like a mistake, it's helping you make progress. Real Leaders CEO Julie Van Ness says, "As in life and relationships, your career is a process of elimination. It's like, 'I don't like this, I don't like that.' But each time brings you closer to what you do love." Co-founder of Dermalogica Jane Wurwand describes this process as a dot-to-dot puzzle: "It's all laid out. The dots are all there, but you can't see what the hell it is until you start making the journey and filling in the space between the dots. You're not going to know what you're doing. You have to join them up in the order that they're written. Otherwise, you won't ever see what is meant to be."

Instead of focusing on all the reasons why you *can't* do something, start experimenting with what you *can* do. What's one small step you could take to begin making progress? It also might be helpful to explore ways to take the pressure off experimenting with your passion. Could you start a side gig while keeping your current job? Put aside monthly savings for a year to build a small cushion to fall back on? Start a smaller-scale version of something and let it build over time? Find consulting work on the side, take a part-time job, get a roommate, barter your services, sell stuff on eBay, teach yourself things on YouTube, find a business partner, launch a crowdfunding campaign? There are heaps of things you can do to make exploring your passion more palatable. The upshot: find a way to make it work instead of convincing yourself you can't do something without even trying.

3. Reframe Risk

When I first had the idea to launch a print magazine, all I could think about were the risks: financial risk, reputational risks, career risks. Even so, something about this magazine just felt . . . right. As I sat in the tension between what my heart wanted to do and what my head told me was too risky, I realized that I was worrying about the minor risks, not the major risks.

Minor risks are things like worrying about potentially failing, disappointing someone, or being judged. If the minor risk actually played out, it might hurt your pride, inconvenience you, or feel disappointing or embarrassing, but in the grand scheme of things, it wouldn't actually *ruin* your life. On the other hand, major risks are things like never living your truth, not spending enough time on the things that matter most to you, compromising your values, not living up to your potential, or settling for a purely mediocre existence—you know, things that would give you serious regrets on your deathbed. Disappointing your parents—microrisk. Not honoring the life your parents gave you by being miserable and stressed the entire time—macrorisk. Feeling judged by others for leaving your high-profile job—microrisk. Wondering on your deathbed what would have happened if you'd done what you actually wanted to do—macrorisk. Too often, we let our fear of the unknown and concern about near-term discomfort prevent us from doing what would lead to long-term contentment and living the life we're truly meant to live.

As you think about your soul success, take a moment to write down all the risks you're concerned about. Which concerns are minor, and which ones are major? If you don't have any major risks, answer any of the following when it comes to the decision you're trying to make:

- What will matter at the end of my life?
- What topic or activity makes me come alive?
- What feels like my truth, like it's mine to do in this life?
- Who do I ultimately want to be, and how do I want to be remembered?

4. Set Learning (Mastery) Goals, Not Performance Goals

When we set professional goals, we often focus on a specific achievement or end result to mark our success and demonstrate our competence: a particular promotion, title, award, sales goal, revenue milestone, or salary. All of these are considered performance goals. On the other hand, learning or mastery goals focus on growing, evolving, and increasing competence. Learning a language, being able to design your website, being a confident public speaker—all of these are learning goals. Psychologists Carol Dweck and Ellen Leggett found that those who set performance goals tend to avoid challenges and learn helplessness in the face of failure. In contrast, those who set learning goals seek out challenges and are more resilient in the face of failure.[9]

Setting learning goals for yourself can help you remain resilient and committed to your passions. For example, when it came to writing this book, I set the learning goals of wanting to grow as a person through the process and hoping that the book will positively impact the readers who pick it up. If I'd set the performance goal of selling one million copies and writing a bestseller, I can nearly guarantee that I would have stopped somewhere along the way once I realized how unlikely those goals were. By setting a learning goal, I've taken the pressure off myself and maintained focus on what genuinely matters to me about this book.

When you think of your professional goals, are they performance goals or learning goals? If you have primarily performance goals, how can you transform them to learning goals? Or if you don't have clear goals, what learning goals can you set for your success?

Soul Success Practice #3: Prioritize Your Quality of Life

At age twenty-one, Courtney Klein sketched an idea for an educational nonprofit on the back of a barf bag on a plane returning from Mexico. That year, she took the idea from a barf bag to a full-scale organization. Klein scaled her venture, New Global Citizen, which focused on empowering high school youths to create change in the world, to fourteen states in thirty-three countries in the coming years. It was kind of a big deal. Klein says, "I was getting a lot of media attention and recognition. I won the Young Alumni of the Year award from ASU, the largest public university in the country, and was recognized as a young CEO to watch."

Klein wasn't exactly thriving despite her success: "I'd been on a bit of a high because I was getting all this love and attention and accolade, but I think I recognized that what gave me juice was not the accolades. If I was honest with myself, it felt superficial. I wasn't in a healthy place. I was working eighty to a hundred hours per week. My health was going down. I had no social life aside from two girlfriends who were also CEOs. It was really isolating. I remember talking to my dad at some point because I was feeling like *If I let go of this thing, what will become of me? My identity is now tied to this organization. Who am I as a human, a woman, a person without it?*

I don't know that I'll survive. My dad said, 'Courtney, we're called human beings, not human doings.'" Klein was coming to the sobering realization that it didn't matter how much she accomplished if it meant compromising the *quality* of her life experience.

If "success" means sacrificing things that matter most to you and the quality of your life, how can we call it success? If you're unhealthy, unhappy, or unfulfilled, does it even matter what your title is or how much money you make? If you're too busy to spend time with your loved ones or too stressed to make beautiful memories, what's the point of it all? New-playbook leaders consider questions like these and define success based on what they need to flourish.

Per Harvard's Human Flourishing Program, the key elements of flourishing include (1) well-being, including good physical and mental health; (2) experiences that nurture connection with others; (3) having purpose and meaning; (4) having integrity around your values, and (5) feeling happy and satisfied.[10] When you compromise these elements in the name of success, it decreases your ability to flourish. Yet how often do you consider these elements in your career? Or how many times have you sacrificed one or more of them in the name of success? You're just so damn busy that something's gotta give, right?

When the siren song of extrinsic success is calling, prioritizing what matters most can be challenging. I've been there. A few years ago, I was headhunted for a pretty big role. CEO title, well-known company, significant pay raise, major influence. My ego was feeling Pretty. Damn. Good. The role would give me access to high-profile people. I'd make more money than ever before. I could prove I was successful on the heels of my first company being shut down. It was all about appearances and traditional (read: toxically masculine) markers of success—status, wealth, and influence.

Well, thank goodness for therapy. When I started thinking about the realities of this new role, it meant a massive workload, more travel, public-facing pressure, higher expectations, and more stress. With the added pressure of the role, I knew I'd fall right back into my old patterns that had destroyed my quality of life during my first stint as CEO: prioritizing my work over all else in the name of success. For the first time in my life, I wasn't thinking about success through the lens of how much I could achieve or how much extrinsic motivation I could accrue. I was thinking about success by asking myself, "Will this lead to me truly flourishing?" I turned down the role, realizing the expectations of the position would strip me of autonomy. I wouldn't be free to pick my kids up from school every day, stop working at 3:30, or take ample vacation time with my family. And given the patriarchal beliefs about men controlling women, autonomy plays a vital role in women's lives. So much so that the Center for Women in Business at Rutgers Business School found that while men typically associate the idea of power with control, women typically associate power with *freedom*.[11]

The third practice of soul success invites you to focus on your quality of life by examining how much freedom you have for the things that matter most to you. Ultimately, it's about asking yourself whether your work stands in the way of or supports your ability to flourish. Can you imagine what would happen if more of us shifted our definition of success from the *quantity* of things we accrue and achieve to the *quality* of our experience? The quality of our work, the quality of how we feel, the quality of our well-being, and the quality of our life. Shouldn't that be how we measure and define success?

Eventually, Klein made this shift in her life. Now working on her third company, when she thinks of success, she says, "I think about happiness and joy a lot more. It's internal more than external. I've had to shed many of the prior notions of being busy all the time as an indicator of success. I have a finite number of conscious hours to spend, and now I'm intentional about asking, 'Does this thing really matter? Or am I doing it because it's an expectation of someone else?' If it's the latter, it's a no-go. I've recalibrated my idea of success not to be defined by financial success, accolades, or titles. All the prior things I used to define success are totally out the window. I'll be on my yoga mat this morning and at the beach with my kids at 4:00 this afternoon. That's success."

I also worked to make this shift, making my decisions based on my quality of life instead of extrinsic motivation. I've turned down opportunities, have felt legit FOMO, don't have a significant social media following, and probably could be considered "more successful" by traditional metrics, *and* I am unequivocally the happiest, healthiest, and most fulfilled I've ever been. I can't encourage you enough to do the same.

Tips for Prioritizing Your Quality of Life

1. Define "Enough" Money

Each of us has a *unique* relationship with money that plays a role in how we think about success. Speaking from experience, when you're struggling to cover the basics of Maslow's hierarchy of needs, money can become your entire definition of success. I've been there and understand the necessity of doing so. *And*, as you make enough money to move up Maslow's hierarchy of needs, I invite you to let go of the story that "more money" should be central to how you define success. More money doesn't equate with greater quality of life. Research has shown that people's happiness rises alongside their income until they make around $100,000. After $100,000, happiness plateaus no matter how much money they make.[12] Even so, how many people base their idea of success on making more money?

One way to help you move away from centering more money in your definition of success is to define enough. What would be a sufficient amount of money for your ideal life? You can reflect on the following to help you define enough:

- How much do you need to cover your basics (rent/mortgage, food, childcare, transportation, etc.)?

- How much do you need for things that support your ability to flourish (travel, gym, health providers, social occasions, hobbies, etc.)?
- What savings goals do you have (kids' education, travel fund, retirement, etc.)?

Once you identify a range of money that would support your ideal life, incorporate it into your vision of soul success and release any further attachment to the need for more.

2. Bring Purpose, Passion, and Quality Together

Ideally, your soul success should involve striving to find the place where a sense of purpose, what you're passionate about, and your quality of life come together. I think of passion as *what* you want to do, purpose as *why* you want to do it, and quality as *how* you want to do it. Each of these elements is critical.

For example, Erin Wade's passion was opening a restaurant. She layered in purpose by pioneering a business model that brought dignity to the food industry. She sought to positively impact her employees' lives and create a replicable model that other business owners could follow. Wade had passion and purpose but soon realized that she was sacrificing her quality of life. She worked too much, didn't get enough time with her kids, and started burning out. So she began committing to new practices to support her quality of life, taking time off, prioritizing a weekly surfing session, and distributing leadership to other executives on her team. Ultimately, she found that sweet spot where purpose, passion, and quality of life overlap.

As Wade discovered, if you're passionate about your work and are making a positive impact but have zero time for your well-being, social connections, or priorities, you'll struggle and eventually burn out. If you have meaningful work and quality of life but aren't passionate about what you're doing, you'll become increasingly disengaged and miss out on the deep satisfaction that comes from getting to work on something that lights you up. If you're passionate about your work and have a good quality of life but don't feel that your work is meaningful, your work won't feel as satisfying or lead to deep contentment.

When Anna Banks, senior VP of personalization and performance marketing for Sephora North America, was between roles, she clarified the critical elements she was looking for: "I determined what my family actually needs and then literally wrote out the list of what I wanted my next role to have. The top of the list was something that's doing good for the world, but I also had things on there like not having a commute and working with nice people." The clearer you get on each element of your soul success, the better your chance of reaching it. Answering the following prompts as you imagine the future can help you start thinking about your ideal work and life:

1. **Why: Purpose/Meaning**
    a. I feel that I'm positively impacting . . .
    b. My work feels meaningful because . . .
    c. I'm proud of . . .
2. **What: Passion/Mastery/Satisfaction**
    a. I get to explore and work on . . .
    b. My work leaves me feeling . . .
    c. I'm inspired to learn more about . . .
3. **How: Autonomy (Well-Being, Social Connection, and Values Alignment)**
    a. I have ample time and freedom for . . .
    b. I don't have to deal with these critical sources of stress . . .
    c. My schedule looks like . . .
    d. I'm never forced to compromise . . .
    e. I feel that I'm genuinely flourishing because . . .

Once you have a clear vision of your ideal life, use it to guide your decisions moving forward. You can also reflect on the following:

- What are the main obstacles between your current and desired ideal states?
- What could you do to begin addressing these key challenges?

Centering all three practices and finding a way to make them come to life is the most profound version of soul success and will help you lead the life you want instead of the life that others want for you. Redefining your definition of success also addresses the toxic definitions of success outlined in the first chapter that harm so many. If you aspire to love your life, aligning your career with what brings your soul alive is one of the most profound ways to do so. The question is, will you rise to the level of your soul's aspirations?

Key Chapter Insights

- The commonly accepted societal definition of success rooted in achievement and extrinsic motivation rarely leads to deep satisfaction or long-lasting contentment. Instead, it has proven to be addictive and leads to increased levels of stress and anxiety but no increased sense of satisfaction later in life.
- Shifting your definition of success to focus on the quality of your experience and intrinsically motivating factors like purpose, pursuing your passion, and having time for things that matter most to you will result in more profound, long-lasting contentment and human flourishing.

Chapter 10

FROM SHORT-TERM PROFIT MAXIMIZATION TO LONG-TERM VALUE CREATION

By 2005, Alison Bailey Vercruysse had turned her passion for making organic granola into a small business. Her company, 18 Rabbits, had distribution through nearly twenty retailers in the San Francisco Bay area and had opened a small kiosk in the Ferry Building.

Soon 18 Rabbits was sold at more than one hundred retailers, and the brand took off when it got national distribution through Peet's Coffee. Of those initial years, Bailey Vercruysse reflects, "I had a really precious, beautiful creation. It was giving me everything I wanted. I was paying myself and traveling to places I wanted to go to. I'd met friends who are still my friends today, and I had a great team I felt energized with."

After the company's success with Peet's Coffee, Bailey Vercruysse brokered additional national distribution deals with hotels, gyms, and other cafés, and the brand was one of the first to get on Amazon's grocery platform. For nearly a decade, 18 Rabbits scaled. However, Bailey Vercruysse says, during this growth, "I started to listen to outside voices about where the brand should go. 'If you want to be successful and sell for $40 million, this is what you need to do. This is the playbook.' When I followed what was supposed to be *the* playbook, that's when it all came crumbling down. It wasn't about the creation, the design, the food, or everything I loved about the business. I lost myself. I was extremely stressed and constantly worried about where the money would come from to do this or that."

Feeling pressured to scale the business as fast as possible by adding more product lines to their offerings, the 18 Rabbits team put up the money to order 500,000 granola bars made from their granola by manufacturer Hearthside Food Solutions. Unfortunately, the manufacturer wasn't able to produce the quality of products it had promised. The first batch of bars Hearthside delivered was nearly inedible, and the manufacturer refused to issue 18 Rabbits a refund. In the end, Hearthside delivered only half of the half-million bars ordered. The financial hit was too much for 18 Rabbits to survive. In 2017, Bailey Vercruysse closed her company for good. The case went to trial six years later, in 2024, and a jury found Hearthside Food Solutions liable for breach of contract. Unfortunately, the assets recovered from Hearthside were only enough to cover Bailey Vercruysse's legal fees.

While a bad actor led to 18 Rabbits' downfall, Bailey Vercruysse also places some of the blame on the pressure she felt to scale her company as quickly as possible based on the traditional playbook's definition of success: "I lost touch with my guiding star and lost my way, and it broke the business."

Bailey Vercruysse's experience illustrates what it looks like to lean into the traditional playbook's idea of success based on short-term, perpetual growth.

The Traditional Playbook: Perpetual Growth for Financial Gain

Milton Friedman's 1970 statement that the social responsibility of business is to increase profits laid the foundation for the traditional business playbook's definition of success. Also in 1970, the SEC started requiring publicly traded companies to report quarterly earnings, forcing those companies to demonstrate results every *three months*.[1] While intended to protect investors, this move resulted in short-termism being baked into the business world as well.

For the last fifty years, the amount of profit and rate of growth have served as the key markers of business success. With venture capitalists and private equity groups demanding outsized rates of return, leaders of private companies, like 18 Rabbits, often feel the need to scale their companies as quickly as possible toward a major liquidity event like an acquisition or IPO, while leaders of publicly traded companies strive to demonstrate growth as quickly as possible to drive up their share price and keep investors happy. The goal is the same across the board: rapid, perpetual growth to generate as much money as possible for a small group of shareholders. And as you might remember, defining success by accruing wealth and power and having a winner-takes-all mentality are core toxically masculine beliefs.

Many business leaders have accepted this definition of success without questioning how absurd it truly is. In 2023, writer Nathalie Robin Justice Gravel helped highlight this dynamic: "If a monkey hoarded more bananas than it could eat, while most of the other monkeys starved, scientists would study that monkey to figure out what the heck was wrong with it. When humans do it, we put them on the cover of *Forbes*." The post went viral, shedding light on how ridiculous the traditional playbook's idea of success is. But it's not just ridiculous; it has caused harm on a global scale.

In 1995, Lynne Twist came face-to-face with some of this harm. With her husband, Bill, and thought leader John Perkins, she traveled deep into the heart of the Amazon rainforest to meet with the Achuar people, an indigenous tribe entirely isolated from the outside world until this point. For years, the Achuar people had watched neighboring tribes enter into contracts with big oil companies promising economic opportunity only to have their land destroyed. At one neighboring site, experts estimated that oil companies were producing more than three million gallons of wastewater per *day*, storing it in unlined pits from which it spread into the soil and waterways. On top of this, it was estimated that nearly seventeen million gallons of oil had spilled from pipelines in the area.[2] All in the name of profit.

Every year, the oil companies encroached closer and closer on Achuar land, and the Achuar were desperate to prevent the destruction of their home. They told Twist, "The most important work you can do to save the Amazon and to support us is to change the dream of the modern world; the dream of consumption, of acquisition. People can't change their everyday actions without changing what they're dreaming for. You actually need to change the dream."[3]

As a result of this interaction, Twist co-founded the Pachamama Alliance. The organization takes people into the heart of the Amazon to learn from the Achuar people and redefine their dream of success to focus on sustainability, spiritual fulfillment, and social justice. Can you begin to imagine what would happen if more and more people changed their dream of success to focus on making a positive impact like this? It would change *everything*.

While the magnitude of changing how society thinks about business success might feel too large to tackle, this change begins with you. As identified by systems change expert Donella Meadows, the two most critical levers that can change an entire system are (1) the mindset out of which the system—its goals, power structure, rules, and culture—arises and (2) the goals of the system.[4] In other words, if you want to change business, change your mindset and the goals you're striving to achieve (read: your definition of success) to align with the world you want to see.

To that end, let's explore new-playbook practices that can help each of us rewrite our dreams of success.

The New Playbook: Long-Term Value Creation

By all traditional metrics, Kuli Kuli Foods is a high-growth start-up. The company was founded in 2011 by CEO Lisa Curtis following her time in the Peace Corps in Niger. Curtis saw the health benefits of moringa while working in a health clinic. She also saw how poorly moringa farmers, mostly women, were paid for their products. When she returned to the United States, she was determined to see if she could create a market for moringa to bring better economic opportunity to the women she'd met while also introducing the world to the healthy properties of the plant.

Outside her full-time job, Curtis started experimenting with making moringa-based protein bars in her kitchen. She found a recipe that passed the muster of her friends and family, got a booth at the farmers market on weekends, and built enough of a following to get distribution at Whole Foods through its local foragers program. Curtis scaled the brand from there, raising more than $10 million in investment and getting into major retailers like Walmart and CVS.

Like founders of traditional-playbook start-ups, Curtis wants her company to grow. Quickly. However, that's where the similarities with the traditional playbook end. Curtis isn't scaling her business to cash out and sail into the sunset on her diamond-encrusted superyacht. No, Curtis is building a company that addresses a societal problem, benefits as many lives as possible, and creates genuine long-term value for society.

One of the critical ways Kuli Kuli Foods is doing things differently is by putting purpose at the heart of the company's growth strategy. The company isn't growing for growth's sake; it's growing to make an even larger impact on people's lives. Curtis founded the company with the vision of creating a market for moringa to provide a true livelihood for disenfranchised moringa farmers. And she's refused to compromise on that mission. With this model, the more the company grows, the more farmers benefit. To date, the company's growth has supported the livelihoods of nearly four thousand women and family farmers, generating nearly $6.5 million in revenue for the moringa farmers who supply its products.

Curtis's dream of creating a company that improves lives doesn't extend just to the moringa farmers. The company strives to benefit as many of its stakeholders as possible, including employees, customers, community, investors, and more. Curtis is one of many new-playbook leaders who's *intentionally* scaling her company to make a positive impact on people and the planet rather than striving for perpetual growth in the name of accruing wealth and power. She's on a mission to demonstrate that this model can work, saying, "I feel like as one of the fewer mission-driven, female-founded companies who has raised VC money, I need to provide an example because I've had a lot of investors say, 'This mission-driven thing is cool, but give me some names of other mission-driven companies that have exited successfully within CPG [consumer packaged goods]. There aren't a lot of examples, and I couldn't come up with any led by women. I think having more examples for others to follow is really critical. It often feels impossible, but it absolutely can be done."

When it comes to following in Curtis's footsteps and redefining success in business to focus on creating long-term value for society, the following practices will help you get started.

Long-Term Value Creation Practice #1: Be Intentional About Why You're Growing

Kathy Bolhous has been the CEO of plastics manufacturer CNG since 2010. In fourteen years, she's grown the company from a $58 million to over a $5 billion valuation. And she's not done yet. Bolhous has aggressive company growth targets for the next few years. But, unlike in the traditional playbook, those targets weren't set to line the pockets of a small number of investors. The CNG team is striving to hit its growth targets to provide financial freedom for the company's nearly two thousand employees.

In 2021, following a major investment by private equity titan KKR, Bolhous announced that CNG would become an employee-owned company. This decision was made in partnership with KKR's co–head of global private equity and founder of Ownership Works Pete Stavros. In the years prior, Stavros had become increasingly passionate about the role employee ownership could play in addressing the widening socioeconomic divide. In the United States alone, the bottom quarter of households have a median net worth of $500, and an estimated 25 percent of workers have *nothing* saved for retirement. On the other hand, stock ownership is one of the most effective ways to generate household wealth, but the richest 1 percent of households own the vast majority of business wealth.[5] Employee ownership helps address this problem. Research has estimated that if 30 percent of companies adopted employee ownership, the wealth of the bottom 50 percent of Americans would *quadruple*, as would the wealth of the median Black household nationwide and those without high school diplomas.[6]

When Stavros and Bolhous discussed the potential of employee ownership to benefit CNG employees, many of whom are hourly manufacturing workers living in the American Rust Belt and attempting to break long cycles of generational poverty, Bolhous was all in. Her talent for scaling her business could lead to something truly impactful.

Now, the company's multiyear growth strategy is focused on its next major liquidity event in the coming years, at which point all employee-owners can cash out with earnings equal to an entire year's salary or more. Everyone on the team, including Bolhous, is clear about *why* they're striving to grow, and the reason is much deeper than making money for investors. Sharing organizational wealth with those responsible for the company's growth has reinvigorated the entire team, tracking with research showing that employee-owned businesses have higher levels of employee engagement, retention, and productivity and that companies that broadly share at least 30 percent of ownership with employees grow faster and are less likely to go out of business.[7]

Both Curtis and Bolhous have aligned their company growth with a larger purpose. The more their companies grow, the more lives they improve. It's a virtuous cycle. Tying company growth to a higher purpose ultimately helps the company grow. Purpose-driven businesses experience 30 percent higher levels of innovation and 40 percent higher levels of employee retention, while eight in ten customers claim to be more loyal to purpose-driven companies.[8]

Aligning your company's growth with making a net positive impact on the world is a key practice for new-playbook leaders. This approach rejects Friedman's idea that "the social responsibility of business is to increase its profits" regardless of the harm to society created along the way. Instead, leaders embrace the idea that the social responsibility of business is to create meaningful value for society. Impact capital executive Diane Henry uses this lens for her investments, saying, "The purpose of innovation isn't for the sake of innovation; it's to do something better than we're currently doing it and have a net positive effect so we're not introducing more new problems than we're solving. How do we use our resources as an instrument of human collaboration to create more value at scale? How do we codify the values we want to see expressed in the world into how we deploy capital and how we build companies?"

Creating meaningful value through your business could include addressing a specific problem or improving people's lives at scale; it could also include creating a business that enables you and others to live your ideal life.

Sharon Rowe took the latter approach. In 1989, Rowe had been thinking about launching a company to address the problem of single-use plastic bags. However, instead of launching a business with dreams of scaling it to a multimillion-dollar enterprise and cashing out someday, Rowe dreamed of growing a business to enable her to live her ideal lifestyle. She wanted to put her family first,

FROM SHORT-TERM PROFIT MAXIMIZATION TO LONG-TERM VALUE CREATION

have flexibility, not work nights and weekends, take four weeks of vacation, have time for self-care, feel financially secure, and solve problems without creating new ones. Rowe built her company, ECOBAGS, to make this lifestyle a reality. Her decision to build a company that ensured she enjoyed her life *while* she was working, not just after retirement, was made all the more profound following her untimely death from pancreatic cancer in 2024 at age 67.

Rowe called her business a "tiny business" and said it grows in alignment with what she valued. She said no to any business decisions that would detract from the lifestyle she loved. The business grew slowly, generating enough money to enable her and a handful of employees to live their ideal lives. Rowe said, "Tiny business is how you make a living, not a killing. Entrepreneurship doesn't need to be a competitive race to the peak, as popular myths and media want you to believe. It can be a pleasurable, educational hike, from point A to point B, step by step to the summit, where you arrive in healthier financial and personal shape than when you began."[9]

Knowing that I'm putting myself at risk of being haunted by Milton Friedman's ghost for the remainder of my days, I invite you to consider the idea that a business doesn't have to perpetually grow to make *more*; businesses can grow to an ideal point where they make enough and then . . . stop growing and sustain over the long term. If a business is creating genuine value for the founders and others associated with it, as in enabling an entire team to live their dream lifestyle, why can't that be enough? Can you imagine what would have happened if Bailey Vercruysse had done so? If she'd stopped aggressively trying to scale 18 Rabbits when she realized that the company was giving her everything she wanted—paying her a decent living and enabling her to travel, meet friends, and feel energized by getting to do work she loved every day? If she'd simply let her "beautiful creation" be *enough*?

Whether it's tying a purpose to your company's products, creating an impactful mission for your organization, or building a company to support an ideal life, having a deeper *why* behind your growth strategy that generates genuine societal value will help you and your organization truly thrive. The more business leaders move away from the harmful dream of short-term perpetual growth at all costs and toward intentional growth driven by creating true value for the world, the better business and the world will become for us all.

Tips for Being Intentional About Why You're Growing

1. Codify Your Why with Your Team

If you've been scaling your business based on the traditional playbook to date and would like to establish a deeper why for your growth strategy, include as many members of your team as possible in the process. Why? Well, for starters, the more brains you have in the room, the stronger the final vision for growth will be. And second, the more people you involve, the more ownership, alignment, and engagement they'll feel in bringing the vision to life.

Beyond including your team in the process, the exercise of writing down why your company is striving to grow (or not) will help *you* get clarity and provide you with a useful tool to communicate the deeper why to your team and other stakeholders.

As you go through this exercise, I'd advise staying away from the common line of thinking that making loads of money so you can siphon off some of it to donate to charity is a good enough *why* for scaling your company. Far too many leaders hide behind philanthropy to justify their company's abhorrent work conditions, extractive practices, or contributions to societal problems. Unless you can confidently say your company isn't causing harm, is benefiting as many stakeholders as possible, is sharing its wealth broadly, and is genuinely creating value for society, your future philanthropy isn't good enough (#sorrynotsorry).

The following questions can help guide your inquiry as you explore your deeper why:

1. Currently, what value does our company create for society and for the people who work here?

2. Can we say with confidence that the work we do is creating a net positive in some way and not contributing to more societal problems? Are there any specific societal problems we know our business is currently addressing?
3. Is there a world where what we're doing right now is *enough*?
4. If we doubled in size next year, who or what would genuinely benefit from our growth? Would anything need to change for our growth to truly benefit a larger group of people or address a societal problem?

2. TIE YOUR WHY TO SUCCESS METRICS

If you're striving to make progress on a core purpose through your brand's growth, define what success toward that goal would look like. Instead of a vague mission statement like "improving lives one product at a time," see if you can create clear, long-term, measurable goals. For example, in 2015, the Eileen Fisher brand set Vision 2020 to codify its purpose, committing to using sustainable materials in 100 percent of the company's products by 2020. From 2015 to 2020, when it came to company performance, Eileen Fisher tracked financial metrics *and* Vision 2020 metrics.

This is a key difference for new-playbook leaders: they don't *solely* measure finances as indicators of organizational success. Yes, they have to sustain financial performance to keep the lights on, but finances are not the only thing they care about. Curtis measures the impact of company operations on the moringa farmers as a key marker of success. Rowe checks in with key elements of her ideal lifestyle to ensure that she's still on track.

Creating clear, measurable goals for your company's higher purpose for growth and prioritizing them as much as you do financial performance will help you truly bake this ethos into your organization's success.

Long-Term Value Creation Practice #2: Strive to Benefit All Stakeholders

Eileen Fisher launched her namesake brand in 1984 with $350 in her bank account. At her first show, she sold over $40,000 worth of clothes, beginning a trend of steady profitability for the brand. The brand's profitability supported its organic growth from year to year. But when the brand started generating more profit than it needed to support growth, unlike most business founders, Fisher didn't see the need to hoard all of the excess wealth: "Once we started having extra profit, the first thought was share it with the employees. They do all the work, it's only fair to share, which I think all companies should have to do. I really do."[10] But Fisher didn't stop there.

As her company grew, Fisher saw opportunities to use the company's success to benefit *all* company stakeholders—customers, community, the environment, vendors, etc. For example, the company started providing grants to up-and-coming entrepreneurs in her community, created take-back centers to recycle and resell clothes, provided leadership training and educational programming for customers, and much more. Essentially, Fisher uses the company's abundance to create as much value for *others* as possible. How revolutionary! To not hoard excess wealth among a small group of people while most others struggle to make ends meet. To use your influence and abundance to lift up those around you, striving to ensure that everyone has enough. How much would the world change if more business leaders adopted a similar ethos?

This concept—the stakeholder model—isn't new. In 1984, University of Virginia business professor Edward Freeman first introduced the idea of stakeholder theory: "If you can get all your stakeholders to swim or row in the same direction, you've got a company with momentum and real power. Saying that profits are the only important thing to a company is like saying, 'Red blood cells are life.' You need red blood cells to have life, but you need so much more."[11]

As Freeman highlights, focusing solely on maximizing wealth for shareholders is a shortsighted way to build a company. If you create

FROM SHORT-TERM PROFIT MAXIMIZATION TO LONG-TERM VALUE CREATION

value only for shareholders while exploiting everyone else, you *might* have short-term results, but the business won't be sustainable over the long run. Employees will quit. Vendors will stop prioritizing orders or providing favorable terms. Customers will write bad reviews or choose to buy from someone else. This approach doesn't acknowledge how interdependent we all are or how critical *every* stakeholder is to a business's success.

New-playbook leaders like Fisher strive to benefit *all* stakeholders. Antoinette Klatzky, VP of programs and partnerships at the Eileen Fisher Foundation, says, "The current capitalist structure doesn't serve us. The next version of capitalism, one that we can get to, serves *all* people. That's what we need to work towards in whatever industry we're working in." Beautifully, striving to serve all people creates greater value for everyone, *including* shareholders. Research has shown that a stakeholder model leads to higher employee retention and engagement; increased customer loyalty and advocacy; enhanced talent acquisition; better brand reputation; and better sustained, long-term financial performance. One case study found that stakeholder businesses outperformed the S&P 500 by a factor of 14 to 1.[12] Put simply, the more value you create for your stakeholders, the more value they'll create for your organization. And the business world is taking note.

In 2019, the Business Roundtable, an industry group including CEOs of the world's largest companies, like Amazon, JP Morgan & Chase, Vanguard, and Johnson & Johnson, released a statement amending the language of its Principles of Corporate Governance, which contain language about the purpose of a corporation: "Each version of that document issued since 1997 has stated that corporations exist principally to serve their shareholders. It has become clear that this language on corporate purpose does not accurately describe the ways in which we and our fellow CEOs endeavor every day to create value for all our stakeholders, whose long-term interests are inseparable."[13] The document was signed by 181 CEOs, publicly committing to lead their businesses for the benefit of all stakeholders.

While the extent to which these companies have followed through remains questionable, the statement was a significant moment indicating that stakeholder theory is gaining traction. In 2021, roughly 90 percent of C-suite executives surveyed by the Conference Board said, "There is a shift underway from stockholder (shareholder) to stakeholder capitalism, and almost 80 percent say the shift is occurring at their firm."[14]

When it comes to how business leaders see their stakeholders, the mindset shifts shown in Table 10.1 help illustrate the difference between the traditional and new playbooks.

The following practices illustrate just some of the ways you can begin thinking about your respective stakeholders.

Employees: Your employees can make or break your company's performance. We've covered many of the specific ways to benefit employees in the workplace section of the book, including practices from employee ownership and providing living wages to supporting your team's mental health and providing more flexibility. Whatever approach you choose, finding ways to help your team realize their potential, add value to their lives, and share the company's success will help your company succeed in the long run.

Suppliers: New-playbook leaders see their suppliers as key partners to build meaningful relationships with and support as much as possible. When it comes to Kuli Kuli Foods' moringa suppliers, Curtis says, "We want to ensure we know where the product is grown and the people who grow it. We want to visit them, hear their stories, see their communities, and really listen to them about what can we do to better support them." Engaging directly with its suppliers to understand their needs, Kuli Kuli launched a community impact fund to provide small grants to its suppliers. Curtis says, "We want this to be the easiest grant they've ever applied for. They just need to send us a paragraph about what their community needs and how can we help, and we give them a grant to do it." By building relationships with

Table 10.1: Short-term Profit Maximizing Mindset vs. Long-term Value Creation Mindset

	Short-term Profit-Maximizing Mindset	**Long-term Value-Creation Mindset**
Employees	My role is to extract the most value for the least amount of money from my employees	My role is to support my employees so we can all share in our success together
Suppliers	My role is to negotiate the best deal for my side at the cheapest cost from our suppliers	My role is to build relationships and find win-win solutions with these valuable partners
Customers	My role is to maximize profits and revenue-generating opportunities from our customers	My role is to be of service and maximize the value that we bring to our customers
Community	My role has very little to do with the community beyond PR opportunities—it's someone else's responsibility	My role is to strengthen and support our community where possible—it's critical infrastructure that our business depends on
Environment	My role is to use and exploit any natural resources available to us to make money	My role is to mitigate any harm our business might cause to the environment and seek opportunities to positively impact it where possible
Shareholders	My role is to make as much money as possible for our shareholders, and they are the only group that deserves to benefit from the company's success	My role is to listen to and learn from our shareholders, with whom I share a portion of the company's success

Kuli Kuli's suppliers, Curtis knows how best to ensure that the suppliers are thriving, which ensures that the suppliers can consistently deliver high-quality ingredients. Everyone wins.

When it comes to your company's suppliers, take the time to sit down with your vendors and get to know them. What are their challenges and needs? How could you benefit each other? Even small things like ensuring that you're paying them on time (or early), referring other customers to them, or writing them a good review online go a long way toward moving beyond a purely transactional exchange to being more relational. The more you do so, the more mutually beneficial these relationships will be.

Customers: Stakeholder businesses strive to bring value to their customers beyond the benefit provided by their product or service. I experienced the power of doing so with housing-swap company Kindred. I'd rented my house out via the company's app during a time when we planned to be on a family vacation. Three weeks before we planned to leave, my father was diagnosed with cancer, and we needed to stay home and cancel the reservation for our house. I sent Kindred's customer service department a note explaining the situation, expecting to be charged some bonkers cancellation fee. Instead, the customer service person cancelled with no fee, and the next week, I received a care package from the company in the mail with calming teas, honey, and a sweet note from their team telling me they were thinking about me as our family dealt with the difficult news about my dad. I was brought to tears by this small gesture and am loyal to the company to this day as a result.

As with Kindred, benefiting your customers might mean going above and beyond when it comes to customer service. You could also offer unique opportunities for learning and enrichment, meaningful ways to connect, platforms to shine a light on their work, and so much more. Simply thinking about your customers as people to delight and create additional value for will help you think through ways to benefit this key stakeholder group.

Community: Businesses flourish when they're located in healthy, vibrant communities, but communities like these don't exist without individual effort. Every business leader has a unique responsibility to strengthen and support the communities where they operate.

To start this journey, co-founder of Zebras Unite and economic and community development leader Mara Zepeda says, "One immediate, practical step is to take a look at your budget spend and ask how much of it is being spent locally. Everything I do now, we tally how many dollars went to local vendors and local businesses and how much went out of state. When your company is thinking about spending, creating local resilience by having as much of that money stay within the city and the state is a huge benefit."

Community engagement specialist VaShone Huff also recommends thinking about the communities your business isn't permanently located in but brings business to: "If you have anything that's mobile or moving, like events or trade shows, or even if it's online, you still have a responsibility to the community. Anytime you go anywhere, try to connect with the local community. There are needs there that are unmet that even your presence can help to impact."

Spending more locally, engaging with community leaders to understand key issues, volunteering, or hosting community gatherings are all great ways your organization can bring more value to your local community and build a stronger foundation for everyone who lives there. Start by asking local community leaders about their key needs and go from there.

The Environment: Every one of us needs healthy ecosystems with clean water and air to sustain our well-being. For many companies, taking the environment into account begins with measuring and negating any harm to the environment that happens as a result of a business's operations. Reducing waste, water usage, energy usage, and carbon emissions are some of the more common ways that companies mitigate the environmental impact of their organization. Others go even further and work to benefit the environment, not just negate harm. Perhaps the most high-profile example of such a company is Patagonia, which not only produces sustainable products that cause less harm to the environment but takes an active role in environmental activism, such as giving a percentage of profits to NGOs that protect the environment and suing President Trump in 2017 to protect Bears Ears National Monument.

When you think of your own company's relationship with the environment, can you say with certainty that your business isn't harming the environment? Are you tracking the environmental impact of your operations? What key steps could you take to work toward truly benefiting the environment, not just reducing your harm?

MOVING AWAY FROM SHAREHOLDER SUPREMACY TO A STAKEHOLDER-focused model is one of the most impactful things company leaders can do to change the world. The model helps business leaders become more aware of their impact, mitigate harm, and benefit society more than ever before.

TIPS FOR BENEFITING ALL STAKEHOLDERS

1. ENGAGE WITH STAKEHOLDERS DIRECTLY

One of the most common mistakes leaders make when it comes to benefiting their stakeholders is *assuming* that they know what their stakeholders want. The best way around this is to engage directly and frequently with your stakeholder groups. Formal surveys are a great place to start but sitting down with your stakeholders to truly listen to them is even better. The more you can strive to co-create solutions *with* stakeholders instead of prescribing solutions *for* them without their input, the more likely it is that you'll create genuine value for everyone involved.

2. ADOPT AN ABUNDANCE MINDSET

As CEO and owner of Minnesota-based Peace Coffee, Lee Wallace faced a major dilemma trying to scale her small company. Fair Trade coffee suppliers forced buyers to purchase coffee in 38,000-pound increments. She says, "It's really difficult for a start-up to be like, 'This year I'm going to sell 38,000 pounds of coffee, and next year I'm going to double that.'"

The solution to Wallace's problem came from the unlikeliest of places: the co-founder of a direct competitor. Bill Harris of Georgia-based Cafe Campesino drove around the United States visiting as many mission-based coffee companies as possible with the idea of creating a coffee-importing cooperative. By collaborating as a group, company owners could smooth out their supply-chain issues and support one another as like-minded Fair Trade organic coffee companies. More than twenty coffee companies signed on as co-owners of the cooperative. Wallace says, "We import as a group and collaborate on everything that happens until it hits our individual roasteries."

This story illustrates an important mindset shift for new-playbook leaders: moving from scarcity to abundance. A scarcity mindset makes business leaders feel that resources are limited and need to be fought over at all times. They view other companies in their industry as competitors to be crushed and constantly seek ways to get more for themselves from their stakeholders. An abundance mindset invites business leaders to feel that there are enough resources to go around. With this mindset, they view "competitors" as potential collaborators and see all stakeholders as partners whom they want to see succeed. The ultimate expression of an abundance mindset comes when business leaders begin to look for win-win solutions for everyone and even begin to internalize their partners' success as linked to their own. The more you can do so as a leader, the more solutions you'll unlock with your partners.

3. Measure Your Impact

Measuring your business's impact on each of your stakeholder groups will help you understand any harm your organization might be causing as well as how you're benefiting each stakeholder. One tool for helping your company do so is the B Impact Assessment, created by the nonprofit B Lab. This is the same assessment that B Lab uses to certify that companies are meeting high standards of social and environmental performance with B Corp certification, but any company can take the assessment for free to benchmark its impact. The assessment examines the company's impact on workers, the community, the environment, and customers and asks questions about company governance structure and accountability.

While quantitative tools like this are a great place to start, it's critical to also measure the *qualitative* aspect of your stakeholders' experience. For example, it doesn't matter how many women you have in leadership roles if they're having a terrible experience in the workplace. Seeking out ways to measure the qualitative *and* quantitative sides of your company's impact will go much further in ensuring that you're in alignment with your goal to benefit all stakeholders and will help you make better decisions. Kindred Organizational Consulting president Kendra Coleman says, "When we talk to our clients, we tell them to consider all of the data. Yes, data includes the financial numbers, but data also includes what you and others are feeling and the behaviors you're observing. Data is multifaceted." Antoinette Klatzky, VP of programs and partnerships at the Eileen Fisher Foundation, says, "Every time we start looking down the rabbit hole of metrics that help us understand our stakeholders, we see all of these different layers of human connection and contribution, what people love and what they care about. All of that helps us make better decisions."

Long-Term Value Creation Practice #3: Strive to Avoid Compromises

Miyoko Schinner launched Miyoko's Creamery in 2014, hoping to bring vegan cheese alternatives to the market. Over the years, Schinner brought in more than $50 million in investment to scale the company's growth. Then, in 2021, she was removed from her company by the board. In response, Schinner said, "Over the last few years since the company has grown, I have had less and less ability to impact the company. I was trying to figure out how to move forward with me somehow working with the company, but I didn't want to just be a puppet for the company."[15]

Unfortunately, situations like Schinner's play out too often. In Curtis's experience, "For female founders or founders of color—anyone who's not a white man with decades of experience—you should worry that if you scale, somebody will kick you out of your company. I've seen a lot of companies scale, and as soon as they get to the double digit of millions and take on private equity money, the investors say, 'We're going to bring in a *real* CEO.'"

Scaling a company in a way that doesn't jeopardize the purpose, values, or founder's long-term vision remains a significant challenge. Diana Propper de Callejon, managing director of investment firm Cranemere, says of this tension, "Trying to achieve a significant social or environmental mission while being financially successful in a short-term investment structure creates a mismatch. I don't think people are honest with themselves as much as we need to be about this conflict. It's hard to do things that create long-term business value and help build a better company—like investing in people and their care, raising wages if they need to be raised, or having broad-based equity plans—even if you know it could lead to better retention, higher productivity, more loyalty, and a more engaged workforce if your investment model forces you to sell your companies in a two- to four-year time horizon. As a board member, it might make sense to support these investments, but with your investor hat on, you have to ask yourself if you will benefit from these investments. It's not because you're not a nice person, but it just financially doesn't make sense if you have an investor who needs to get out in three or four years. Stakeholder and shareholder interests can be in conflict."

One way to navigate the conflict between scale and values is to follow in Eileen Fisher's footsteps and organically scale your company over the long term. Over forty years, Eileen Fisher sustainably grew to hundreds of millions in annual sales. The brand *could* have scaled much faster, but Fisher rejected the idea of taking the company public or bringing in investors: "I don't want to bring in outsiders. I want to keep the company intact with the people who've grown it."[16] By finding a sustainable path to profitability, keeping her company private, not bringing in outside investors, and being okay with steady growth over the long term, Fisher wasn't forced to make compromises when it came to her values.

While Fisher's model works for some, not everyone has a profitable business model straight out of the gate or can commit to such long-term timelines. This is especially true when your company purpose addresses a societal problem that you're passionate about and you want to scale as quickly as possible to increase your impact, as in Curtis's case. To navigate this challenge, Curtis is pioneering a model to avoid compromises: "The number-one thing is controlling the board. I was up-front and adamant from the beginning that this is my company and my purpose. I want to grow this thing, and I want to exit in a way that benefits employees and farmers and investors. I want to do it my way, and I don't want to be kicked out. We designed a five-person board: myself, my co-founder, two independents that we elect who we think are experts in the field that can add value to the conversation that our investors can decline, and one investor. We nominate them, and our investors ratify that. None of the VCs have governing rights."

Beyond the board, Kuli Kuli also changed its legal structure from a C Corp to a Benefit Corporation. For Curtis, the board and legal structure of the company were nonnegotiable. She insisted on these elements while fundraising, even if it meant losing investors. In one case, Curtis closed the final million-dollar commitment to complete her Series B round. Shortly after committing to closing the round, the investor started asking questions about board seats, legal structure, and mission. Curtis says, "Finally I was like, 'We're not budging.' They responded, 'Then we're not investing.' We effectively kicked them out of our round in the final hour. It almost broke me. I remember coming home and telling my partner, 'I can't handle this anymore. I don't know if this is the right thing to do.' He just told me, 'You can do this. You've made it this far. You've got five out of six million. You're going to close. Just stick to it.' So I did. It took way longer than I wanted, but we got a really wonderful investor, and our round ended up being oversubscribed."

By not compromising on the key structural elements that help her stay true to her purpose with all outside capital partners, Curtis feels that she's been able to scale her values-driven brand without compromise. She hopes this model can help others looking to do the same.

For a new-playbook company, being intentional about capital partners, company structure, and timeline as you grow can help you avoid painful trade-offs in the future. While decisions like these might be more complicated or make your growth take a little longer, they're well worth it in the end, often making the difference between a company's higher purpose surviving or thriving in the long term.

Tips for Scaling Without Compromise

1. Be Intentional About Your Board

Per Curtis's model, board structure plays a critical role in staying true to your company's higher purpose as it scales. The co-founders of Biggby Coffee, one of the fastest-growing coffee franchises in the United States, are working on building the ideal board for their company to ensure that their values and purpose don't get compromised in the future. Their current plan is to create a seven-person board, giving five of the board seats to key representatives from each of their stakeholder groups: employees, coffee growers, community, environment, and customers. The other two board seats will be held by the co-founders for a time and then will pass to the executive directors of each founder's personal foundation.

When you think about your company's board, instead of stacking it with investors and high-profile people who lend "credibility" to your venture, imagine it as an external representation of what your company values most. How can your board not only support your vision and the impact you want to create but also advance your aspirations? Which stakeholders should be represented? What governing principles will ensure an equitable distribution of power? The more you consider these types of questions, the more likely your company won't be forced to compromise on key priorities down the line.

2. Explore Benefit Corporation Status

Becoming a Benefit Corporation, which is a legal structure for your business just like being an LLC or S Corp, is another way to avoid compromises. Being a Benefit Corporation is different from being a B Corp. Being a B Corp means you've been certified by B Lab as meeting certain impact metrics, akin to being certified organic. Being a Benefit Corporation releases you as a leader from having a "fiduciary responsibility" to shareholders. Benefit Corporation leaders must "take into consideration anyone that is materially affected by that company's decision-making, like workers, customers, local communities, wider society and the environment," and commit to creating general public benefit defined either as "a material positive impact on society and the environment, or as the obligation to operate in a responsible and sustainable manner depending on the state/province of incorporation."[17]

Companies like Cotopaxi, Dr. Bronner's, Allbirds, Patagonia, and, of course, Kuli Kuli Foods have all become Benefit Corporations. Curtis says, "This allowed us to write our purpose into our legal DNA. If you were investing in us, you were investing in the whole vision."

3. Seek Values-Driven Long-Term Capital Partners

While the investment space is chock-full of institutions seeking 10x returns as quickly as possible, there *are* capital partners out there who support new-playbook ideals. Two things to investigate when it comes to potential investors are their definition of success and their time horizon. Morgan Simon, founding partner at Candide Group, is an example of a capital partner who flips the script on what "success" means for her company's investments. The firm mostly builds custom portfolios for families and foundations that want their money working for social justice but also leads two debt funds, Olamina and Afterglow, focused on US community development and climate justice, respectively. Candide Group strives to ensure that communities play a key role in envisioning their own futures. To help it do so, the firm created representative community advisory boards that determine whether an investment will be sufficiently impactful and address something the world truly needs. These advisory boards have the majority of the decision-making power for Candide's fund vehicles.

In addition to success metrics and values alignment, capital expert Propper de Callejon feels that finding investors with a long-term time horizon is one of the best ways to support the intentional growth of a company. Her work at Cranemere focuses on making long-term investments that allow companies the space to create a social or environmental impact and be financially successful in the long run.

Seeking capital partners who truly integrate impact into their goals and see the benefit of making long-term investments will help reduce much of the pressure to compromise your purpose in the near term.

4. Explore Perpetual Purpose Trusts

In September 2022, Patagonia founder Yvon Chouinard released a statement titled "Earth Is Now Our Only Shareholder," which outlined an unprecedented decision he'd made for his $3 billion company. Chouinard explained, "While we're doing our best to address the environmental crisis, it's not enough. We needed to find a way to put more money into fighting the crisis while keeping the company's values intact. One option was to sell Patagonia and donate all the money. But we couldn't be sure a new owner would maintain our values or keep our team of people around the world employed. Another path was to take the company public. What a disaster that would have been. Even public companies with good intentions are under too much pressure to create short-term gain at the expense of long-term vitality and responsibility. Truth be told, there were no good options available. So, we created our own. Instead of 'going public,' you could say we're 'going purpose.' Instead of extracting value from nature and transforming it into wealth for investors, we'll use the wealth Patagonia creates to protect the source of all wealth. Here's how it works: 100% of the company's voting stock transfers to the Patagonia Purpose Trust, created to protect the company's values; and 100% of the nonvoting stock has been given to the Holdfast Collective, a nonprofit dedicated to fighting the environmental crisis and defending nature."[18]

Chouinard's announcement put a spotlight on what are known as purpose trusts. Founder and CEO of MSC Industries Mara Zepeda, who has been exploring alternative business structures for years, sees purpose trusts as a key tool for leaders who want to ensure that their vision and values live on beyond them: "Family trusts are what we generally think of when we think of trusts. They allow for the protection of wealth to be handed over generations, have all sorts of tax implications, and create a tremendous sense of privacy. This structure is used by basically every wealthy family to protect and grow their wealth and ensure it gets handed down from generation to generation. That same structure of trusts can be deployed among groups of unrelated individuals [read: like a business] through a purpose trust structure." If you have a long-term vision for your company, exploring the purpose trust structure is one of the best ways to ensure that your values won't be compromised down the road.

CHANGING THE DREAM OF MODERN SOCIETY BEGINS WITH YOU. As a business leader, every decision you make impacts more people than you know. When you make decisions that create genuine long-term value for society, benefit all stakeholders, and refuse to compromise your values and larger purpose, you're rewriting the narrative about success and what business can do for the world.

Key Chapter Insights

- The traditional playbook's definition of business success based on perpetual growth and rapid scale has caused immeasurable harm on a global scale, including broadening the socioeconomic divide, environmental harm, and increased workplace stress.
- Embracing a new dream of business success rooted in long-term value creation builds more resilient, better-performing companies while also benefiting society in the long run.
- Companies focusing on long-term value creation prioritize meaningful business growth, strive to benefit all company stakeholders, and work to avoid compromises by being intentional about their governing principles, legal structure, and growth partners.

CONCLUSION

WELL, FRIEND, HERE WE ARE AT THE END OF THIS JOURNEY. As I thought about ending our time together, I realized that my deepest hope is that this end is actually the beginning. The beginning of you making impactful changes in your life based on the book's practices that resonated most with you. The beginning of continued dialogue and new ideas as you chew on these concepts with others. The beginning of building new relationships with as many of you as possible and helping you connect with others. And I hope it's the beginning of your journey toward reimagining what's possible with your life and your work. Because change happens when we embrace new ideas about what's possible.

Patriarchy, toxic masculinity, shareholder supremacy, and harmful, extractive business practices—*none* of these things are foregone conclusions. They were all once mere ideas that only gained traction because people *chose* to believe in them. Beautifully, this also means they can lose their power when we stop believing in them.

We're already seeing traditional systems beginning to crumble. More people are demanding that businesses pay attention to their impact. More workers are refusing to settle for abusive, toxic workplaces. More business leaders are aligning their ideas of success with adding value to society. The business world is changing;

this change will be expedited if more people refuse to settle for the status quo and demand a better way. Author and thought leader Akaya Windwood says, "I think the next five to ten years are going to be tumultuous because these systems we've been working toward breaking down aren't going to fall down neatly. So it becomes really important, particularly for women, to ask ourselves, 'What am I here to do? What's mine to do?' Then, only do that."

No matter how big these issues feel, your actions matter. As futurist Libby Rodney puts it, "We're in such a world of macroconflict and challenges we've almost forgotten that the micro means anything; yet the micro means everything. The energy you show up with at a coffee shop to greet someone, the way you volunteer outside of work, the way you run your team inside of an organization, all these micro things are the ripple effect that's going to change the macro eventually in a ten-year time frame. We're so disillusioned when we think we have no agency. Take the macro issues, break them into microactions, and start there."

Every time you stay true to yourself, refuse to settle, and choose a better way, you're taking a microaction that will usher in profound change. Every time you shift your leadership toward being more holistic, authentic, optimized, and sustained; change your workplace to be more beneficial, dignified, and unified; or make progress toward changing your dream of what success means to you, you release the powerful hold these old systems have on all of us. In addition, these changes will improve your life, enhancing your individual and business performance as well as your well-being and quality of life. It's the ultimate win-win-win.

Beyond the benefits to your own life, each time you refuse to play by the traditional rules, you honor the women who came before us. The women who endured being the first woman in their office, industry, or role; the ones who faced immeasurable challenges, harassment, and bias to break barriers and shift the business world to accept women. These women sacrificed and persevered so future generations wouldn't be subjected to the same status quo. Each of us can honor their sacrifice by refusing to abide by our current status quo and, instead, focus on redefining it for the next generation. I hope this is the beginning of your journey toward doing so.

ACKNOWLEDGMENTS

To you, my incredible reader, I am more grateful than you will ever know. Without you, this book won't make an impact. You're the reason I aspired to write this book in the first place. You've given me the profound gift of feeling like the work I love to do in the world has meaning.

This entire book was a community effort. More people than I can adequately acknowledge were a part of its journey, lending support, experiences, and wisdom that made it possible. Here are just *some* of those I wish to thank from the bottom of my soul.

Every lovely human who gave me your time, insights, and hard-won lessons to inspire this book: Akaya Windwood, Alfa Demmellash, Alison Bailey Vercruysse, Ann Shoket, Anna Banks, Antoinette Klatzky, Ayla Schlosser, Caroline Duell, Carter Stepanovsky, Cat Perez, Christina Hachikian, Courtney Klein, Deepa Purushothaman, Diana Chapman, Diana Propper de Callejon, Diane Henry, Eileen Fisher, Elaine Dinos, Emily Lutyens, Erin Wade, Garnie Nygren, Gayle Jennings-O'Byrne, Hannah Drain Taylor, Jane Wurwand, Julie Van Ness, Kat Taylor, Katherine Goldstein, Kathy Bolhous, Katlin Smith, Kendra Coleman, Khalila "K.O." Olukunola, Kristy Wallace, Lee Wallace, Libby Rodney, Lisa Curtis, Liz Allen, Liz Richardson, Mara Zepeda, Mary Meduna-Gross, Maryam Sharifzadeh, Megan McDonald, Melanie Dulbecco, Michelle Cirocco, Michelle Finocchi, Michelle Lemming, Michelle Pusateri, Morgan Simon, Nicole Snow, Parneet Pal, Robyn Sue Fisher, Rose Marcario,

ACKNOWLEDGMENTS

Saloni Doshi, Sharon Rowe, Sheryl O'Loughlin, Steph Gripne, Steph Olson, Susan Alban Wolfe, Susan Griffin-Black, Susan McPherson, Tara Milburn, Taryn Bird, Twanna Harris, Vanessa Roanhorse, VaShone Huff, Vicki Saunders, Yscaira Jimenez, and Zahra Kassam. Thank you for challenging the status quo, being willing to fail, blazing new trails, and building new models that are creating a better world for us all. It has been the honor of my life to know you, witness your work, learn at your feet, call you my friends, and share your work with the world. Also, to every thought leader, author, and researcher whose work I learned from and referenced, thank you for everything you've done to advance these critical conversations.

To my wonderful agent, Jessica Faust. Thank you for leading the change and seeing value in my idea from day one.

To my extraordinary editor, Emily Taber, thank you for helping me see the potential of this book and helping me rise to meet it time and time again. To Kimberly Meilun, thank you for believing in my vision and advocating on my behalf to bring me into the PublicAffairs community. To the entire publishing team at Hachette Book Group, PublicAffairs, and Basic Ventures, I am humbled by the opportunity to be included as one of your authors.

To Jane Wurwand and Deepa Purushothaman, who picked me up, dusted me off, and pointed me in the right direction, and to Suzanne Kingsbury, who took my "promising" proposal and helped me turn it into something real.

To the entire Conscious Company Media family—our team, community, investors, readers, suppliers, and more—who played such a critical role in shaping my life and perspective. Specifically, thank you to my co-founder, Maren, for starting the journey with me and the SOCAP Global team for keeping the journey going.

To the Fireflies—Aniyia, VaShone, and Jocelyn—thank you for the inspiring weekly chats throughout COVID that helped me evolve, feel inspired, and dream of a better way.

To my first boss, Whitney Kollar—thank you for taking a chance on me and modeling such integrated leadership.

ACKNOWLEDGMENTS

To the Stakeholder Business team—Kent, Mark, and Nathan—thank you for doing the critical work of building community and inspiring others to think about how much better business can be. And to every business leader who's pushing the envelope and trying to build a better world through business, like the entire SB Society crew, you're creating the world I dream of. Keep going. You're not alone, and your work matters more than you know.

To my children's incredible caretakers in the last few years, Kari, Melanie, and Cydne, thank you for giving me the space to write this book, knowing that my children were safe and cared for. It's a gift whose depths are hard to explain.

To our neighborhood crew, you've taught me what it means to live in a community. Thank you for Tuesday nights, impromptu gatherings in the park, and contributing to a thriving neighborhood built on trust, connection, and joy.

To my therapist, Lynn, thank you for untangling the knotted parts of my soul, helping me love myself without validation, and catalyzing my healing journey. This book wouldn't exist without your guidance, and my life will never be the same after working with you. And to Jen Sellers, thank you for generously coaching me years ago, helping me to keep my head above water when I felt like I was going under.

To my brother from another mother, Nathan, thanks for Nashing with me, chasing bonkers ideas together, and pushing me to demand more from business. You're a constant source of inspiration, thought leadership, and friendship.

To the incomparable Jocelyn, for inviting me to show up authentically for the first time, being the string to my balloon, trusting my intuition, and giving me the profound gift of getting to change lives and do work I love with one of my best friends. You are a gift to the world.

To my Hannah, for being my hype woman, thoughtfully replying to my nonsensical brainstorming texts about the book, saying the perfect thing every time I doubted myself on this journey, and being such a bright, gorgeous light in the lives of everyone who's lucky enough to know you.

ACKNOWLEDGMENTS

To the soul friends who've held me in my grief, loved the unhealed parts of my soul, filled my life with laughter, helped me see my blind spots, and become some of my very favorite parts of my life: HDT, Gan, Jonesy, Pavia, Musaki, and MacdougallyDoo, I love you unconditionally.

To my family unit: Jeff, Katie, Nora, Hazel, Ali, Brian, Lucy, Schaffer, Kerry, Mom, Dad, Jack, Atalaya, and Scott. Thank you for all the love. To my siblings-in-law, thank you for your friendship and gifting our family with wonderful nieces and nephews who light up all our lives. Kerry, thank you for raising my beloved partner and for stepping up time and time again to take care of our children so lovingly. Mom and Dad, thank you for the gift of life, for encouraging me to use my wings to fly, and for being the extraordinary Nana and Gda who are a constant part of our kids' lives. Wild Thing, thanks for being my first friend and constantly pushing the bar higher, inspiring me to chase in your footsteps. Jack and Atalaya, thank you for making me a mom, being profound teachers, reminding me to play, being the source of endless laughter, and giving me something bigger to ensure that I never give up striving to build a better world. And to my beloved Scott. From the very beginning, I knew we would build a beautiful life together, but I never imagined all that we have. Thank you for all the little things—taking the kids to the park so I could write, waking up early to get our family train on the tracks, and gently checking in on my progress—and thank you for the big things—encouraging me when I was steeped in doubt, being my constant adventure buddy, loving the full spectrum of all that I am, supporting my dreams in every way, being a rock-solid logistical army of two, and showing me what a healthy, deeply loving relationship looks like for more than fifteen years. I love you, always.

Finally, to every woman who shows up with courage and grace, who persists and endures, who stumbles and picks themselves back up, who reaches out to others to help guide them through the mess, who holds their sisters in their sorrow in the face of a world that tells us we're not enough and worth less . . . I see you. You are more than enough, and I honor every single one of you.

NOTES

Introduction

1. "2023 Deloitte Global Workplace Burnout Survey," Deloitte, 2023; "Compounding Pressure: The Impact of Work Stress on Well-Being," American Psychological Association, 2021.
2. "Well-Being Stats: Women in the Workplace Show a Need for Change," Gallup, June 22, 2023.
3. "2023: Women in the Workplace Study," Lean In, 2023.
4. Tetyana Pudrovska, "Gender, Job Authority, and Depression," *Journal of Health and Social Behavior* 55, no. 4 (December 2014): 425–441.
5. Heather Kramar, "2 in 5 Workers Say Job Biggest Factor Influencing Mental Health," *HCAMag*, June 5, 2024.

Chapter 1: It's Not You. It's the System.

1. bell hooks, *The Will to Change: Men, Masculinity, and Love* (New York: Atria Books, 2004).
2. Elise Loehnen, *On Our Best Behavior: The Seven Deadly Sins and the Price Women Pay to Be Good* (New York: Dial Press, 2023).
3. Kevin Foss, "What Is Toxic Masculinity and How It Impacts Mental Health," Anxiety and Depression Association of America, November 14, 2022.
4. Valerie Rein, *Patriarchy Stress Disorder: The Invisible Inner Barrier to Women's Happiness and Fulfillment* (Pittsburgh, PA: Golden Brick Road Publishing House, 2019).
5. Emily Nagoski and Amelia Nagoski, *Burnout: The Secret to Unlocking the Stress Cycle* (New York: Ballantine Books, 2019).
6. Gabor Maté and Daniel Maté, *The Myth of Normal: Trauma, Illness, and Healing in a Toxic Culture* (New York: Avery, 2022).
7. Keith Roberts, *The Origins of Business, Money, and Markets* (New York: Columbia University Press, 2011); James Allen, James Root, and Andrew Schwedel, "3000 Years of Business History in Two Minutes," Bain & Company, June 22, 2017.
8. Gabriela Huerta, "Countries with the Most Female CEOs," *CEO Magazine*, March 8, 2024; Emma Hinchliffe, "Share of Fortune 500 Companies Run by Women Reaches Record 10 Percent," Yahoo Finance, June 4, 2024.

9. Ian Bezek, "10 Largest Private Equity Firms," *U.S. News & World Report*, July 24, 2024; Nathan Reiff, "10 Biggest Companies in the World by Revenue," Investopedia, June 20, 2024.

10. "A Decade of Stagnation: New UNDP Data Shows Gender Biases Remain Entrenched," United Nations Development Programme, June 12, 2023.

11. "Gender Discrimination Affects 42% of Working Women," LeClerc & LeClerc LLP, June 2022.

12. "Report: 94% of Women in Tech Say They're Held to a Higher Standard Than Men," VentureBeat, April 15, 2022.

13. Katherine Haan, "Gender Pay Gap Statistics," *Forbes*, March 1, 2024.

14. Jennifer Liu, "Men Were More Likely to Get Raises in 2022," CNBC, December 13, 2022.

15. Emily Field, Alexis Krivkovich, Sandra Kügele, Nicole Robinson, and Lareina Yee, "Women in the Workplace 2023," McKinsey & Company, October 5, 2023.

16. Amy Woodyatt, "UN Report Highlights Global Gender Bias Trends," CNN, June 12, 2023.

17. Kelly Shue, "Women Aren't Promoted Because Managers Underestimate Their Potential," Yale Insights, September 17, 2021.

18. Maryam Kouchaki, Keith Leavitt, Luke Zhu, and Anthony C. Klotz, "Research: What Fragile Masculinity Looks Like at Work," *Harvard Business Review*, January 27, 2023.

19. Matthew J. Streb, Barbara Burrell, Brian Frederick, and Michael Genovese, "Social Desirability Effects and Support for a Female American President," ResearchGate, January 2008.

20. "2024: Women in the Workplace Study," Lean In, 2024.

21. "Feedback Bias: The Data Driving Inequitable Workplace Feedback," Textio, 2024.

22. C. H. Dupree, "Words of a Leader: The Importance of Intersectionality for Understanding Women Leaders' Use of Dominant Language and How Others Receive It," *Administrative Science Quarterly* 69, no. 2 (2024): 271–323.

23. M. E. Heilman, A. S. Wallen, D. Fuchs, and M. M. Tamkins, "Penalties for Success: Reactions to Women Who Succeed at Male Gender-Typed Tasks," *Journal of Applied Psychology* 89, no. 3 (2004): 416–427.

24. Eve Rodsky, *Fair Play: A Game-Changing Solution for When You Have Too Much to Do (and More Life to Live)* (New York: G. P. Putnam's Sons, 2019).

25. Tom McCarthy, "The Never-Ending Battle over the Best Office Temperature," BBC Worklife, June 19, 2016.

26. Elsie Boskamp, "35+ Compelling Workplace Collaboration Statistics," Zippia, February 7, 2023.

27. National Academies of Sciences, Engineering, and Medicine, *Sexual Harassment of Women: Climate, Culture, and Consequences in Academic Sciences, Engineering, and Medicine* (Washington, DC: The National Academies Press, 2018).

28. Milton Friedman, "A Friedman Doctrine—the Social Responsibility of Business Is to Increase Its Profits," *New York Times*, September 13, 1970.

29. Michael Sainato, "UN Report: Amazon, Walmart, and DoorDash Pay So Low That Workers Can't Afford Basic Needs," *Guardian*, November 2, 2023.

30. Sravya Tadepalli, "Amazon Workers Face Alarming Injury Rates Despite Promises of Safer Conditions," Prism Reports, November 6, 2023.

31. Shannon Hall, "Exxon Knew About Climate Change Almost 40 Years Ago," *Scientific American*, October 26, 2015.

32. Nina Totenberg, "Supreme Court to Decide Fate of Purdue Pharma Settlement Shielding Sacklers from Opioid Lawsuits," NPR, December 4, 2023.

33. Carey Gillam, "Monsanto Manipulates Journalists and Academics. How Do We Know? We Have the Documents," *Guardian*, June 2, 2019.

34. Rakesh Kochhar and Stella Sechopoulos, "How the American Middle Class Has Changed in the Past Five Decades," Pew Research Center, April 20, 2022.

35. Daniel de Visé, "Top 1% of American Earners Now Hold More Wealth Than the Entire Middle Class," *USA Today*, December 6, 2023.

36. Lindsay Kohler, "Over 4 out of 5 People Say Their Stress Primarily Comes from Work," *Forbes*, April 23, 2024.

37. "Understanding the Stress Response," Harvard Health Publishing, July 6, 2020.

38. "The Biggest Environmental Problems of Our Lifetime," Earth.Org, July 13, 2023.

39. Harriet Agerholm, "One in Five CEOs Are Psychopaths, According to a New Study," *Business Insider*, September 12, 2016.

40. Jeanne Sahadi, "The Silent Struggle of CEOs: Depression and Mental Health at the Top," CNN, September 30, 2018.

41. Elizabeth Grace Saunders, "6 Causes of Burnout, and How to Avoid Them," *Harvard Business Review*, July 2, 2019.

42. "What Causes Mental Illness?," WebMD, March 28, 2023.

Chapter 2: From Imbalanced "Masculine" Leadership to Holistic Leadership

1. M. E. Heilman, C. B. Block, and R. F. Martell, "Sex Stereotypes: Do They Influence Perceptions of Managers?," *Journal of Social Behavior and Personality* 10 (1995): 237–252.

2. Hemant Kakkar and Niro Sivanathan, "How Dominant Leaders Go Wrong," *Scientific American*, March 1, 2017; Donald Sull, Charles Sull, William Cipolli, and Caio Brighenti, "Why Every Leader Needs to Worry About Toxic Culture," *MIT Sloan Management Review*, January 11, 2022.

3. America This Week Tracker, Harris Poll, 2023.

4. Unlocking Eve-Harris Poll, Harris Poll, 2023.

5. Jim Harter, "The Percentage of Employees Who Feel Their Employer Cares About Their Wellbeing Plummets," Gallup, March 9, 2022.

6. "Why in the COVID Era Is the Wellbeing of Workers and Workplaces Not Improving?," The Adecco Group, last modified April 2021.

7. LinkedIn Glint, "Employee Well-Being Report," LinkedIn, 2022.

8. Harter, "The Percentage of Employees."

9. Matthew Hutson, "8 Truths About Intuition," *Psychology Today*, December 2019.

10. "Trust in Leadership: Global Leadership Forecast 2023," DDI World, 2023.

11. Stephen Trzeciak, Anthony Mazzarelli, and Emma Seppälä, "Leading with Compassion Has Research-Backed Benefits," *Harvard Business Review*, February 27, 2023.

12. Sandra K. Collins and Kevin S. Collins, "Risk, Resistance, and Psychological Distress: A Longitudinal Analysis with Adults and Children," *Journal of Abnormal Psychology* 112, no. 3 (2003).

13. "Mental Health at Work: Managers and Money," UKG.

Chapter 3: From Assimilated Leadership to Authentic Leadership

1. Dinesh Bhugra and Matthew A. Becker, "Migration, Cultural Bereavement and Cultural Identity," *Journal of Health and Social Behavior* 43, no. 3 (2002).

2. Gabor Maté and Daniel Maté, *The Myth of Normal: Trauma, Illness, and Healing in a Toxic Culture* (New York: Avery, 2022).

3. Julia Moskin, "Barbara Lynch, a Leading Boston Restaurateur, Is Accused of Workplace Abuse," *New York Times*, April 20, 2023; Cait Munro, "Female Founders Face Backlash for Toxic Workplace Cultures," Refinery29, March 6, 2020.

4. Ana Patrícia Duarte, Neuza Ribeiro, Ana Suzete Semedo, and Daniel Roque Gomes, "Authentic Leadership and Improved Individual Performance: Affective Commitment and Individual Creativity's Sequential Mediation," *Frontiers in Psychology*, May 7, 2021.

5. Duarte et al., "Authentic Leadership and Improved Individual Performance."

6. Cong Wang, Jidong Yao, and Lei Gao, "Leaders' Emotional Intelligence and Subordinates' Psychological Safety: The Role of Leaders' Positive Emotions," *Heliyon*, February 15, 2024.

7. Elizabeth Grace Saunders, "6 Causes of Burnout, and How to Avoid Them," *Harvard Business Review*, July 2, 2019.

8. Bronnie Ware, *The Top Five Regrets of the Dying: A Life Transformed by the Dearly Departing* (Carlsbad, CA: Hay House, 2012).

Chapter 4: From Overextended Leadership to Optimized Leadership

1. "Data Deep Dive: A Decline of Women in the Workforce," U.S. Chamber of Commerce, November 30, 2022.

2. Jill E. Yavorsky, Lisa A. Keister, and Michael Nau, "Women in the One Percent: Gender Dynamics in Top Income Positions," *American Sociological Review* 84, no. 1 (2019).

3. Juliana Menasce Horowitz, "How Americans See the State of Gender and Leadership in Business," Pew Research Center, September 27, 2023.

4. Elizabeth Grace Saunders, "6 Causes of Burnout, and How to Avoid Them," *Harvard Business Review*, July 2, 2019.

5. Emily Nagoski and Amelia Nagoski, *Burnout: The Secret to Unlocking the Stress Cycle* (New York: Ballantine Books, 2019).

6. Dolores Fernández-García, María Olga, Jesús Castro-Calvo, Vicente Morell-Mengual, Rafael Ballester-Arnal, and Verónica Estruch-García, "Academic Perfectionism, Psychological Well-Being, and Suicidal Ideation in College Students," *International Journal of Environmental Research and Public Health* 20, no. 1 (2023): 85.

7. "Digital 2024: Global Overview Report," DataReportal, 2024.

8. "How Social Media Is Affecting Your Mental Health," McLean Hospital.

9. Jonathan Rothwell, "What Are the Social Effects of Television?," *New York Times*, July 25, 2019.

10. Kayla Good and Alex Shaw, "Why Kids Are Afraid to Ask for Help," *Scientific American*, July 1, 2023.

11. Summer Allen, *The Science of Generosity: How and Why It Is Good for You* (Berkeley, CA: Great Good Science Center, 2018).

12. Xuan Zhao and Nicholas Epley, "Surprisingly Happy to Have Helped: Underestimating Prosociality Creates a Misplaced Barrier to Asking for Help," *Psychological Science* 33, no. 10 (2018).

13. "Why It's So Hard to Say No to an Invitation," American Psychological Association, December 2023.

Chapter 5: From Sacrificial Leadership to Sustained Leadership

1. Gabor Maté and Daniel Maté, *The Myth of Normal: Trauma, Illness, and Healing in a Toxic Culture* (New York: Avery, 2022).

2. Consensus Conference Panel, "Recommended Amount of Sleep for a Healthy Adult: A Joint Consensus Statement of the American Academy of Sleep Medicine and Sleep Research Society," BMC Medicine, 2015.

3. Harvard Medical School Division of Sleep Medicine, "Sleep and Mental Health," Harvard Medical School, 2021.

4. Eva Selhub, "Nutritional Psychiatry: Your Brain on Food," *Harvard Health Blog*, September 18, 2022.

5. "Nutrition's Role in Mental Health: What You Eat Can Help Improve Mood, Sleep, and More," McLean Hospital, May 24, 2024.

6. A. P. Jha, E. A. Stanley, A. Kiyonaga, L. Wong, and L. Gelfand, "Examining the Protective Effects of Mindfulness Training on Working Memory Capacity and Affective Experience," *American Psychologist* (2010).

7. Emily Nagoski and Amelia Nagoski, *Burnout: The Secret to Unlocking the Stress Cycle* (New York: Ballantine Books, 2019).

8. Ashish Sharma, Vishal Madaan, and Frederick D Petty, "Exercise for Mental Health," *Primary Care Companion to Journal of Clinical Psychiatry* 11 (2006).

9. "Benefits of Physical Activity," Centers for Disease Control and Prevention, April 24, 2024.

10. Kai Lam, Leah Sterling, and Edward Margines, "Effects of Five-Minute Mindfulness Meditation on Stress and Anxiety," Semantic Scholar, 2015.

11. Jamie Ducharme, "Even Short Workouts Can Improve Health—Here's How to Make the Most of Them," *Time*, December 27, 2022.

12. "Our Epidemic of Loneliness and Isolation: The U.S. Surgeon General's Advisory on the Healing Effects of Social Connection and Community," US Department of Health and Human Services, 2023.

13. Andrew Dugan, "Over 1 in 5 People Worldwide Feel Lonely a Lot," Gallup, July 10, 2024.

14. Renée Onque, "Yale Happiness Expert: The No. 1 Thing You Can Do to Be Happier," CNBC, February 12, 2024.

15. Brené Brown, interview with Karen Walrond, *Unlocking Us with Brené Brown*, March 9, 2022,

16. Brown, interview with Karen Walrond.

17. Stephen Trzeciak, Anthony Mazzarelli, and Emma Seppälä, "Leading with Compassion Has Research-Backed Benefits," *Harvard Business Review*, February 27, 2023.

18. Robert Emmons, "Why Gratitude Is Good," *Greater Good Magazine*, November 16, 2010.

Chapter 6: From Harmful Workplaces to Beneficial Workplaces

1. Ruth Margalit, "The Death of Moritz Erhardt and Keynes's Mistake," *New Yorker*, August 22, 2013.

2. "Nearly 3 Million People Die of Work-Related Accidents and Diseases Every Year," International Labour Organization, November 26, 2023.

3. Steve Crabtree, "Global Study: 23% of Workers Experience Violence and Harassment," Gallup, December 14, 2022.

4. Kapo Wong, Alan H. S. Chan, and S. C. Ngan, "The Effect of Long Working Hours and Overtime on Occupational Health: A Meta-Analysis of Evidence from 1998 to 2018," *International Journal of Environmental Research and Public Health* 16, no. 12 (June 2019): 2102.

5. David Cooper and Lawrence Mishel, "America's Vast Pay Inequality Is a Story of Unequal Power," American Bar Association, January 6, 2023.

6. Neli Esipova, Julie Ray, and Ying Han, "750 Million Struggling to Meet Basic Needs with No Safety Net," Gallup, June 16, 2020.

7. Jennifer Lubell, "Low-Wage Work Exacerbates Health Inequities," American Medical Association, June 13, 2022.

8. "Persistent Low Wages Linked to Faster Memory Decline in Later Life," Columbia University Mailman School of Public Health, August 3, 2022.

9. Kim Parker, Ruth Igielnik, and Rakesh Kochhar, "Unemployed Americans Are Feeling the Emotional Strain of Job Loss," Pew Research Center, February 10, 2021.

10. "2023 Work in America Survey: Workplace Health and Well-Being," American Psychological Association, 2023.

11. "2023 Work in America Survey."

12. K. Uehli, A. Mehta, et al., "Sleep Problems and Work Injuries: A Systematic Review and Meta-analysis," *Sleep Medicine Reviews* 18 (2014).

13. "2023 Work in America Survey."

14. Prospira Global, "Women and Girls: Empowerment Through Mental Health," Kate Spade New York Foundation, 2023.

15. Renée Onque, "49% of Workers Fear Being Open About Mental Health Status at Work," CNBC, September 13, 2022.

16. Kim Parker and Juliana Menasce Horowitz, "How Americans View Their Jobs," Pew Research Center, March 30, 2023.

17. "Denver Nonprofit Transitions to 4-Day Work Week with No Reduction in Productivity," CBS News, April 18, 2022.

18. Mark Travers, "A Psychologist Explores the Shorter Workweek Paradox," *Forbes*, February 7, 2024.

19. Massachusetts Institute of Technology, "Living Wage Calculator: Methodology," Living Wage Calculator.

20. Daniel Krasner, Rachael Doubledee, and Matthew Nestler, "Only 3% of America's Largest Companies Encourage Living Wages for Supply Chain Workers—but These 5 Companies Are Leading on the Issue," JUST Capital, 2023.

21. Economic Policy Institute, "CEO Pay Declined in 2023 but They Still Made 290 Times as Much as the Typical Worker; CEO Pay Has Soared 1,085% Since 1978," Economic Policy Institute, September 13, 2023.

22. "Mental Disorders," World Health Organization, June 8, 2022.

23. A. J. Skiera, "Workplace Mental Health a Priority for Today's Workers," Harris Poll, May 17, 2022; "2023 Work in America Survey."

24. Robert Kegan, Lisa Lahey, Andy Fleming, Matthew L. Miller, and Inna Markus, *An Everyone Culture: The Deliberately Developmental Organization* (Brighton, MA: Harvard Business Review Press, 2016).

25. Salvador Ordorica, "Why and How to Center a Workplace Culture Around Learning and Development," *Forbes*, November 11, 2022.

26. Carol Dweck, "How Companies Can Profit from a Growth Mindset," *Harvard Business Review*, November 2014.

27. Denise McLain and Bailey Nelson, "How Effective Feedback Fuels Performance," Gallup, January 19, 2024.

Chapter 7: From Disenfranchised Workplaces to Dignified Workplaces

1. Robert Glazer, "Command-and-Control Leadership Is Dead. Here's What's Taking Its Place," Inc., August 12, 2019.

2. Anjali Tiwari and Radha R. Sharma, "Dignity at the Workplace: Evolution of the Construct and Development of Workplace Dignity Scale," *Frontiers in Psychology* 10 (2019).

3. Nate Dvorak and Ryan Pendell, "Want to Change Your Culture? Listen to Your Best People," Gallup, March 6, 2019.

4. Yanhe Deng, Yifei Zhang, and Yijie Zhu, "Autonomy Need-Based Experiences and Hope and Fear Components of Autonomy Strength," *Personality and Individual Differences* 202 (February 2023).

5. Second Chance Business Coalition, 2024; Cheryl Winokur Munk, "Workers Without Degrees Are Not Getting as Many Good Job Offers as It Seems," CNBC, February 19, 2024.

6. Second Chance Business Coalition.

7. Mervyn Dinnen, "How Recognition Improves Employee Wellbeing and the Bottom Line," Workhuman, September 5, 2024.

8. Robert Roy Britt, "Return to Work: Why Making the Office Feel More Like Home Could Be Good for Business," U.S. Chamber of Commerce, September 24, 2020.

9. Deng et al., "Autonomy Need-Based Experiences."

10. Renée Onque, "49% of Workers Fear Repercussions for Being Open About Their Mental Health at Work," CNBC, September 13, 2022.

11. CultureX, "ROWE Business Results," ROWE, 2024.

12. Tapas K. Ray and Regina Pana-Cryan, "Work Flexibility and Work-Related Well-Being," *International Journal of Environmental Research and Public Health* 18, no. 6 (March 2021): 3254.

13. Emily Field, Alexis Krivkovich, Sandra Kügele, Nicole Robinson, and Lareina Yee, "Women in the Workplace 2023," McKinsey & Company, October 5, 2023.

Chapter 8: From Individualistic Workplaces to Unified Workplaces

1. "State of the Global Workplace: 2024 Report," Gallup, 2024.

2. A. Bowers, J. Wu, S. Lustig, and D. Nemecek, "Loneliness Influences Avoidable Absenteeism and Turnover Intention Reported by Adult Workers in the United States," *Journal of Organizational Effectiveness: People and Performance* 9, no. 2 (2022).

3. Elsie Boskamp, "35+ Compelling Workplace Collaboration Statistics," Zippia, February 7, 2023.

4. Boskamp, "35+ Compelling Workplace Collaboration Statistics."

5. Boskamp, "35+ Compelling Workplace Collaboration Statistics."

6. Kirsten Weir, "A Sense of Belonging Is Crucial for Employees," American Psychological Association, June 26, 2024.

7. Akaya Windwood and Rajasvini Bhansali, *Leading with Joy: Practices for Uncertain Times* (New York: Berrett-Koehler Publishers, 2022).

8. M. Li, S. Peng, and L. Liu, "How Do Team Cooperative Goals Influence Thriving at Work: The Mediating Role of Team Time Consensus," *International Journal of Environmental Research and Public Health* 19, no. 9 (2022): 5431.

9. Ernst & Young, "The Business Case for Purpose," *Harvard Business Review* Report, 2020.

10. Boskamp, "35+ Compelling Workplace Collaboration Statistics."

11. Leeron Hoory, "The State of Workplace Communication in 2024," *Forbes*, March 8, 2023.

12. Elizabeth Grace Saunders, "6 Causes of Burnout, and How to Avoid Them," *Harvard Business Review*, July 2, 2019.

13. "Seeking and Finding Fairness at Work," UNC Kenan-Flagler Business School, October 1, 2020.

14. "Seeking and Finding Fairness at Work."

Chapter 9: From Social Success to Soul Success

1. "Alcohol Researchers Localize Brain Region that Anticipates Reward," National Institute on Alcohol Abuse and Alcoholism, August 3, 2001.

2. University of Rochester, "Achieving Fame, Wealth and Beauty Are Psychological Dead Ends, Study Says," ScienceDaily, May 19, 2009.

3. Daniel H. Pink, *Drive: The Surprising Truth About What Motivates Us* (New York: Riverhead Books, 2011).

4. University of Rochester, "Achieving Fame, Wealth and Beauty Are Psychological Dead Ends, Study Says."

5. Meg Selig, "10 Powerful Benefits of Living with Purpose," *Psychology Today*, August 23, 2021.

6. Tony Schwartz and Christine Porath, "Why You Hate Work," *New York Times*, May 30, 2014.

7. Naina Dhingra, Andrew Samo, Bill Schaninger, and Matt Schrimper, "Help Your Employees Find Purpose—or Watch Them Leave," McKinsey & Company, April 5, 2021.

8. Pink, *Drive*.

9. C. S. Dweck and E. L. Leggett, "A Social-Cognitive Approach to Motivation and Personality," *Psychological Review* 95, no. 2 (1988).

10. The Human Flourishing Program, "Our Flourishing Measure," Harvard Institute for Quantitative Social Science, 2024.

11. Colleen M. Tolan, Deepa Purushothaman, and Lisa S. Kaplowitz, "How to Improve Women's Advancement Programs," *Harvard Business Review*, July 22, 2024.

12. Michele W. Berger, "Does Money Buy Happiness? Here's What the Research Says," *Knowledge at Wharton*, March 28, 2023.

Chapter 10: From Short-Term Profit Maximization to Long-Term Value Creation

1. *Annual Report of the U.S. Securities and Exchange Commission, 1970*, U.S. Securities and Exchange Commission, 1970.

2. Peter Korn, "A Village in Ecuador's Amazon Fights for Its Life as Oil Wells Move In," Natural Resources Defense Council, April 4, 2018.

3. Rachel Zurer, "The Extraordinarily Committed Life of Lynne Twist," SOCAP Global, January 6, 2018.

4. Donella Meadows, "Leverage Points: Places to Intervene in a System," Donella Meadows Project.

5. "The Rationale," Ownership Works, 2024.

6. Thomas Dudley and Ethan Rouen, "The Big Benefits of Employee Ownership," *Harvard Business Review*, May 13, 2021.

7. Paul D. Woodard, "The Benefits of Being an Employee-Owned Company," Bregman, Steinfeld & Landau LLP, October 30, 2017; Dudley and Rouen, "The Big Benefits of Employee Ownership."

8. "2020 Global Marketing Trends: Bringing Authenticity to Our Digital Age," Deloitte, 2020; Ernst & Young, "The Business Case for Purpose," *Harvard Business Review* Report, 2020.

9. Sharon Rowe, *The Magic of Tiny Business: You Don't Have to Go Big to Make a Great Living* (Oakland, CA: Berrett-Koehler Publishers, 2018).

10. Haley Draznin, "Eileen Fisher Built a Fashion Empire. Her Employees Now Own Nearly Half of It," CNN, January 6, 2020.

11. R. Edward Freeman, *Strategic Management: A Stakeholder Approach* (Cambridge: Cambridge University Press, 2010).

12. Rajendra Sisodia, Jag Sheth, and David Wolfe, *Firms of Endearment: How World-Class Companies Profit from Passion and Purpose* (Upper Saddle River, NJ: Pearson Education, 2014).

13. "Statement on the Purpose of a Corporation," Business Roundtable, 2019.

14. "Towards Stakeholder Capitalism: Highlights from the December 2021 Report," Conference Board, December 2021.

15. Anna Starostinetskaya, "Miyoko Schinner Removed as CEO From the $260 Million Vegan Cheese Brand That Bears Her Name," *VegNews*, February 20, 2023.

16. Theo Francis, "Inside Eileen Fisher's Employee Stock Plan," *Wall Street Journal*, January 22, 2007.

17. "Benefit Corporation," B Lab U.S. & Canada, 2024.

18. Yvon Chouinard, "Earth Is Now Our Only Shareholder," Patagonia, September 14, 2022.

INDEX

ableism, 16
abundance mindset, 197, 256–257
Accenture, 150
accountability, 69–70, 103, 203
achievement addiction, 214
Achuar people, 242
acknowledging others, 173–174
active listening, 172–173
ADHD, 115, 129
advocacy, 175–181
Afterglow, 263
Alban, Susan, 174–175
Albright, Madeleine, 10
Allbirds, 262
Allen, Liz, 183–184
All Good Body Care, 224–226
allyship, 179–181
Alphabet, 16
Amazon, 16, 23, 240, 251
American Medical Association Council on Medical Service, 139
antifemininity, 13, 18, 33
anxiety, 93, 115, 116, 132, 139, 214
Anxiety and Depression Association of America, 13
Apple, 16
Asana, 3, 156
assimilation, 50–53, 57(table), 79
assumptions, questioning, 169–170
attachment, 51–52
attention span, 84–85
attentiveness, 39
authenticity, 51–52, 53–56, 68, 76, 78–79, 85–86

authentic leadership
 vs. assimilated leadership, 57(table)
 benefits of, 56
 cultivating emotional regulation, 73–76
 example, 53–56
 honoring your truth, 62–70
 leading from values, 57–62
 overview, 79
 questioning the norm, 70–73
 seeking the right environment, 76–78
autobiographical listening, 173
autonomy frustration, 164
autonomy satisfaction, 181–182

Bailey Vercruysse, Alison, 239–240, 247
Bank of America Merrill Lynch, 138
Banks, Anna, 236
Barry Wehmiller (BW), 155, 164–165
Bear Ears National Monument, 256
Bear Stearns, 212, 215
behaviors, letting go of unhealthy, 88–90
Ben-Ami, Aner, 224
Beneficial State Bank, 55, 193
beneficial workplaces
 bolstering everyone's economic well-being, 149–151
 example, 140
 finding solutions to feedback, 141–145
 normalizing and supporting mental health, 151–155
 normalizing healthy practices, 145–148
 nurturing continued learning and growth, 155–158
 overview, 158–159

INDEX

Benefit Corporations, 260–261, 262
benefits packages, 165–166
Berkshire Hathaway, 16
Bhansali, Rajasvini, 197
Biggby Coffee, 261
Bird, Taryn, 83–84, 153
B Lab, 258, 262
Blackstone, 16
Black women, 17, 52
boards, 261–262
Bolhous, Kathy, 50, 51, 61, 167–168, 204, 244–246
boundaries, setting and committing to, 100–104
Brown, Brené, 125
Built to Last (Collins and Porras), 200
bullying, 142, 145
burnout, 4, 25–26, 38, 76, 83, 145, 164, 194–195, 206
business
  advent of, 16
  books about, 53
  command-and-control model, 163, 188
  contemporary design of, 16–17, 22
  culture, 138–139, 145–146
  employee-owned, 245–246
  exclusion of women from, 50–51
  impact assessment, 257–258
  influence of patriarchy on, 16–27, 79
  "masculine" traits valued in, 19
  profit-at-all-cost mentality, 163–164, 188
  purpose in, 220
  shareholder theory, 22
  tiny, 247
Business Roundtable, 251–252

Cafe Campesino, 257
calling people in, 68
Candide Group, 224, 262–263
capital partners, 262–263
career mixology, 185
caretaking responsibilities, 82–83, 95, 109–110
Carlyle Group, 16
Center for Women in Business, 233
CEO roles
  compensation structures, 151, 174–175, 201

  executives with stay-at-home partners, 83
  men in, worldwide, 16
  mental health impacts, 3–4
  physical health impacts, 2–3
  psychopaths in, 25
  women in, worldwide, 2, 16
  See also leaders and leadership
Chang, Lily, 223
change, 77–78, 242
Chapman, Diana, 75, 156
Charter Next Generation (CNG), 50, 167–168, 204, 244–245
check-ins
  personal, 154
  values, 61–62, 201
choice, 181–187
Chouinard, Yvon, 263–264
chronic disease, 15
chronic stress, 24, 25
Cia (employee), 2, 168
Cirocco, Michelle, 170
Clearlake Capital Group, 16
Clemente (refugee), 181
Clif Bar, 3
climate change, 23, 24, 58, 96, 224, 263
CNG. *See* Charter Next Generation
Coleman, Kendra, 86, 223, 258
collaboration, 193, 194–195, 201–206
collective success, 205
collective trauma, 14–15
collective wisdom, 203–204
college-degree requirements, 170, 222–223
colonialism, 16
command-and-control business model, 163, 188
communication, clear, 203
community
  creating, 97
  finding your people, 120–121
  lack of, 25, 26
  as stakeholder, 255
  support circles, 121–122
comparisons, 70
compassion, 38, 131–133
compensation structures, 151, 174–175, 201
compliments, 119–120
compromises, avoiding, 258–264

INDEX

Conference Board, 252
conflict, 39–40, 101, 133
connection
  cultivating genuine, 195–197
  flourishing and, 232
  nurturing genuine, 118–122
Conscious Company (periodical), 1–2, 34
Conscious Company Leaders Forum, 3, 11
Conscious Company Media, 9, 62, 65, 85, 100, 127, 189–190, 211
Conscious Leadership Group, 75, 156
content consumption, 93–94
contribution management, 181–182, 185
control
  power associated with, 233
  releasing need for, 99–100
Coralus, 76, 85
corporations, purpose of, 251
Cotopaxi, 262
COVID-19 pandemic, 5, 82–83, 93, 108, 124, 127, 130, 211
Cranemere, 259, 263
criminal records, 170
C-suite roles, 18, 25, 219, 252. *See also* CEO roles
cultural norms, 15
curiosity, 75–76, 203–204
Curtis, Lisa, 117, 243–244, 246, 249, 252, 254, 259, 260–261, 262
CVC Capital Partners, 16
CVS, 243

daily moments of joy, 125–126
Darn Good Yarn, 182
Deci, Edward, 214, 218
decision-making
  career, 184–185
  collaborative, 201–206
decompression time, 98
Decurion, 154
deforestation, 24
deliberately developmental organizations (DDO), 154
Deloitte, 2, 70–71
Delta Institute, 96
Demmellash, Alfa, 5, 35, 64, 69, 195, 212–213, 215
depression, 4, 25, 93, 115, 116, 128–129, 139, 214

Dermalogica, 5, 59–60, 226, 228
difficult conversations, 41–42
dignified workplaces
  example, 165–167
  giving people more voice and choice, 181–187
  overview, 187–188
  respecting and valuing everyone, 167–175
  understanding experiences/preferences of others, 179–181
  using your privilege to support others, 175–181
dignity, 163–165, 169, 175–176
Dinos, Elaine, 219–220, 223
discrimination, 15, 17, 25, 26, 142, 153
disenfranchised workplaces, 162–165
diversity, equity, and inclusion (DEI), 167, 175
Division of Sleep Medicine, 114
dopamine, 214
Doshi, Saloni, 228
Double Shift, 82
double standards, 18–20, 26
Drain Taylor, Hannah, 6, 46, 145, 173–174
Dr. Bronner's, 151, 262
Duell, Caroline, 224–226
Dulbecco, Melanie, 71–72, 151, 156, 181, 185, 194, 199, 200–201, 204
Dunbar, Scott, 2, 127–128
Dupree, Cydney Hurston, 19
Dweck, Carol, 156, 230

Earthwise, 143
ECOBAGS, 247
EcoEnclose, 228
Economic Policy Institute, 151
economic security, 138–139, 149–151
EFWO (Everything Fucking Works Out), 227
18 Rabbits, 239–240, 241, 247
Eileen Fisher, 5, 34, 172, 197–198, 249, 250, 259–260
Eileen Fisher Foundation, 186, 251, 258
Ellevate Network, 21, 83
Emmons, Robert, 132
Emotional Brain Training, 152
emotional labor, 20, 104
emotional regulation, 57(table), 73–76

INDEX

empathy, 38, 43, 131
employee engagement, 38, 167
employees, as stakeholders, 252
employee stock ownership plan (ESOP), 197–198
energy/impact matrix, 90–92, 91(fig.)
environment
   as stakeholder, 255–256
   workplace, 57(table), 76–78
Environmental Defense Fund, 36–37
EO Products, 5, 35, 59, 111, 140
EQT, 16
Equal Employment Opportunity Commission, 142
Erhardt, Moritz, 138
Erica (project manager), 169
essentializing, 88, 90–94, 91(fig.)
Ethical Swag, 143
experiences, understanding others', 179–181
extrinsic motivation, 212, 214, 218, 233
Exxon, 23

failure, embracing, 226–227
fairness, 206
Fair Play (Rodsky), 20
Farrigan, Tracey, 150
feedback, 43, 141–145, 157
feminine traits, 32, 34–35, 47
feminism, resistance to use of word, 10
figuring it out as you go, 227–229
finances, therapy and, 130–131
finding your people, 120–121
Finocchi, Michelle, 121
Fisher, Eileen, 5, 34, 172, 197–198, 250–251, 260
Fisher, Robyn Sue, 73–74
Fleming, Andy, 154
flexible policies, 185–187
flourishing, 218, 232
flow state, 225
focus, 84
freedom, 233
Freeman, Edward, 250–251
Friedman, Milton, 22–23, 241, 246, 247
full-time, redefining, 148

Gallup, 157
game-tape review, 43

gender discrimination, 17
gender roles, 18–20, 32–33, 104
General Atlantic, 16
Giggey, Amy, 173
"girl in the corner," 171–172
Givi, Julian, 103
Glasmeier, Amy, 150
goals
   creating shared, 197–201
   learning vs. performance, 230–231
   measurable, 249
Goldstein, Katherine, 82
Gonzalez, Cesar, 126
gratitude, 132, 173–174
Griffin-Black, Susan, 5, 35, 59, 111–112, 119, 140, 144, 172
Gripne, Stephanie, 149
growth
   intentionality about, 244–249
   mindset, 156
   opportunities, 39–40
guilt, 82, 125

habits, letting go of unhealthy, 88–90
Hannah (friend), 113
happiness, 218, 234
harassment
   sexual, 21, 137, 141–142
   workplace, 142, 145
harmful workplaces, 138–139, 158
Harris, Bill, 257
Harris, Twanna, 52, 217–218
Harris Poll, 59, 94, 166
Harvard Medical School, 114
Harvard Study of Adult Development, 119
Harvard University, 212, 232
health conditions
   assimilation and, 52, 79
   chronic disease, 15
   compassion and, 131–132
   economic security and, 139
   exercise and, 115–116
   loneliness and, 118–119, 192
   self-sacrificing and, 109–111
   social acceptability concerns and, 15
   stress-related, 2–3, 4, 9, 24, 116
   workplace safety and, 138
Hearthside Food Solutions, 240
Hellman and Friedman, 16

INDEX

help
    asking for, 95–100
    seeking professional, 127–131
Henry, Diane, 146, 246
heteronormativity, 16, 20–21
hierarchy, 163–165, 168–169
hiring protocols, 169–170
Hispanic women, 17, 137
Holdfast Collective, 264
holistic leadership
    cultivating balance and discernment, 45–47, 46(table)
    cultivating healthy traits, 36–40, 38(table)
    examples, 34–35
    overview, 48
    releasing toxic traits, 40–45, 43(table)
Homeroom, 99, 141–142, 193, 203, 217
hooks, bell, 12
household responsibilities, 19–20, 104
Houser, Chad, 3
Huff, VaShone, 52, 65–66, 255
Human Flourishing Program, 232
human resources (HR), 145

identity, privilege and, 177–179
impact assessment, 257–258
Impact Finance Center, 149
income inequality, 23–24
Indigenous women, 17, 121
Indigo Ink, 143, 196, 204
individualistic workplaces, 191–193, 207
injuries in the workplace, 138, 145–146
Insight Partners, 16
intentionality
    about board, 261–262
    about growth, 244–249
Interface, 219
internal validation, 173–174
intrinsic motivation, 156, 218
intuition, 38

Janah, Leila, 123
Jeff (brother), 124
Jeff (BW employee), 164–165
Jennings-O'Byrne, Gayle, 165–166, 184–186
Jess (friend), 129
Jimenez, Yscaira, 170, 222–223
job loss, 139
Johnson & Johnson, 251
joy, prioritizing, 122–127
JP Morgan & Chase, 251
judgment, 131–132
Justice Gravel, Nathalie Robin, 241

Kassam, Zahra, 35, 51, 107–109
Kate (membership manager), 190
Kate Spade New York Foundation, 83–84, 146, 153
Kegan, Robert, 154
Ken (BW employee), 155–156
Kindred, 254
Kindred Lane, 220
Kindred Organizational Consulting, 86, 223, 258
KKR, 16, 245
Klatzky, Antoinette, 172, 186–187, 251, 258
Klein, Courtney, 231–232, 233
Knutson, Brian, 214
Korey, Stephanie, 52–53
Kuli Kuli Foods, 117, 243–244, 252, 254, 260–261, 262

LaborX, 170, 223
Lahey, Lisa, 154
Latinas, 17, 137
Laurie (investor), 2
leaders and leadership
    assimilated, 50–53, 57(table)
    authentic, 53–79, 57(table)
    balanced traits, 46(table)
    exclusion of women from, 18
    healthy traits, 37–40, 38(table)
    hierarchical, 163–165
    holistic, 34–47
    imbalanced "masculine," 32–33, 48
    individual, 191–192
    optimized, 85–105
    overextended, 82–85
    power analysis, 178–179
    psychological harm caused by, 139
    sacrificial, 109–111, 134
    sustained, 111–134
    toxic traits, 42–45, 43(table), 83
    See also workplaces
Leading with Joy (Windwood and Bhansali), 197

INDEX

learning goals, 230–231
learning opportunities, 155–158
Leggett, Ellen, 230
Legworks, 148
Lemming, Michelle, 151–153
Leonard Green, 223
"Let the River Run" (song), 10
LinkedIn, 94
TheLi.st, 97, 192
Listening Like a Leader program, 155–156, 157–158
listening to understand, 144
Living Cities, 96
living wage, 150–151
loneliness, 118–119, 192
long-term value creation
  avoiding compromises, 258–264
  being intentional about growth, 244–249
  benefitting all stakeholders, 250–258
  example, 243–244
  overview, 264–265
  vs. short-term profit-maximizing, 253(table)
The Lost Art of Connecting (McPherson), 97
Lost Boys of Sudan, 181
Lutyens, Emily Mochizuki, 2, 121, 126, 148
Lynch, Barbara, 52
Lynn (therapist), 128, 212

Macdougall, Jocelyn, 11, 12, 54–56, 121, 177–178
macrorisks, 229–230
Maddie (employee), 171
male-centered workplaces, 20
managers. *See* leaders and leadership
Marcario, Rose, 221
marginalized identities, 14, 17, 26, 52, 66, 139, 192–193, 259
Markus, Inna, 154
masculine traits, 32–33
mastery, 225, 230–231
Maté, Daniel, 15, 51–52, 109–110
Maté, Gabor, 15, 51–52, 109–110
matriarchal societies, 12
Matt (lawyer), 191
McDonald, Megan, 175–176
McKinsey, 217
McPherson, Susan, 97

Meadows, Donella, 242
meaning. *See* purpose
meditation, 118
Meduna-Gross, Mary, 125–126
meetings, one-on-one, 182–183
Meetup, 121
Mellin, Laurel, 152
men
  advent of business and, 16
  in CEO roles, 16
  gender roles, 18–20, 32–33
  influence of patriarchy on, 12–13
  power associations, 233
  stress and, 4
  toxic masculinity, 13
mental health
  burnout and, 4, 25–26
  content consumption and, 93–94
  flourishing and, 232
  manager effects on, 47
  normalizing and supporting workplace, 151–155
  nutrition and, 115
  professional help for, 45, 127–131
  psychological safety, 139, 202–204
  rest and, 146–148
  stigma, 152, 153
  stress and, 3–5
  women's, 153
Meta Platforms, 16
Michelle (overextended leader), 81–82, 83
microaggressions, 17, 177, 187
microrisks, 229–230
Microsoft, 16
Milburn, Tara, 143
Miller, Matthew, 154
Minangkabau people, 12
mindfulness, 115
mindset
  abundance, 197, 256–257
  growth, 156
  relational, 197
  scarcity, 197, 257
  shifting, 97, 103, 129–130
  transactional, 196–197
MIT Living Wage Calculator, 150
Miyoko's Creamery, 258–259
money, defining "enough," 234–235
Monsanto, 23

INDEX

MontiKids, 35, 51, 107–109
moringa farmers, 243–244
Mosuo people, 12
motherhood, 82–83
motivation
    extrinsic, 212, 214, 218, 233
    intrinsic, 156, 218
movement, 98–99, 115–116, 118
Moving the Needle, 121, 222
MSC Industries, 264
MSC Strategies, 65
Murthy, Vivek H., 118

Nadi Olson, Stephanie, 51, 110–111, 146, 218, 228
Nagoski, Amelia, 15, 116
Nagoski, Emily, 15, 116
Nana Jones Granola, 89
Native American women, 17, 121
Native Women Lead, 121
needs
    attachment, 51–52
    authenticity, 51–52
    individual, 167
    Maslow's hierarchy of, 174, 234
    onboarding process and, 183–184
    risks of ignoring, 109–111
Neiman Marcus, 3
neurotransmitters, 115
New Global Citizen, 231
New York Times, 22, 74, 142
Nina (events manager), 190
norms, questioning, 57(table), 70–73
nutrition, 114–115
NVIDIA Corporation, 16
Nygren, Garnie, 90, 228

objectification, 21
O'Connor, Sandra Day, 10
office temperatures, 20
Office Yoga, 154
Olamina, 263
O'Loughlin, Sheryl, 3
Olukunola, Khalila "K.O.," 66–68
onboarding, intentional, 183–184
one-on-one meetings, 182–183
optimized leadership
    embracing support, 95–100
    example, 85–87

overview, 104–105
    releasing what doesn't serve you, 87–94, 91(fig.)
    setting and committing to boundaries, 100–104
overassimilation, 52–53
overextended leadership, 82–85
ownership, shared, 197–199
Ownership Works, 245

Pachamama Alliance, 242
pain points, identifying, 97–99
Pal, Parneet, 84–85, 92, 116, 131, 132
paper ceiling, 222–223
parental leave policies, 20–21
passions, pursuing, 224–231, 235–237
Patagonia, 221, 256, 262, 263–264
patriarchy
    defined, 11, 12
    gender roles, 32–33
    influence of, 12–13
    influence on business, 16–27, 79
    resistance to use of word, 9–11
    "smashing the patriarchy," 11
    societal expectations of women, 82–83
    trauma of, 13–15, 65
    violence of, 177–178
pausing, 74–75
pay equity, 174–175
Peace Coffee, 256–257
Peet's Coffee, 239
Perez, Cat, 137–138, 142
perfectionism, 88, 99–100
performance goals, 230–231
Perkins, John, 241–242
Perryville Women's Prison, 169
physical activity, 98–99, 115–116, 118
physical health. *See* health conditions
Pink, Daniel, 225
Playa Xinalani, 126–127
Plum Organics, 3
pollution, 24
Polman, Paul, 60
post-traumatic stress disorder, 153
power
    men's idea of, 233
    privilege and, 178–179
    toxic masculinity and, 13, 22–27
    women's idea of, 233

INDEX

preferences, understanding others', 179–181
Principles of Corporate Governance, 251–252
private equity firms, 16, 51, 223, 241, 245, 259
privilege, understanding personal, 175–181
professional development, 157–158
professional help, 45, 127–131
profit-at-all-cost mentality, 163–164, 188
Propper de Callejon, Diana, 217, 259, 263
psychological safety, 139, 202–204
psychopaths, 25
PTO, 146–148
Purdue Pharma, 23
purpose
    flourishing and, 232
    passion and, 235–237
    seeking, 219–224
    sense of, 97, 218, 220–221
    shared, 199–200
purpose-driven companies, 219–220, 246
purpose trusts, 263–264
Purushothaman, Deepa, 2–3, 70–71, 95
Pusateri, Michelle, 89

quality of life, 231–232, 235–237
questions
    meaningful, 120
    for one-on-one meetings, 183
    open-ended, 173

Rachel (editor-in-chief), 100–101
Real Leaders, 92, 228
recognition, 173–174
red flags
    to honoring your truth, 69–70
    to questioning the norm, 72–73
ReEngineering HR, 66
reflection, 115
ReGen Ventures, 221
regrets, 78
Rein, Valerie, 14
relational mindset, 197
relationships
    co-workers, 196
    essentializing, 92–93
    with money, 234–235

relational, 197
transactional, 196–197
Renegade Partners, 174–175
Resonate, 45, 178
respect, 167–175, 203–204
Ressler, Cali, 186
rest, 84–85, 146–148
Results-Only Work Environment (ROWE), 186–187
Rhode Island School of Design, 107
Rice, Condoleezza, 10
Richardson, Liz, 143, 196, 204
Rising Tide Capital, 5, 35, 64, 195, 215
risk, reframing, 229–230
Roanhorse, Vanessa, 92, 95–96, 103, 121, 123, 127
Roanhorse Consulting, 92, 96
Rodney, Libby, 59, 94, 166, 268
Rodsky, Eve, 20
Rosenstein, Justin, 3
Rowe, Sharon, 246–247, 249
Rutgers Business School, 233
Rwanda, 153
Ryan, Richard, 214

sacrificial leadership, 109–111, 134
safety in the workplace
    economic, 138–139, 149–151
    physical, 138, 142, 145–146
    psychological, 139, 202–204
salary caps, 151
Salesloft, 68, 179
salon dinners, 122
Santos, Laurie, 119
Saudi Aramco, 16
Saunders, Vicki, 76, 85–86, 90, 92
scaling without compromising, 258–264
scarcity mindset, 197, 257
scheduling joy, 126
Schinner, Miyoko, 258–259
Schlosser, Ayla, 45–46, 61, 121, 178, 223
SEC, 241
second-chance employees, 170
second shift, 20
self-awareness, 74
self-care, 113–118
self-sacrificing, 109–111
self-suppression, 52
self-worth, 104, 212, 214

INDEX

Selhub, Eva, 114
Sephora North America, 236
Serenbe Development, 90, 228
serotonin, 115
sexual harassment, 21, 137, 141–142
shareholder supremacy, 22–27, 138–139, 241
Sharifzadeh, Maryam, 126–127, 154
Shark Tank (TV show), 107
SheEO, 85
Shoket, Ann, 97, 192
short-termism, 241–242, 253(table), 265
Simon, Carly, 10
Simon, Morgan, 223–224, 262–263
Simple Mills, 88, 118, 199–200
sleep, 114
Smith, Katlin, 88, 118, 199–200
Smitten Ice Cream, 73–74
Snow, Nicole, 182
SOCAP, 65
social acceptability, 15
social connection, 118–122, 192
social isolation, 26
social media, 93–94
social success, 212–215, 237
societal expectations, 82–83
Solstice Energy, 58, 146
soul success
  examples, 215–218
  overview, 237
  prioritizing quality of life, 231–237
  pursuing passions, 224–231
  seeking more purpose and meaning, 219–224
Spade, Kate, 3–4
Speirs, Steph, 57–58, 121, 146
stakeholders
  benefitting, 250–252, 256–258
  community, 255
  customers, 254
  employees, 252
  engaging with, 256
  environment, 255–256
  impact assessment, 257–258
  short-term vs. long-term mindset, 253(table)
  suppliers, 252, 254
stakeholder theory, 250–251
status quo, questioning, 57(table), 70–73

Stavros, Pete, 245
Stepanovsky, Carter, 68, 179–180, 184
strengths, 39
stress
  business culture and, 138–139
  chronic, 24, 25
  economic security and, 139
  health conditions caused by, 2–3, 4, 9, 24
  hormones, 116
  internal, 15
  loneliness and, 192–193
  perfectionism and, 88
  physiological effects of, 15
  prevalence of work-related, 140
  women vs. men, 4
strong ties, 196
structure, 205
success
  in boundary setting, 102–103
  collective, 205
  defining, 215
  long-term value creation, 243–265, 253(table)
  sacrificial conditioning towards, 109–111
  short-term profit-maximizing, 241–242, 253(table), 265
  social, 212–215, 237
  soul, 215–237
  toxic definitions of, 22–27
  tying your why to metrics of, 249
suicide, 3–4, 25
superfriending, 121–122
suppliers, 252, 254
support
  building your own circle of, 121–122
  embracing, 95–100
  nurturing genuine connection, 118–122
sustained leadership
  committing to the basics, 113–118
  cultivating compassion, 131–133
  examples, 111–113
  nurturing genuine connection, 118–122
  overview, 133–134
  prioritizing joy, 122–127
  seeking professional help, 127–131
Sweet, Julie, 150
systems change, 242

INDEX

Taiwan Semiconductor Manufacturing, 16
Talent to Team, 46, 145, 173
Taylor, George, 66–67
Taylor, Kat, 193
teamwork, 194–195, 196
Televerde Foundation, 169–170
temperatures, office, 20
Tesla, 16
Teuta (friend), 129
Texoma Health Foundation, 151–152
therapy, 45, 127–131
"think manager, think male" phenomenon, 32
Thomas Bravo, 16
Thompson, Jody, 186
thriving wage, 149
time off, 146–148
tiny business, 247
Tom (BW employee), 162–163, 164–165
TOMS, 219
Torani, 71–72, 156, 181–182, 185, 194, 200–201
toughness, 13, 18, 83
toxic masculinity, 13, 16, 18, 53, 83, 95, 96, 110, 213–214
transactional mindset, 196–197
transparency, 204–205
trauma
   assimilation, 51–52
   collective, 14–15
   defined, 14
   of patriarchy, 13–15, 65
Tribal Good, 52
TRU Colors Brewery, 67
Trump, Donald, 256
trust, 202–203
truth, 57(table), 62–70, 78
Turner, Brock, 14
Twist, Bill, 241–242
Twist, Lynne, 3, 241–242

unfairness, 25, 26, 206
unhealthy lifestyles, 89
unified workplaces
   collaborative decision-making, 201–206
   creating shared goals, 197–201
   cultivating genuine connection, 195–197
   examples, 193–195
   overview, 206–207
Unilever, 60
United Nations, 17
Universal Declaration of Human Rights, 163
University of Virginia, 250

validation
   external, 213–215, 219
   internal, 173–174
values
   aligning truth with, 64, 68
   capital partners and, 262–263
   conflict between scale and, 259–261
   core, 77, 200–201
   flourishing and, 232
   leading from, 57(table), 57–62
   shared, 200–201
   unalignment with, 25–26, 85
valuing everyone, 167–175
Vanessa (editor-in-chief), 190
Vanguard, 251
Van Ness, Julie, 92–93, 228
victimization, 21
violence, 138, 177–178
voice
   finding, 68–69
   giving people more, 181–187
vulnerability, 38, 67–68

Wade, Erin, 99–100, 121, 126, 141–143, 144, 193–194, 203–204, 205, 215–217, 235
wage gap, 17, 151
Walker, Andrea, 55
Wallace, Kristy, 21, 83, 96
Wallace, Lee, 256–257
Walmart, 23, 243
Walrond, Karen, 125
Warberg Block, Kari, 143
Washington Post, 142
weak ties, 196
weaponized incompetence, 206
We Are Rosie, 51, 110, 146, 228
well-being, 112–113, 117–118, 133–134, 140, 149–151, 154–155, 232
white supremacy, 16
Whitney (boss), 36–37, 161
Whole Foods Markets, 1, 243

why
  team codification of, 248–249
  tying to success metrics, 249
  understanding, 117–118
Windwood, Akaya, 5, 35, 53, 69, 77–78, 127, 131, 194, 197, 268
Winfrey, Oprah, 10
Wocstar Capital, 165–166
The Wolf of Wall Street (film), 23
women
  in CEO roles, 2, 16
  collective trauma, 14–15
  exclusion of in business, 50–51
  exclusion of in leadership, 18
  gender roles, 18–20, 32–33
  influence of patriarchy on, 12–13
  internalized patriarchy, 13–15
  mental health, 153
  power associations, 233
  societal expectations of, 82–83
  stress and, 4
Women in Sustainability, 120–121
Women of Renewable Industries and Sustainable Energy, 120
Women's Earth Alliance, 121
Women's Executive Forum, 223
Women's Venture Fund, 66
workforce
  women dropping out of, 82–83
  women in, 52

Working Girl (film), 10
working parents, barriers for, 20–21
work-life balance, 147–148
workloads, excessive, 25, 26, 194–195
workplace(s)
  beneficial, 141–149
  customizable, 166–167
  dignified, 165–188
  disenfranchised, 162–165
  dynamics, 161–162
  flexibility, 185–187
  harmful, 138–139, 158
  individualistic, 191–193, 207
  normalizing healthy practices in, 145–148
  safety, 138–139, 142, 202–204
  toxic, 76–77, 162
  unified, 193–207
World-Changing Women's Summit, 54–55, 65–66
Wurwand, Jane, 5, 59–60, 95, 226, 228
Wurwand, Raymond, 60

Yale University, 119

Zebras Unite, 255
Zen as a Service (ZaaS), 154
Zepeda, Mara, 255, 264

Credit: Photo courtesy of the author.

Meghan French Dunbar is a serial entrepreneur, business journalist, speaker, and leadership expert whose work focuses on making business better for all. Her work has touched the lives of over a million people worldwide, including co-founding the first nationally distributed print magazine in the US focusing on impact-driven business, *Conscious Company* magazine. She's a sought-after speaker on women's leadership and the future of business, and writes for leading business outlets like *Inc., Business Chief,* and *Forbes* magazines. Through her current ventures, she works with leaders of major brands like Coach, Kate Spade, Biggby Coffee, and more. She lives in Boulder, Colorado, with her husband, Scott, and two children. For more about Meghan and supporting book material, please visit meghanfrenchdunbar.com.